'Great stuff. Lot of interesting research.
Connections. Thoughts. Blasphemies.'
Terry Gilliam

Who was the real Brian? Who was the real Jesus? Who
was the real Bishop of Southwark? Did the Romans
build the Jerusalem Aqueduct? Were the Magi wise?
Was Brian's father really Nortius Maximus and were
the People's Front of Judea, splitters? All the crucial
questions this book attempts to answer.

'A wild, chaotic, bronco-busting ride in an out-of-control
fairground, but hang on in there – it's worth it.'
Terry Jones

THE LIFE OF BRIAN ~~Jesus~~

Julian Doyle

Matador
5 Weir Road
Kibworth Beauchamp
Leicester LE8 0LQ, UK
Tel: 0116 279 2277
Email: books@troubador.co.uk
Web: www.troubador.co.uk/matador

ISBN 978-184876-628-0

British Library Cataloguing in Publication Data.
A catalogue record for this book is available from the British Library.

Other contact and information can be found at
www.juliandoyle.info

Printed in the UK by TJ International, Padstow, Cornwall

Matador is an imprint of Troubador Publishing Ltd

To Graham Chapman
who was Brian Cohen
and Joshua ben Joseph
who was Jesus Christ

Contents

Foreword

Prepare to leave your assumptions, suppositions, familiar notions and points of view far behind as you set off with Julian Doyle on this joyfully mischievous journey of discovery and self-discovery.

The first thing to say is that Julian is a polymath.

I first met Julian when Terry Gilliam and I invited him to help produce *Monty Python & The Holy Grail*. Julian turned himself into Line Producer and then Director of Photography for the Black Knight sequence.

He went on to edit *Monty Python's Life of Brian*, *Monty Python's Meaning of Life*, *Jabberwocky*, *Time Bandits*, *Brazil*, and *Wind in the Willows*. He also directed the special effects for many films, and wrote and directed his own movies, *Love Potion* (1987) and *Chemical Wedding* (2008).

He then turned himself into a theatre dramatist, and wrote a play, *Twilight of the Gods*, about Wagner's relationship with Nietzsche, which was as intelligent and informative as any fun play could possibly get. I have only just discovered that before he went into films he was a research scientist!

The great thing about Julian is that he doesn't have any assumptions or pre-suppositions, but he does have points of view. He has lots of them. This book is an exploration of his mind. Like the original film, this book is likely to outrage and irritate a lot of people, but it is never dull. It is full of surprising and interesting ideas.

Although it centres around the world of Jesus as reflected in *The Life of Brian*, it embraces the career of Richard Dadd, the nature of Masonary, the Jewish identity. It asks startling questions such as: Was Jesus really crucified? Did the Christians pinch the symbol of the fish from the Pythagoreans? At one point he presents a fascinating explanation of Bosch's mysterious picture of Christ being adorned with the crown of thorns, and then the next moment he is examining the significance of numbers in the Bible story.

It's a wild, chaotic, bronco-busting ride in an out-of-control fairground, but hang on in there - it's worth it.

Terry Jones
25 September 2010

Backword

Julian Doyle, like many others who worked on Monty Python's *Life Of Brian*, has clearly not recovered from the experience. To be honest, Julian's mental state has worried us all over the years. Having worked with him on *Monty Python and The Holy Grail* and *Jabberwocky* I urged the others to have him put quietly in an institution, rather than endure any more of his offensive Anne Boleyn impersonations. But no-one listened and now look what's happened. He's written a disgusting book and used our likenesses to try and sell it. I was sent a complimentary copy and, to be honest, I threw it in the bin, as instructed by Sarah Palin. My lawyers are currently looking at a copy and rather enjoying it.

Michael Palin
October 2010

Acknowledgements

Thanks to Jeremy Thompson who turned black into white and Perrine Moran who turned unreadable into readable and Gerry Conroy who turned wrong into right.

Introduction

THE DEBATE

They didn't look like trouble. The Bishop of Southwark, the Right Reverend Mervyn Stockward in all his glorious, purple gowns and Christian broadcaster Malcolm Muggeridge in mustard jacket and tie, but like the Spanish Inquisition they came to attack and condemn the film, 'Monty Python's Life of Brian' as blatant blasphemy.

Defending themselves were Monty Python's Michael Palin and John Cleese. But by the end of the discussion the Right Reverend pointed his massive cross, like Abraham Van Helsing warding off Dracula, at the blasphemers and announced that the two sinners would "get their thirty pieces of silver."

Malcolm Muggeridge on the other hand took the stand that "There is nothing in this little squalid number that could possibly affect anybody because it's much too tenth rate for that."

This attack certainly made the wonderfully 'nice' Michael Palin show some extraordinary (for him) anger. As he recalls, "We had done our homework, thinking we were going to get into quite a tough theological argument, but it turned out to be virtually a slanging match. We were very surprised by that. I don't get angry very often, but I got incandescent with rage at their attitude and the smugness of it."

The anger came from the inability to argue against such a comment. What were Michael and John supposed to say – "it is a good film or its a great film etc, etc…" How can the filmmakers themselves actually say that? But now 30 years later we do have the ammunition to deal with these scornful and derisive remarks.

In 2007 'Life of Brian' was voted, 'the funniest comedy ever' in Channel Four's '50 Greatest Comedy Films'. And then the British Film Institute declared it to be the 28th best British film of all time.

And here are some of the comments on the Youtube clip of the debate.

crisis123456789: 'There's nothing in this little squalid number that could possibly affect anybody' Then why the hell are you arguing against it being shown???

Sliptodance: When I die I hope I remember how important Monty Python has been for me.

MLennholm: They should have told those pompous stuck up buggers "Just like the Beatles, we ARE bigger than Jesus"

Ullghoirt: The Life of Brian is both funny and thought provoking. Well done, Monty Python!!! The God debate is still going on today, so at least we're still "All individuals and not letting anyone tell us what to do."

LienPT: God wants us to laugh…God wants us to be happy! Why do conservative people *have* to insist speaking for a God they seem to know so poorly...?

intermender: This debate is still going on! Why is religion so suspiciously fragile? One of the funniest movies ever made!

MrSparky1913: If only the Bishops were so forthcoming in Ireland to unmask the sex abusing priests. They really think they are someone! Remove that collar Bishop. It means nothing.

mortalhellion: Palin should have said, "Yes, I am the messiah. Now fuck off!" Many hardcore religious simply lost their sense of humor.

emzii92: Bloody old, pretentious, stick up their arses men. Get a sense of humor! Cleese and Palin well done.

FandPrulethesky: Religion is the best and worse thing sometimes. Well done Cleese and Palin.

These types of comments are being made consistently over the past 20 years, so I think we can now definitively say that Muggeridge's scathing, personalized criticism is wrong. The film is not tenth rate or infantile but funny and lasting.

Talking of personalized criticism let's get down in the gutter with them. Here is another, more personalized, comment on Youtube:

Ketersimax: What a hypocrite! That priest with the purple shirt is gay and an alcoholic.

This in fact is true, the Bishop of Southwark's obituary reads: *'His capacity for alcohol was prodigious, but it never impaired his mental facilities; the more wine he drank, the sharper his memory became.'*

As the bible says: *'Be on your guard against the yeast of the Pharisees, which is hypocrisy. There is nothing concealed that will not be disclosed, or hidden that will not be made known. What you have said in the dark will be heard in the daylight, and what you have whispered in the inner rooms will be proclaimed from the roofs.' (Luke 12:1)*

And so the Gay movement did just that and ousted the Right Reverend. Here I must slap my wrists for dropping to their level of mud slinging and want to add that being gay does not in my mind make him a good or bad Christian, in fact I know Mervyn Stockwood did some very good work in his Diocese. And in a later section about the identity of Jesus I will investigate the groups who believed that Jesus himself was involved in homosexual activities.

But let us tackle the main thrust of the Right Reverend's argument. Was the film 'Life of Brian' blasphemous?

Many considered it was. 'Life of Brian' received its world premiere in New York on 17th August 1979, the same week as Apocalypse Now and The Muppet Movie. In the USA, freedom of speech and religious choice are enshrined in the Constitution. Or so it was thought.

The opening salvo in what became a heated and often surreal war of words appeared on August 19th from Rabbi Abraham Hecht, president of the Rabbinical Alliance of America, who claimed to speak for half a million Jews. Writing in Variety Magazine, he declared, *"Never have we come across such a foul, disgusting, blasphemous film before."* Hecht went on to make public his view that 'Brian' *"was produced in hell."* After Hecht's denunciation, outraged religious leaders queued up to vent their spleen to any hack with a microphone, in stark contrast to other more liberal churchmen who defended the film's right to be shown.

The Protestant voice of protest belonged to Robert EA Lee of the Lutheran Council, whose tirade against 'Brian' *"crude and rude mockery, colossal bad taste, profane parody. A disgraceful assault on religious sensitivity"*, was broadcast across 1,000 radio stations. Not to be outdone, the Catholic film-monitoring office rated 'Brian' 'C' for 'Condemned' and implored its flock not to visit theatres where it was playing, it being a sin to do so. With massive protests against the movie from all denominations of Christianity, and Judaism, John Cleese joked with Michael Palin, "We've brought them all together for the first time in 2000 years!"

Naturally, the protests and marches only served to heighten 'Brian's' media profile and so increase its box-office take. Nothing sells better than when it comes attached to the whiff of notoriety. With such free publicity, the original plan to open Brian on 200 screens nationwide snowballed to nearer 600. As John Cleese joked on an American TV show, *"They have actually made me rich."*

But some countries acted to prevent any success. The film was banned in Norway, and so it was marketed in Sweden as, *'The film that is so funny that it was banned in Norway!'* Ireland banned the film for blasphemy and banned director, Terry Jones' next film 'Personal Services'. Terry went on to say, *"I'm not sure if I have made a good film if the Irish don't ban it."*

On November 8, 1979 'Life of Brian' opened in London and, in spite of hymn-singing demonstrators outside, went on to break box-office records in its first week, smashing the previous house record set by 'Jaws'. The film was backed by an advertising campaign in which each Python recruited, either a relative or friend e.g. Gilliam's mum, Michael Palin's dentist, to present their own radio spot. John Cleese's 80-year-old mother, Muriel, read an appeal to listeners, claiming that she was 102-years old and kept in a retirement home by her son, and that unless enough people see his new film and make him richer, he will throw her on to the streets where she will assuredly perish. The ad won a delighted Muriel an award for best radio entertainment commercial of 1979.

But in the rest of Britain, 'Brian' became a victim of regional censorship. There is a loophole in British law to protect the spread of disease. Local authorities have the power to close cinemas for health reasons, and they used this extraordinary clause to ban 'Life of Brian' because it was unhealthy. As Michael Palin recalls, *"I suppose they thought it would spread diseases in cinemas."*

So 'Life of Brian' was banned in Harrogate, parts of Surrey, East Devon where councillors refused even to watch it, arguing that, *"You don't have to see a pigsty to know that it stinks"* and Cornwall where, after one screening, a local councillor stated, that all the participants in the film should be locked up in Broadmoor Criminal Lunatic Asylum.

Terry Gilliam noted, "In Britain, it was banned in certain towns; what that meant was that people in those towns organized coaches and went to the neighbouring town where it was showing. But in the States they banned it in the Bible belt and nobody went to see it. One has to conclude that the British can't be controlled and the Americans can – that's what we learnt over that."

In 1997 Swansea Council finally permitted the film to be shown in cinemas in aid of Comic Relief. Informed that the ban had been lifted, Eric Idle told the press, "What a shame. Is nothing sacred?"

Finally Aberystwyth in Wales lifted its local ban in 2009 when, extraordinarily, Sue Jones-Davies the actress who played Judith (the Welsh tart!) in the film was elected mayor of the town.

But one thing the Monty Python team all agree on, (except one: who might have a different perspective from Heaven) is that 'Life of Brian' could not be made today.

Obviously it was difficult even then to raise the money for the film. Originally Barry Spikings, then production head of EMI, agreed to back the film with a budget of $4 million. Sets built for the Zeffirelli's television series *Jesus of Nazareth* were still standing near Monastir in Tunisia, and were earmarked for the film, which was due to begin shooting in April 1976 with Terry Jones directing.

I still remember the moment with incredulity. The crew had signed contracts and were packed and ready to leave on Saturday to fly to North Africa. Then on the Thursday before, EMI pulled out! To our dismay EMI's 69-year-old chief executive, Lord Bernard Delfont had read the script! Shocked, he famously declared, *"What are they trying to do, crucify me?"* So EMI paid a hundred thousand dollars to get out of their commitment!

The Pythons found themselves marooned in pre-production limbo and there began a desperate scramble to raise the funds. They went to the studios but as Eric Idle describes "It was like trying to sell 'Spring Time for Hitler.'" But by coincidence, Eric was friends with Beatle, George Harrison, a Python fan with a private library of records and films of just about everything the group had done. He admitted that when the Beatles were breaking up, it was watching

Monty Python's Flying Circus that kept him sane. George personally offered to finance the film. When asked later why he put such a lot of his own money into such a dangerously, foolish venture, George just said, in his gentle Liverpool voice, "I wanted to see the movie."

As Eric Idle teased, "This must be the most expensive cinema ticket ever bought!"

All this is reflected in the end song where Eric Idle sings the classic, 'Always Look on the Bright Side of Life'. If you look up the lyrics of the song they end with the Chorus, with Eric as Mr. Cheeky, adlibbing in brackets.

> *And always look on the bright side of life...*
> *(Come on guys, cheer up!)*
> *Always look on the bright side of life...*
> *(Worse things happen at sea, you know.)*
> *Always look on the bright side of life...*
> *(I mean – what have you got to lose?*
> *You know, you come from nothing*
> *you're going back to nothing.*
> *What have you lost? Nothing!)*

In fact if you listen to the film there is actually more adlibbing by Eric, saying the last lines of the film.

> *"Who do you think pays for all this rubbish?*
> *They'll never make their money back – I told them.*
> *I said to them, Bernie,*
> *I said, they'll never make their money back."*
> (Bernie – being Lord Bernard Delfont)

But George Harrison (the man who paid for all this rubbish) had the last laugh when he found himself in the first class lounge at Kennedy airport with Sir Bernard Delfont. He could not resist going up to Bernie and asking if he had heard that 'Brian' had gone into profit. George thanked him profusely – (all the way to the bank).

So was the film blasphemy and is it true that it could not be made today? Or is it both respectful and, as I will argue, the most accurate film ever made of the time of Christ?

Here I suppose we should ask what exactly is blasphemy? Being totally impartial, let's take the dictionary definition.

'Blasphemy is irreverence toward holy personages, religious artifacts, customs, and beliefs. The Abrahamic religions condemn blasphemy vehemently. Some countries have laws to punish blasphemy. These laws may discourage blasphemy as a matter of blasphemous libel, vilification of religion or a religious insult.'

The word is hardly mentioned in the Holy Books. Leviticus 24:16 states that those who speak blasphemy *"shall surely be put to death."* Another verse that directly concerns the sin reads as follows:

*'Thou shalt not take the name of the Lord thy God in vain; for the
Lord will not hold him guiltless that taketh his name in vain.'
(Exodus 20:7)*

These quotes raise one particular problem with blasphemy. Clearly *'Thou shalt not take the name of the Lord thy God in vain,'* has no relevance to atheists who obviously do not have a 'Lord thy God', as they don't have a God at all, so how can you take his name in vain? In this case, one has to say that blasphemy can only be a crime to a believer in God. Those who do not have a God are presumably exempt.

The only other Gospel reference to blasphemy is in Luke.

*'And whosoever shall speak a word against the Son of man, it shall
be forgiven him: but unto him that blasphemeth against the Holy
Ghost it shall not be forgiven.' (Luke 12:10)*

This is rather confusing and difficult to interpret. It probably means that, you will be forgiven if you blaspheme Jesus, or perhaps 'everyman', depending on who you think the 'Son of Man' is, but not if you blaspheme the Holy Ghost or Spirit of God or in a better translation, the 'Breath of God'. It cannot mean the Holy Trinity, as this extraordinarily weird concept was not developed at this stage in Christian history. (The trinity is God the Father, God the Son and God the Holy Ghost, which for a monotheistic religion is all a bit odd.) So somebody (it does not say God or Man) is not going to forgive you if you blaspheme against – a 'particular kind of Ghost' – a Holy one. Which I presume means God.

So that's it, in terms of the Bible, but now we come to the official religious organizations, that follow a particular God. Blasphemy is condemned as a serious, or even, the most serious, sin by all the major creeds and Church theologians. Thomas Aquinas writes that, *'It is clear that blasphemy, which is a sin committed directly against God, is more grave than murder.'* Wow, that makes it pretty serious.

The Book of Concord calls blasphemy *'the greatest sin that can be outwardly committed'*.

Christ Almighty! Worse than genocide?

(Oops! Did I blaspheme there?)

The Baptist Confession of Faith says: *'Therefore, to swear vainly or rashly by the glorious and awesome name of God…is sinful, and to be regarded with disgust and detestation.'*

The Heidelberg Catechism answers question 100 about blasphemy by stating that, *'No sin is greater or provokes God's wrath more than the blaspheming of His Name'*.

All these seem to be referring to swearing using God's name, as becomes clear from Calvin who found it intolerable: *'when a person is accused of blasphemy, to lay the blame on the ebullition of passion, as if God were to endure the penalty whenever we are provoked.'*

'Ebullition of passion' like, *'Christ, that cake is bloody luvly.'* Or when you accidentally hammer your thumb and yell, *'Jesus b___ Christ!'*

So whereas the Bible hardly mentions blasphemy, the Christian organizations go for it big time as a method of control and authority.

Official Islam appears to function in the same way. Not much in the Qu'ran, which just advises Muslims to shun those who find fault with Allah (again it sounds like atheists are exempt because they don't find fault with Allah – they just cannot find Allah at all). There is no punishment suggested in the Qu'ran for blasphemers just those who wage war against Allah and his Messenger.

But then again the religious authorities have gone mad and created a crazy creed of behaviour, Sharia Law. Blasphemy here is any irreverent behaviour toward holy personages, religious artefacts, customs, and beliefs that Muslims respect. The penalties for such behaviour vary by jurisdiction, and can include fines, imprisonment, flogging, amputation, crucifixion, hanging or beheading. Muslim clerics may call for the murder of an alleged blasphemer by issuing a fatwa, making murder legal under Sharia law, which has now made it a punishable crime under Sharia law to:

Speak ill of Allah.

To find fault with Muhammad.

To slight any prophet who is mentioned in the Qu'ran,

To speculate about how Muhammad would behave if he were alive.

To draw a picture to represent Prophet Muhammad or any other prophet, or to make a film which features a prophet.

To write Prophet Muhammad's name on the walls of a toilet.

To name a teddy bear Muhammad or any other prophet's name.

To find fault with Islam.

To say that the Qu'ran is full of lies.

To believe in transmigration of the soul or reincarnation or to disbelieve in the afterlife.

To find fault with or to curse apostles, prophets or angels.

To express an atheist or a secular point of view or to publish or to distribute such a point of view.

To pray for Muslims to become something else.

To whistle during prayers.

To flout the rules prescribed for Ramadan.

To publish an unofficial translation of the Qu'ran.

For anyone to damage a Qu'ran or other books of importance to Islam.

To spit at the wall of a mosque.

This all-embracing crime is similar to Christianity during the Spanish Inquisition, and if Allah believes any of this he is a very sad case. But of course none of this rubbish is in the Qu'ran, just in the heads of some of the Mullahs, who have forgotten the original tolerance of Islam. Just take Moslem Spain where Christians, Jews and Muslims lived happily together for 700 years till the Christian invasion. Or take the example of the great Saladin.

When the crusaders first occupied Jerusalem in 1099 they killed thousands, including women and children. When Saladin recaptured the city, there was no killing and no desecration of holy places, and Christian pilgrims were allowed free access to their places of worship.

Far from becoming drunk with power, Saladin seemed to feel that his new responsibilities demanded more and more restraint. At the famous siege of Acre, Richard the Lion Heart violated an agreement and slaughtered the city's entire 3,000-man garrison. Saladin apparently forgave Richard this villainy and during a later skirmish in front of Jaffa, Richard's horse was killed under him and

Saladin sent him a steed to replace it, with the message: "It is not right that so brave a warrior should have to fight on foot."

Saladin always preferred negotiation and diplomacy to fighting. War to him was a necessary means of reaching certain objectives—a last resort when arbitration had failed.

Unlike the savage Christians, Saladin was especially chivalrous towards women and children. During an attack on the Castle of Kerak, Saladin learned there was a wedding party underway inside. He politely inquired in which wing it was being held, and then directed his catapults elsewhere. The bride sent out cakes and other samples from the wedding feast.

Perhaps Saladin was the only humane and compassionate conqueror in the whole of human history?

But lets look at it from God's perspective. An ordinary, intelligent adult human being would find name calling, childish, stupid and irrelevant. An ignorant thug would take offence and retaliate.

"Who you calling a thug?"

"You, you ignoramus."

And bang! I would have a busted nose.

Which is your God? Someone who is so stupidly oversensitive that he can't take a bit of name-calling? If that is true then he is obviously not worth worshipping. Give up on him and find a more intelligent and adult God.

Perhaps we just have the wrong attitude towards God. Yannis Andricopoulos, in his book 'The Greek Inheritance' explains that the mischievous Greek Gods:

> '...lacked the essential qualities of Gods – aloofness, imperiousness, disciplinarianism, retributivness. They did not personify 'pure good' and could never claim, even if they tried, to be the guarantors of a morally ordered universe or the source of moral obligation. Unscrupulous and wretched, they often offended human decency and were severely reproached for their misdeeds by the humans.'

So if the Judeo-Christian God is jealous: stops us eating from the apple of knowledge or participates in genocide and mass murder, we humans should be critical of him. You think genocide is too strong?

'Then the Lord said to Joshua, "Hold out toward Ai the javelin that is in your hand, for into your hand I will deliver the city." So Joshua held out his javelin toward Ai. As soon as he did this, the men in the ambush rose quickly from their position and rushed forward. They entered the city and captured it and quickly set it on fire.

When Israel had finished killing all the men of Ai in the fields and in the desert where they had chased them, and when every one of them had been put to the sword, all the Israelites returned to Ai and killed those who were in it. Twelve thousand men and women fell that day—all the people of Ai. For Joshua did not draw back the hand that held out his javelin until he had destroyed all who lived in Ai. But Israel did carry off for themselves the livestock and plunder of this city, as the Lord had instructed Joshua.

So Joshua burned Ai and made it a permanent heap of ruins, a desolate place to this day. He hung the king of Ai on a tree and left him there until evening.' (Joshua 8:18)

This murderous spree, condoned by God, continues throughout the book of Joshua, from town to town, killing men, women, children and babies; and hamstringing the horses (cutting their tendons) till all the Canaanites are wiped out.

I really think that us present day humans should, at least, have the same rights that the ancient Greeks had, to attack any immoral and disgraceful action by anybody's God. In other words to blaspheme! (Check Appendix 5 for an extraordinary experiment.)

On the cover we ask, 'does God believe in blasphemy?' It may sound like a joke but I think we can prove that he does not because, if the Bible is true, and written by God, then we have this verse in Mark:

'The high priest asked him, "Are you the Christ, the Son of the Blessed One?"

"I am," said Jesus. "And you will see the Son of Man sitting at the right hand of the Mighty One and coming on the clouds of heaven."

The high priest tore his clothes. "Why do we need any more witnesses?" he asked. "You have heard the blasphemy. What do you think?"

They all condemned him as worthy of death. Then some began to spit at him; they blindfolded him, struck him with their fists, and said, "Prophesy!" And the guards took him and beat him.'
(Mark 14:61)

So it is quite clear that Jesus was put to death because the authorities believed he was blaspheming. I can only conclude that any Christian who accuses anyone of blasphemy must be totally insensitive to the memory of Jesus and by implication to God!

Before we begin a small caveat, this book is not a research document and therefore references are not always given but all information can be found in the books listed in the bibliography. But I must warn you, from the books used for research one was described by the Vatican as, *'Fantastic speculation to new levels of absurdity.'* Another by the respected Jewish author, Arthur Koestler, was attacked by the Israeli ambassador, as *'An anti-Semitic action financed by the Palestinians.'* And the man who translated a third into English, was arrested by Church Authorities, tried for heresy, found guilty and strangled to death. His body was then burnt at the stake. His name was William Tynsdale, and the book he translated into English was the Holy Bible. I hope I will survive the publication of this one.

1

IN THE BEGINNING

In the beginning were the Shepherds. Well the film did initially begin with the Shepherds but we cut the scene before the film was released. What was the Shepherds scene? It was a portrayal of the Christmas Carol, 'While shepherds watch their flocks by night all seated on the ground an Angel of the Lord came down and glory shone around.' Why was it cut? Well let's look at it.

ERIC, TERRY AND MIKE AS SHEPHERDS

1. EXT. HILLSIDE NEAR BETHLEHEM NIGHT
Three shepherds sit round a campfire watching their sheep. Scattered around
are other distant campfires.
MIKE PALIN: I love sheep.
TERRY JONES: So do I. Terrific animals. Terrific.
MIKE: No trouble.
TERRY: No, no trouble.

ERIC IDLE: *Except at shearing. They can play up a bit then, can't they?*

MIKE: *Oh, yeah, but I like that sort of little burst of frenzy they have then, you know. I like it when they get a little bit angry. Shows they're human.*

ERIC: *Oh, yeah. I— I— I'm not saying I dislike them at shearing, you know, but they can be a bit of a handful, can't they?*

MIKE: *Well, so would you be if you had a great pair of scissors snippin' away while someone held your back legs apart. You'd wiggle a bit. You'd kick up a bit of a fuss.*

ERIC: *Yeah, I— I'm not saying I just expect them to stand around in the fields and nibble the grass and look a bit pretty. I— I'm not saying that.*

TERRY: *Oh, but they are pretty, aren't they?*

MIKE: *Yeah.*

Behind them as they talk a mysterious light falls upon a distant hillside and an Angel flies down.

TERRY: *I mean, look at that one over there against the sky. The white of the coat, the little black face against the twinkling stars beyond.*

MIKE: *Yes. Aww. Terrific. Terrific animals. I think, of all God's creatures, sheep have the best offspring.*

TERRY: *Oh, yes. Terrific animals. Terrific.*

ERIC: *Yeah. They're so sure-footed.*

MIKE: *And quick-witted.*

ERIC: *Are they quick-witted?*

MIKE: *Yeah. Yeah. Oh, yeah, they're quite, uh, quick-witted.*

TERRY: *Always cheerful.*

ERIC: *Well, except at shearing.*

MIKE: *Why are you always on about shearing?*

ERIC: *I'm not always on about it, Morris.*

MIKE: *Of all the moments in their little lives, you unerringly put your finger on the one moment where they lose a little bit of dignity. Well, I regard that as cheap, quite honestly.*

TERRY: *Oh, look! Look. One of them's looking up at us. He knows we're talkin' about him.*

ERIC: *Don't get me wrong. I actually like their behaviour at shearing. I actually like them when they get a little bit cross. I find that endearing.*

2

MIKE: *That's the fantastic thing. They're beautiful to look at, well-disposed, quite quick-witted, and yet, tough as nails.*
TERRY: *You know, I can't think of anything I'd rather do than watch sheep.*

The distant Angel flies back up with the magical light. The shepherds oblivious continue.

ERIC: *The only other animals that I would be remotely interested in watching would be cats.*
MIKE: *They don't have flocks of cats.*
ERIC: *No, I— I'm not saying they do.*
MIKE: *Can you imagine a herd of cats waiting to be sheared? Meow! Meow! Woo hoo hoo.*
TERRY: *Shh! Shh! I heard something over there.*
MIKE: *Wolves?*
TERRY: *Could be.*
MIKE: *Where?*
TERRY: *Over there.*
Mike picks up a stone and flings it. There is a thump.
MIKE: *Take that, you buggers!*
JOHN CLEESE: *Oowhh.*
TERRY: *That's not a wolf.*

John and Graham as shepherds appear out of the darkness.

GRAHAM: *What did you do that for!?*
MIKE: *I thought he was a wolf.*
GRAHAM: *You hit him right in the face!*
MIKE: *Well, he shouldn't come snooping 'round like that.*
GRAHAM: *You wait till you hear what we've just seen! The most incredible things just happened!*
JOHN: *Don't tell 'em. Owhh.*
GRAHAM: *We were on the hillside over there when this amazing-*
JOHN: *Don't tell them! They broke my bloody nose!*
GRAHAM: *Can't I tell them about the amazing …*
JOHN: *No! Oohh.*
GRAHAM: *Well, they said we were to tell everybody!*

JOHN: *Not people who break your bloody nose! Come on.*

They head off towards Bethlehem.

ERIC: *Where are you going?*
GRAHAM: *Bethlehem.*
JOHN: *Nowhere! Good night.*
MIKE: *That's right! Leave your sheep! Leave them to the wolves! Call yourselves*
    shepherds?! You're a disgrace to the profession!
TERRY: *What a rotten thing to do.*
MIKE: *Yeah.*
TERRY: *To go and leave those little helpless furry bundles alone on the hillside.*
MIKE: *So they can go down to Bethlehem and get drunk.*

They drop into silence. Eric looks at his wristwatch, (if he had one) then looks up.

ERIC: *Is it A.D. yet?*
MIKE: *Quarter past.*

Here I suppose I should describe the process of how this scene ended up on my proverbial cutting room floor. Perhaps I should add, as this becomes relevant, that we do not actually throw rolls of film on the cutting room floor, other than in anger. All cuts and trims are logged, boxed and moved to vaults where they should be kept indefinitely. This unfortunately, for reasons we will deal with later, has not happened with 'Life of Brian.'

Anyway those of you who are not interested in film structure should skip this section and move on to the meat of the chapter.

For you film students, still reading, here goes.
To cover the main body of the dialogue of the shepherds scene you basically need 3 shots:

Shot 1. Wide shot of our shepherds seated by their fire.
Shot 2. A close shot of all three shepherds talking.
Shot 3. A shot of the sheep they are looking at. This is called a 'cut away' as we
    can use it to cut away from one take of the shepherds talking to another.

Now we have to use Shot 2 for the shepherds' dialogue, close enough to see their faces for the comedy. But the ideal shot to do the gag of the Angel coming down behind them, is in fact Shot 1, the wide shot. Unfortunately we can only use this shot to establish the scene, we cannot stay on it, as this would harm the comedy. So Terry Gilliam was going to have to superimpose the animated angel on to the background of shot 2.

To see the hill behind the shepherds, you really need to shoot this scene Day for Night. Unfortunately if you shoot Day for Night the fire looks strangely dull. There is a moment at dusk when the fire is bright and you can still see the background hills but this only lasts half an hour – not long enough to shoot the scene. So we actually shot at night. The fire looks fine but there is absolute blackness behind the shepherds. At a strategic moment a light was put onto the hill behind. Unfortunately lighting the hill brought it forward, so it looked like it was just behind our shepherds heads. Remember there was no CGI in those days, so in hindsight we should have shot the scene in a studio with a painted background or better still a model background, which Terry G. could then animate his angel on to.

I edited the scene together and played the whole film back in London, with as yet no angel. The film seemed to be working, so we played it to an audience; generally friends. As you can imagine they enjoyed the film and laughed plenty at the shepherds scene (still without angel). Several friends have since said to me that they were really sorry the shepherds were not in the final cut because they enjoyed it so much.

There is a problem with accepting people's laughter at the opening of a Python film as it does not relate to how funny the scene is. What actually happens is that, the audience, laugh in expectation, even if what they are watching is not that funny. For instance when I edited Terry Gilliam's 'Timebandits' and we ran it to an audience there were a couple of gags in the opening scene. The audience 'over' laughed at these, in expectation that this was going to be a funny, 'Python type' film. Then as the film developed into the adventure (it was not a comedy) you could feel the audience starting to worry about where the next laugh was. I removed or played down the gags at the front so that expectations were not raised.

You always have to be careful about what the audience is laughing at. I was asked to go to Hollywood to re-cut the film of the Pythons' stage show, 'Monty Python Live at the Hollywood Bowl'. We had watched the first cut in London and it was not working. One sketch, 'Crunchy Frog' didn't seem to get a laugh at all. It was suggested that I remove it. Out in Hollywood I looked at 'Crunchy Frog' – it seemed to be working fine. Then I realized that it was the scene before Crunchy Frog that was not right. But because the scene before that was good, the audience laughed through the bad scene but were being killed by the time they got to 'Crunchy Frog'. I took out the bad scene and 'Crunchy Frog' worked great. There is actually a nice example of this in 'Brian'. After the 'Biggus Dickus' scene ends, with all the guards laughing (and all the audience hysterical by this point) Brian escapes and runs up a tower. To show that the tower is unfinished we cut to a workman at the top of the tower, hammering. He drops the hammer to show how high we are. The audience who are so wound up by the 'Biggus Dickus' scene, that they burst out laughing. Never in the history of cinema has a man dropping a hammer received such a big laugh.

Back to the shepherds; Terry Gilliam put the animated Angel on to the shot. The idea that this small fluttering thing was going down to a distant hill was not obvious – as there just was no depth in the shot. It looked more like a little fairy coming on to the Shepherds' shoulders. It received the same laughs, or maybe a few less, than before as the angel addition was all a little confusing. So as the shepherds was just one of the two opening pre-credits scenes and did not actually involve Brian directly, it was cut.

Now returning to the blasphemous nature of 'Brian' and its accuracy let's have a look at the shepherds sketch and see how it fits into the biblical story as told in the Holy Book. For clarity, I had better start with a quick history of the Bible.

The story of Jesus is told in the four books of the Gospels, which were written no earlier that AD 65 (30 years after his death) and probably as late, if not later, than AD 100 (63 years after his death). He does appear in other Christian Gospels that were originally held as Holy Scripture, the Gospel of Thomas, The Gospel of Phillip, of Magdalene, of Nicodemus, etc. But when the New Testament was formulated these were not selected and an attempt was made to destroy them. Luckily a monk in Egypt, rather than destroy his Holy Scriptures, buried them in sealed jars. These were found in 1945 and became known as the Nag Hammadi Scrolls. Some of these Gospels offer a different point of view, which we shall refer to later.

The four Gospels that start the Bible's New Testament are named, Matthew, Mark, Luke and John, although these names are fabricated as they were originally untitled and the names suddenly appear around AD 180. Matthew, Mark and Luke are called the synoptic Gospels because they seem to be from a common source with John much later. If you place them in order,

Mark is the first, with Matthew and Luke being slanted re-writes of Mark. From this, you can tell the way Christianity was developing. For instance in Mark, Jesus is clearly a Jew but by the time of John you have phrases like "Jesus said to the Jews" as if He were not Jewish.

Later we shall be dealing with occult imagery, so you need to know that the imagery for Mark is a Lion: look at St. Mark's Square in Venice, the main feature is a lion on a plinth. John is an eagle, Luke is a bull and Matthew is a human with wings. On cathedrals where you see statues of the Apostles, these four are shown with books.

The only Gospel that tells the shepherds' story is Luke.

'And there were shepherds living out in the fields nearby, keeping watch over their flocks at night. An angel of the Lord appeared to them, and the glory of the Lord shone around them, and they were terrified. But the angel said to them, "Do not be afraid. I bring you good news of great joy that will be for all the people. Today in the town of David a Saviour has been born to you; he is Christ the Lord. This will be a sign to you: You will find a baby wrapped in cloths and lying in a manger." Suddenly a great company of the heavenly host appeared with the angel, praising God and saying, "Glory to God in the highest, and on earth peace to men on whom his favour rests."

When the angels had left them and gone into heaven, the shepherds said to one another, "Let's go to Bethlehem and see this thing that has happened, which the Lord has told us about." So they hurried off and found Mary and Joseph, and the baby, who was lying in the manger.'

As Luke and Matthew derive from Mark (the original), any story that is not in Mark but appears in Matthew and Luke must be viewed a little sceptically. And, in fact neither of the original Gospels, Mark or John, contain any story of Jesus' early years. Both start at John the Baptist baptizing Jesus, with Jesus already 30 years old. So one has to wonder why the shepherds have been introduced into the later Gospels.

Whereas Jesus' birthplace is never mentioned in the original Mark, both Luke and Matthew try to place his birth in Bethlehem. Why? Because the Messiah, it was said by the prophets, would be born in Bethlehem in Judea of a virgin (although this is a mistranslation – the Old Testament word just means 'young woman') and be of the bloodline of the Biblical King David.

So both Luke and Matthew have him born of a Virgin in Bethlehem and from the line of David, all the requirements to be the Messiah, which somehow the original Mark seems to have missed. But this is not all; unfortunately these Nativity stories contradict each other on all counts.

Firstly, the genealogy that traces Jesus back to King David does not match as Jesus has different grandfathers on his father's side.

Secondly Matthew has our Holy couple married at the time of the birth, while Luke says that Joseph went to Bethlehem with Mary:

'…who was pledged to be married to him and was expecting a child.'

Thirdly they live in different places. Luke has them living in Nazareth and travelling to Bethlehem where they can't find anywhere to stay, while Matthew has them living in Bethlehem and escaping to Egypt. It is only after their return from Egypt that they go to live in Nazareth.

In Luke they do not escape to Egypt at all. He has them active in Israel while the child is still an infant.

But the worse contradiction of them all is exposed by the 'shepherds scene'. The last words of the scene should be correct.

"Is it AD yet?"
"Quarter past!"

The Anno Domini dating system was devised in 525 by Dionysius Exiguus. It was decided to restart the dating of the world; just like Pol Pot did later in Cambodia, from the beginning of the Khmer Rouge. Both Pol Pot and Rome were making an attempt to wipe out the previous history by burning books as well as half their populations in witch-hunts and killing fields.

There is however a rather daft mistake in our system of dating. There is no year zero! So the dating runs uninterrupted from 1 BC straight to AD 1 which means firstly that there is a year missing in all our historical records and that we celebrated the millennium recently one year too early. It should have been on the eve of 2000 to 2001 not 1999 to 2000.

So the shepherds got it wrong: it was not *'quarter past AD'*; in fact the time would have been *'one year and a quarter hour past AD'*. But here, 'Life of Brian' is still more accurate than the infallible word in the Bible, as Luke and Matthew make an awful hash of the dating.

Matthew's Gospel makes a big play of Herod the Great, who on hearing that Jesus has been born, goes out and kills all the innocent children in an attempt to wipe out this King of the Jews. But Herod the Great was a much maligned, historical character, who we know died in 4 BC. So Matthew is out by more than 4 years if not more.

And Luke what date can we assume from him?

'In those days Caesar Augustus issued a decree that a census should be taken of the entire Roman world. This was the first census that took place while Quirinius was governor of Syria, and everyone went to his own town to register. So Joseph also went up from the town of Nazareth in Galilee, to Bethlehem in Judea, the town of David, because he belonged to the house and line of David. He went there to register with Mary, who was pledged to be married to him and was expecting a child.'

The census of Quirinius was an important event at the time in that it was the precursor to a property and poll tax on the Judeans. It is used by Luke to explain why Mary and Joseph travelled to Bethlehem the town of his birth at that particular time, (when she was in labour) and ended up giving birth in the correct town for the Messiah.

But I am afraid this is all so totally wrong. Firstly the tax was on property and wealth so where you were born was obviously irrelevant. The idea that Joseph left his property in Nazareth to go to Bethlehem and stay in a stable like a pauper, can only have one interpretation. That Joseph was trying to conceal his real wealth in Nazareth. He was a tax evader! I wish I could advance this theory, as I like it a lot, but I'm afraid there is another fact that makes it fall. Nazareth is in Galilee, and the Romans did not tax Galilee, at the time of the census.

The census occurred because after Herod the Great died in 4 BC Israel was divided; with Judea ruled by his son Archelaus and Galilee by another son Antipas (Herod Antipas is the Herod of the crucifixion). Archelaus ruled so badly that he was banished by Caesar to Vienne in Gaul in AD 6. Judea was then put under the direct rule of the Roman Governor of Syria, none other than Publius Sulpcius Quirinius. He then undertook a census, but not the population of the whole world under Caesar's instruction; and not even the population of Israel, but just the population of Judea. Galilee was not his domain and was still taxed by Herod Antipas. So we can date the census no earlier than AD 6 when Quirinius took over control of Judea or possibly as late as AD 7.

Whoops! Someone is definitely wrong here, either Matthew, Luke or Dionysius Exiguus who set the date of Jesus' birth at AD 1. If Dionysius is right then Matthew and Luke are wrong but if Matthew is right then Luke and Dionysius are wrong. And vice versa, if Luke is right then Matthew is wrong. I am sorry to say the Bible has a glaring error. But wait, is the Bible allowed to be wrong? I don't think it is. Is it blasphemy to point out that it is absolutely and definitely wrong? Very likely, because to say the Bible is wrong is offensive to Christians. Can I be found guilty of blasphemy for this statement? Yes! Definitely. I must therefore offer myself up for a hefty fine or imprisonment. At least I should be grateful that today I won't be burnt at the stake. There are though two possible solutions to my dilemma. Firstly, that all blasphemy laws be repealed, or secondly that God performs a post-dated miracle and makes Herod not die till the census of Quirinius. All things are possible to God so don't be surprised (now that the error has been pointed out to Him) if next week, the history books all have this revision suddenly magically appear in them.

Given the considerable contradictions in the Bible about the Nativity – they go to Egypt – they don't go to Egypt. Herod kills all the babies – Herod isn't alive to kill anyone, etc. I suppose we have to ask ourselves, at this early stage, if Jesus was ever born at all? Whether he even existed?

Besides the Christian Gospels, there are only four major non-Christian writers of the late 1st and early 2nd centuries, who according to the Church mention Jesus: Josephus, Tacitus, Suetonius and Pliny the Younger. However, these are generally references to early Christians rather than to a historical Jesus. Here I shall deal with a few examples as some give a clear picture of Israel at the time. The most important is the Jewish historian Josephus and because he is so vital to my argument, I have given his full, fascinating life story in Appendix 1. Josephus was born in Israel just after Jesus' death, and was involved in the war against the Romans in AD 66. Josephus wrote up his experiences in the 'Jewish Wars' and later composed a history book, 'The Antiquity of the Jews'. Between them he mentions Herod the Great, John the Baptist, Pontius Pilate and also tells us exactly what life was like in Israel at the very time of Christ, which is why he is so vital to my argument. But does Josephus mention Jesus? Judge for yourself whether this is written by a dedicated believer in Judaism.

> *'About this time came Jesus, a wise man, if indeed it is appropriate to call him a man. For he was a performer of paradoxical feats, a teacher of people who accept the unusual with pleasure, and he won*

over many of the Jews and also many Greeks. He was the Christ. When Pilate, upon the accusation of the first men amongst us, condemned him to be crucified, those who had formerly loved him did not cease to follow him, for he appeared to them on the third day, living again, as the divine prophets foretold, along with a myriad of other marvelous things concerning him. And the tribe of the Christians, so named after him, has not disappeared to this day.'

Concerns have been raised about the authenticity of the passage, and it is widely held by scholars that, at least, part of the passage has been altered by a later scribe. The language clearly does not sound like Josephus, a Jew, but more like a Christian writing at the time of Constantine, 350 years later. In fact not a single writer before the 4th century – not Justin, Irenaeus, Clement of Alexandria, Tertullian, Cyprian, Arnobius, – in all their defences against pagan hostility, make a single reference to Josephus' wondrous words, which clearly suggests that they were forgeries created at a later date. Some of you may be surprised that Christian scribes were up to forging historical documents. Oh yes, we shall be dealing with these forgeries, which, even exist, in the actual Gospels themselves.

It is suggested that evidence for Jesus comes from the Roman historian Tacitus who when writing about the Fire of Rome in AD 64, blamed it on: *'followers of Christos a person convicted by Pontius Pilate during Tiberius reign.'* Some scholars suggest that even this was added to Tacitus by Christians, at a later date. Actually I believe it is original, but Tacitus does not tell us that these people were Christians. They could well be Jews who were followers of a Christ, which is the Greek word for Messiah, and as John Cleese says in the film, *"He is the Messiah and I should know I've followed a few."* There were lots of people claiming to be the Messiah. One scholar suggests it is Judas the Galilean and that this is the man crucified by Pilate and considered the Messiah by some Jews. What we can say from recent research is that there were people fanning the flames in Rome and they were believers in the 'End of Days', a belief amongst some Jews who thought the Messiah had come. The main reason I personally think Tacitus wrote this section is because he adds in the same paragraph *'it is a most mischievous superstition.'* Not something a Christian would write. But I'm sure Tacitus had no first hand knowledge of Judea at the time.

There are some, well-researched, theories suggesting Jesus never existed. Daniel Unterbrink, in his book 'Judas the Galilean' explored the similarities between Jesus and this other first-century rabbi whose followers were Sacarii zealots. He not only suggests sacarii is the origin of the name Judas Iscariot but found both men cleansed the Temple in Jerusalem, were involved in a Barabbas-style prisoner release, were proclaimed Messiah in Galilee, and both founded new philosophies. Josephus, wrote extensively about the life of Judas the Galilean.

> *'Judas the Galilean was the author of a Jewish sect. These men agree in all other things with the Pharisaic notions; but they have an inviolable attachment to liberty, and say that God is to be their only Ruler and Lord. They also do not value dying any kinds of death, nor indeed do they heed the deaths of their relations and friends, nor can any such fear make them call any man Lord.'* (Antiquities 18:23)

Now although Josephus recorded the crucifixions of two of Judas' sons in AD 45 and the stoning of another, Menahen, in AD 66, he incomprehensibly forgets to tell us how Judas the Galilean himself actually died. And while Josephus does not describe a single action of Jesus he suddenly remembers to tell us of his crucifixion at the hands of Pilate. Unterbrink believes the 'Jesus' passage in Josephus was a substitution for the death of Judas the Galilean. Although this can explain the Christos reference in Tacitus, he goes further and suggests that Jesus was simply a title for Judas the Galilean, and that the Christian Church's Jesus did not actually exist.

Another theory from Timothy Freke and Peter Gandy, in their book, 'The Jesus Mystery', also suggest Jesus never actually existed because of the fact that not one action or belief that Jesus is purported to say or do is original. They are all from the Mystery Religions of the time. The Mysteries are based on the ancient Egyptian death and resurrection God, Osiris, which was spread through the Mediterranean by the Pythagoreans. Water into wine, riding on a donkey with palm leaves waved, turning the other cheek, etc etc.. These writers believe Christianity was a product of Paul a man who never met Jesus but took this Jewish cult to the Gentiles in Rome.

When you take all the information together, in the end it is just personal judgment as to whether you believe he existed, there is no absolute evidence one way or the other. I myself believe he did exist but recognize the validity of the dissenters. I suppose in the end I have three main reasons for believing in him.

1.   Even though history has been doctored, there is one ancient ethnic group called the Mandaeans who in fact believe Jesus existed but are rather disparaging about him. The Mandaeans still speak Aramaic and they accord special status to John the Baptist. They do not consider John to be the founder of their religion but revere him as one of their greatest teachers. Interestingly Mandaeans maintain that Jesus was a false messiah, who perverted the teachings entrusted to him by John.

2.   My second reason is that Mary Magdalene, whom the Roman Church have desperately tried to discredit and would love to write out of history, remained a historical character in the South of France where evidence suggests she lived and died.

3.   My last reason is that a version of Josephus appeared called the Slavonic Josephus. It has sections that, like the original Greek version, have been doctored but there are other passages, of which the Greek text shows no trace. These sections were not written by a Slavic scribe but have been shown to be translations from Greek, not only by the construction of the sentences, but also the Greek original for the curtain of the temple (katapetasma) is retained. The main point is that some of these references are not flattering to Jesus, and secondly, it has John the Baptist functioning as a prophet during the time of Archelaus, (before AD 6). This totally contradicts the Bible because John and Jesus were meant to be the same age and yet in the Slavonic Josephus, John is already an adult at the time of the census that is supposed to have occurred at Jesus' birth. So why would this be forged by a Christian – unless he was an idiot.

But although I believe he did exist I am pretty sure that no angels singing, 'Hosanna in the Highest' descended on a band of sleepy shepherds on a hillside just outside the 'little town' of Bethlehem. So this is as good a reason as any to cut it from the film.

2

THREE WISE MEN

Well not quite 'Wise' men and not necessarily 'Three'. The Bible actually does not say how many there were. The idea that there were three is assumed from the fact that they bring three presents, gold, frankincense and myrrh. Mind you Mike wanted four wise men:

> *The fourth one being continually shut up by the others, who always refer to themselves as the Three Wise Men. 'Four'. 'Ssh!*

The story comes from Matthew and as with the shepherds it is not in the original source Gospel, Mark, so one has to wonder where it came from? There are so many weird and wonderful points that I will quote the section in full. The text is from a recent translation – not the King James version where 'Magi' were incorrectly translated as 'Wise men.'

> *'After Jesus was born in Bethlehem in Judea, during the time of King Herod, Magi from the east came to Jerusalem and asked, "Where is the one who has been born king of the Jews? We saw his star in the east and have come to worship him."*
> *When King Herod heard this he was disturbed, and all Jerusalem with him. When he had called together all the people's chief priests and teachers of the law, he asked them where the Christ was to be born.*
> *"In Bethlehem in Judea," they replied, "For this is what the prophet has written:"*
> *'But you, Bethlehem, in the land of Judah, are by no means least among the rulers of Judah; for out of you will come a ruler who*

will be the shepherd of my people Israel.'

Then Herod called the Magi secretly and found out from them the exact time the star had appeared. He sent them to Bethlehem and said, "Go and make a careful search for the child. As soon as you find him, report to me, so that I too may go and worship him."

After they had heard the king, they went on their way, and the star they had seen in the east went ahead of them until it stopped over the place where the child was. When they saw the star, they were overjoyed. On coming to the house, they saw the child with his mother Mary, and they bowed down and worshiped him. Then they opened their treasures and presented him with gifts of gold and of incense and of myrrh. And having been warned in a dream not to go back to Herod, they returned to their country by another route. When they had gone, an angel of the Lord appeared to Joseph in a dream. "Get up," he said, "take the child and his mother and escape to Egypt. Stay there until I tell you, for Herod is going to search for the child to kill him." So he got up, took the child and his mother during the night and left for Egypt, where he stayed until the death of Herod. And so was fulfilled what the Lord had said through the prophet: "Out of Egypt I called my son."

When Herod realized that he had been outwitted by the Magi, he was furious, and he gave orders to kill all the boys in Bethlehem and its vicinity who were two years old and under, in accordance with the time he had learned from the Magi.'

So many fascinating things in this, one wonders where to start. Perhaps with the opening shot of 'Life of Brian' in the form it was released. A star is animated across the screen.

It is followed by three men on camels. The star comes to a halt over Bethlehem. Now this looked really odd when we did it because stars don't move and then suddenly stop in mid flight! Stars don't actually move anyway, it is the earth that moves making stars travel East to West like the sun. Even the moon and the planets, which may change position from day to day, still mainly move in one night East to West, which is true even for comets. I remember seeing Halley's comet in 1982 and being somewhat disappointed, as it didn't actually whiz across the sky with its tail trailing behind it. It just sat there slowly moving with all the other stars and the tail did not trail behind but pointed towards the sun. I happened to fly to Spain at the time and when I arrived, there was the comet, still hovering in the same place. I suppose what I was expecting was more like a shooting star. Anyway to return to our Biblical star, this little wonder first goes to Jerusalem; stops while they visit Herod the Great; then continues on its journey, till it picks out the stable in Bethlehem. Not a bad trick but surely if anything so amazing happened it would be recorded somewhere. Astronomy and Astrology where important to the ancients and most of the histories written at the time tell us of any strange astral events because they were considered omens. Halley's comet for instance was witnessed as early as 240 BC. And around the time of the Nativity a comet is recorded as appearing over Rome in 12 BC when Marcus Agrippa died. The Chinese also documented this same comet, which we now know, was Halley's comet which has a 75 year cycle. Even our Josephus records the return of Halley's comet in AD 66 at the outset of the Jewish revolt against the Romans and was considered an omen that led to the destruction of the Temple.

But perhaps I am taking it all too literally. You will see from the Matthew quote above that, several times he says that this fulfils such and such a prophecy. And I think the probable reason for the star is just that it fulfils a prophecy in Numbers 24:17

'A star shall come forth from out of Jacob, and a sceptre shall rise out of Israel.'

We know this was a famous text because a later Jewish leader in AD 130 used it to suggest his legitimacy to lead. Of course the star could have just been a miraculous phenomenon visible only to the Magi, and no one else, and obviously if God could manage this tremendous feat and even succeeded in having the star stop over Bethlehem, it would still hardly give the Magi a clue about exactly which stable was hiding the Holy Infant. Therefore the idea of the wise men getting the wrong stable is not at all far fetched. In fact it would be very likely.

But enough about the star, let's deal with the intriguing issue of these wise men who, it says came from the East. They are described only as Magi. And what is a Magi you may well ask? Well if they are arriving from the East they could be coming from Persia where the people are followers of the ancient Zoroastrian religion. And what is a Zoroastrian priest called? A Magi! Followers of Mazda, and here I don't mean the car but Ahura Mazda, the Wise God, The Lord of Wisdom, a divinity who was proclaimed by the prophet Zoroaster as God.

So these guys are not Jews at all but Priests of a totally different religion who worship a totally different God. The religion still exists today, the followers of which are called Parsi. And what are the basic tenants of this religion?

(1)   Belief in one universal and transcendental God.
(2)   Moral and cosmic dualism.
(3)   Prevalence of the eternal law of truth.
(4)   Existence of the bounteous good spirit.
(5)   Operation of the law of consequences.
(6)   Immortality of the soul or afterlife.
(7)   The final triumph of good over evil.

Hang on, this sounds familiar! Maybe the Magi came to convert Jesus to the worship of Mazda, after all Zoroastrianism is of great antiquity. It served as the state religion of Persia (modern Iran) for many centuries, until Islam gradually marginalized it, although it was unable to dethrone the Zoroastrian festivals, which are still celebrated in modern Iran. The political power of the Iranian dynasties lent Zoroastrianism immense prestige in ancient times, and some of its leading doctrines were adopted by other religious systems.

One intriguing belief is number (2) on our list, moral and cosmic dualism. This belief led to the acclaiming, by Magi, of the birth of twin brothers as highly significant. So if the Magi looked into the manger and saw two baby boys they would have instantly dropped to their knees in prayer. Twins! Now you do think I have lost my marbles! But wait: give me a moment to see if there is any evidence for the existence of a twin.

There was in the past a heresy that proposed a twin for Jesus, so I am not the only one to have lost my marbles. There were other believers in the twin idea and some were burnt at the stake.

To believe in the idea of a twin, first we would need evidence that Jesus had a brother. Well, in the Bible it clearly says in the original book of Mark:

> "Isn't this Mary's son and the brother of James, Joseph, Judas and Simon? Aren't his sisters here with us?" And they took offence at him. Jesus said to them, "Only in his hometown, among his relatives and in his own house is a prophet without honour." (Mark 6:3)

These brothers are also mentioned in Matthew 13:55. So he definitely had brothers and sisters, which makes the Roman Church's pronouncement that Mary died and went to Heaven still intact, some trick! The Church attempts to wriggle out of the Biblical evidence by saying things like 'they were Joseph's sons of a previous marriage', or 'Jesus considered everybody, especially the Disciples, as brothers'. Sorry guys, the Biblical statements don't say that; and in fact Acts of the Apostles states quite clearly:

> 'Those present were Peter, John, James and Andrew; Philip and Thomas, Bartholomew and Matthew; James son of Alphaeus and Simon the Zealot, and Judas son of James. They all joined together constantly in prayer, along with the women and Mary the mother of Jesus, and with his brothers.' (Acts 1:13)

Jesus' brother James became the leader of the group after Jesus' death and is considered to be the Teacher of Righteousness mentioned in the Dead Sea scrolls. And sons of other brothers lived on. It was known that a group called the 'Desposyni' had been negotiated with the early Church of Rome. Who the Desposyni were was kept secret till 1964 when Vatican insider, Father Malachi Martin resigned and went to live in New York where he published certain unwelcome facts. One was that, 'Only those persons in the bloodline with Jesus through his mother qualified as Desposyni.'
(Appendix 4 – more revelations from Malachi Martin)

So which brother could be the twin? There is a disciple mentioned in the Bible named Thomas. Now Thomas is not a name; thomas actually comes from the Aramaic word for twin (similar to the Hebrew). Does our Mr. Twin have a proper name? In John's Gospel there is the story of Lazarus: when Jesus is told that Lazarus is dead Thomas gives this peculiar statement.

'Then Thomas, called Didymus said to the rest of the disciples "Let us also go that we may die with him."' (John 11:16)

We will question this weird suicidal statement later but at least for now we have a name for Thomas, he is called Didymus! Or is he? Sorry, no, because didymus is in fact the Greek word for TWIN! So Thomas Didymus translates as Mr. Twin who is called Twin!! This is a lot like 'Brian who is called Brian' either a tautology (an unnecessary or unessential repetition of meaning, using different words that effectively say the same thing twice) or more likely, an attempt to omit the twin's actual name. The plot thickens. Nowhere in the Bible are we given his proper name. Either it was never there or it has been removed.

But we do have other Gospels, as mentioned in the beginning. Many of these were found in 1945 and named the Nag Hammadi Scrolls. One is the Gospel of Thomas! This begins with the statement:

"These are the secret sayings that the living Jesus spoke and Didymus Judas Thomas recorded."

Syrian tradition also states that the apostle's full name was Judas Thomas, or Jude Thomas or Judas the twin.

Judas Thomas! Jesus does have a brother called Judas. Can this possibly be Jesus' twin brother? What about going from the other direction, not who was Jesus twin but who was Thomas' twin. No Biblical text identifies who the twin is of Thomas Didymus, but in the Book of 'Thomas the Contender', again one of the Nag Hammadi Scrolls there is a pretty clear statement by Jesus:

"Now, since it has been said that you are my twin and true companion, examine yourself..."

Halley's comet; Magi with hidden agendas; twins; oh what fun! Could there be more in this one Chapter of Matthew's Gospel, to raise the eyebrows?

You bet your bottom dollar there is! And this time you will really think I have gone totally mad. To protect myself from this claim I need to explain why we believe certain things. My degree was in the sciences and science works by spotting an unexplainable event, coming up with a variety of hypotheses, testing them by experiment and proving one, which then becomes the law. That is until someone finds another anomaly to the law, for which you have to advance a new hypothesis. One of my subjects was Geology where there is the rule of 'conformity', which states that if water freezes today at 0 degrees centigrade then way back in the Ice Age, water still froze at 0 degrees centigrade. So we assume the laws of physics were the same then as they are now. But we can't prove that, it just seems very, very likely. There was also a theory when I was a student that, a meteorite had caused the end of the dinosaur age. I thought it was a reasonable theory but many geologists and biologists pooh-poohed the idea. Slowly more and more evidence has been collected that supports this theory and it is now the accepted norm. But there is no actual scientific experiment we can perform to absolutely prove it.

With history we have the same problem. We can't prove anything. For instance a theory existed that four thousand years ago animalistic humans walked around in skins and banged each other on the head with clubs. So an anomaly pops up, such as discovering the Pyramids are over four thousand years old! One hypothesis advanced is that men from another planet must have built them. An alternative theory is that there were advanced civilizations that existed four thousand years ago and these earthlings used their astounding knowledge and technical ability to build the Pyramids. Which do you believe? You pays your money and you takes your choice. But we tend to work from this premise: which is the most likely? Unfortunately, however attractive the alien theory is, we have now found more evidence that such advanced civilizations did exist. One other problem related to history is that it involves individuals, so by definition it must involve a lot of generalizations. Take a statement like 'the original British were forced into Wales by the invading English', which is generally true, but Wally the Briton decided to stay and make friends with the English. So Wally is an exception. This book makes lots of these generalizations.

Okay, hold on to your seats, this is the theory.
The Magi are originally very ancient descendents of intelligent Giants who lived in Britain. After a meteorite catastrophe, which wiped out most of mankind, the Magi built observatories to watch the skies for future potential hits. They brought people to Britain from less knowledgeable societies to teach them to be Watchers. At a certain point, perhaps having sighted a worrying astrological event, they seem to have left Britain and travelled to Mesopotamia and as Far East as China where they were considered supreme beings.

How's that for a theory? Okay I worded it in the most sensational way I could. I wish I could claim it as my theory but it comes from the research of Knight and Lomas and is reasoned in several books, the first being, 'Uriel's Machine'. Their research stems from:

1. An investigation into archaic Masonic ritual.
2. Their successful attempt to build a stone circle.
3. An analysis of several ancient British sites.
4. A reinterpretation of one of the earliest books ever written and found amongst the Dead Sea scrolls, the 'Book of Enoch'.

I can't reproduce their argument here as it takes a book and a half to list it all. But here are a few little teasers.

THE MAGI WERE VERY ANCIENT

From the term Magi derives the word 'magic and 'magician' in English, 'Magico' in Spanish, 'Magie' in German and 'Mag' in Chinese. How come, at the root of all these languages, (many of which are ancient) are Magi? Could Magi be more ancient than the Pyramids? I would remind you that magicians are traditionally shown in many cultures wearing pointed hats with astrological symbols on them. Magi we know were keen observers of the stars, wise enough to predict eclipses etc.

THE MAGI WERE ORIGINALLY GIANTS

I was in a Temple in Bangkok where there was a mural of a battle. The Thai guy I was with said it was the 'War with the Giants'. I studied the fresco carefully and realized, one side had men, who were slightly bigger than the others. There's the clue, giants may not be our mythical 'Jack and the Beanstalk' type giants but just very tall people in comparison with the local population. We know for instance that northern tribes of Europe were particularly tall in comparison with the people of the Mediterranean and would have been considered giants.

The Irish have myths about early inhabitants who were giants. But where else do these giants appear? What about the Bible?

> *'The Nephilim were on the earth in those days—and also afterward—when the sons of God went to the daughters of men and had children by them.' (Genesis 6:4)*

What are the physical features of the Nephilim? The Bible tells us.

'We saw the Nephilim there (the descendants of Anak come from the Nephilim). We seemed like grasshoppers in our own eyes, and we looked the same to them.' (Numbers 13:33)

Obviously Giants. Also from Genesis 6 comes this odd statement.

'When men began to increase in number on the earth and daughters were born to them, the Sons of God saw that the daughters of men were beautiful, and they married any of them they chose.'

I thought God had only one Son. Who were these other 'Sons of God'? Perhaps this is a description, by primitive people, of tall, more advanced individuals. An example of this is Cortez arriving in Mexico and being considered a God by the Aztecs.

A METEORITE NEARLY WIPED OUT MANKIND

Following the Sons of God statement comes this. Genesis 6:6

'The Lord was grieved that he had made man on the earth, and his heart was filled with pain. So the Lord said, "I will wipe mankind, whom I have created, from the face of the earth."'

This is followed by the story of Noah's flood. Myths of such an event exist around the world and it is even central to Masonic ritual. These are the common characteristics: the sea rose till it covered even the mountains; those who survived were in a boat, an arc, a raft or a canoe (red Indians); it goes dark and rains for many days; a rainbow signifies the end, and they land their boats on a high mountain.

Geneticists tell us that mankind almost suffered extinction. Only 20,000 people survived, not enough to fill a football stadium. We also know that a worldwide event did suddenly wipe out many animal species. American palaeontologist, P. S. Martin wrote, '

'Animals that had been native for millions of years disappeared under circumstances that were suspiciously sudden....

The loss of over 30 genera of large mammals including mammoths, saber-tooth tigers, mastodons, North American horse, tapir, ground sloth and many other species of large animals in north America alone.'

Lake Van 1,670 meters above sea level and not far from Noah's landing place (Mount Ararat) is unbelievably a salt lake! Not only this but to the East lies the Caspian Sea, the largest land locked body of water containing salmon, herrings as well as porpoises and seals! Yet it has never been connected to the oceans. In South America, Lake Titicaca is 3 kilometres up in the Andes yet it contains marine fish such as sea horses. Could these be 'rock pools' left by the invading sea? But how could this be when there isn't enough water to cover the land mass and how could a Noah survive?

On July 9, 1958, a large earthquake struck Alaska which triggered a massive landslide, creating a mega-tsunami wave that rose to a maximum height of 1,720 feet (516 m) at the head of Lituya Bay. The extreme height of the wave and the mechanism of its generation were puzzling. There were questions as to whether there was sufficient water volume in the bay for such an extreme wave to be generated and to reach such an enormous height. But we know it happened because we have witnesses. At the time, there were fishing boats anchored near the entrance to the bay. One boat survived. William Swanson and Howard Ulrich later provided accounts of the fearful event. The wall of water coming towards them: the lifting of the boat like a giant surf ride; the depositing of the boat high up the mountain.

LITUYA BAY SHOWING THE GIANT WAVE PATH THAT SWEPT TREES OFF TO 1720 FEET

So we have a mechanism, a survival method and roughly a time when it happened. Somewhere around the extinction of the mammoths around 10,000 years ago. Is there any record of a strange event at that time?

There was a massive wobble in the earth's magnetic field around 7000 BC signifying a massive geological event. But more specifically, when events like major volcanoes occur there is an increase in nitric acid in the atmosphere. This is recorded in the polar ice layers. There is one such massive increase in atmospheric nitric acid in the year 7640 BC.

Was it a meteorite? The clue comes from the original native stories of the flood. One story from the Ute tribe says how, *'the sun was shivered into a thousand fragments which fell to earth.'*

The Australian Aborigines tell of *'seven sisters who fell from a hole in the sky'*.

But from Peru, a survivor who was not in a boat but high in the Andes and obviously saw the whole event, gives us the clearest picture.

> *'...the animals were staring in the direction of the sun. When he lifted his hand to his eyes, he saw a cluster of stars surrounding the sun even in daylight. He took his family high into the mountain and just as they reached the summit the waters of the sea rose up in a mighty wave and swamped the land and the sun was hidden by a great darkness. It was many days before the waters receded.'*

In 1994 an identical event occurred when comet Shoemaker-Levy 9 broke up into fragments as it passed near Jupiter's gravity and finally the pieces, with diameters no more than two kilometres wide and glowing like a string of pearls, crashed into Jupiter creating plumes of debris and fireballs larger than the Earth.

Evidence that seven fragments of a comet hit Earth around 7500 BC has been shown by Edith and Alexander Tollman of the Institute of Geology, Austria. They studied the distribution of Tektites, which are igneous rocks that have been scattered into the atmosphere, freezing suddenly in the upper layers creating flattened and rounded spheres. They are known to be the products of high-energy comet impacts. From these studies we know exactly where the seven pieces struck, five in the sea! And we can calculate what would have happened.

Their arrival would appear like burning mountains. Heat then massive tsunami. Darkness from the dust and water vapour thrown into the atmosphere. The water vapour cools and drops as torrential rain for days. Significant rainbows appear as the sun breaks through! Sound familiar?

Piecing all this information together is the grandfather of Noah, Enoch. Found amongst the Dead Sea scrolls is the ancient book of Enoch, strangely used in Masonic rituals which predate its appearance,

> *'and I saw seven stars like great mountains and burning with fire… descend and cast themselves down from heaven… And the spirit of the sea was driven forward amid the mountains… then the water began to run down and the earth became visible… and darkness retired and light appeared.'*

Give or take a few errors in the calendar, the 10,000th anniversary of this event is the infamous ancient prediction of the end of the world, 2012.

THE MAGI BUILT OBSERVATORIES

In Britain there are over two thousand stone circles and many astrologically aligned burrows. Knight and Lomas built their own and realized these megalithic celestial calculators could accurately predict the positions of stars in the night skies, moon cycles, equinoxes and solstices. Additionally, they could measure the size of the earth, the distance to the moon and even forecast the arrival of comets.

One site, which predates the Pyramids of Ghiza by at least 1000 years, is the Thornborough henge (North Yorkshire). Researchers at Newcastle University have found the site is one of the earliest major monuments aligned to the constellation Orion. These 5,500-year-old earthworks, north of Ripon, like the Egyptian pyramids mirror the three stars of Orion's belt in the constellation of Orion. The banks of the henge are coated in brilliant white gypsum to appear star-like. Senior lecturer at the university, Dr Jan Harding said a three dimensional model was used to confirm the stellar alignments of the henge, which dates back to the Neolithic period. Now would you believe, the word Nephilim although of uncertain origin, is believed by some scholars to be similar to the Aramaic word nephila, which is the name of the constellation of Orion, and therefore Nephilim seems to mean 'those from Orion'. Could they be our British Watchers who built the replica of Orion at Thornborough?

MAGI BROUGHT PRIMITIVES TO BRITAIN TO TEACH THEM ASTRONOMY

The Bible lists the birth and deaths of the descendants of Adam. But Enoch is the only one who does not die.

> 'When Enoch had lived 65 years, he became the father of Methuselah... Enoch walked with God; then he was no more, because God took him away.' (Genesis 5:21)

Where did God take Enoch? Here we need to look at the Book of Enoch. It consists of quite distinct sections. The first 3 are:

> The Book of the Watchers (Enoch 1 – 36)
> The Book of Parables of Enoch (1 Enoch 37 – 71)
> The Book of the Heavenly Luminaries. (Enoch 72 – 82)

(It has also been suggested that another Dead Sea scroll should be added here, 'The Book of Giants'.)

The first part of the Book of Enoch describes the fall of the Watchers, the angels who fathered the Nephilim. The remainder of the book describes Enoch's visit to Heaven in the form of travels, visions and dreams, and his revelations. Knight and Lomas have calculated that Enoch was taken by an Angel (that Enoch calls Uriel) to Britain. They calculate this from Enoch's description of the day's length over the year.

(Around the Mediterranean day lengths hardly change). He also sees the light of the sun travel around the Northern horizon, which we see in Britain but any further North the sun would not set at all. In Britain, Uriel shows Enoch how to be a Watcher and understand the way the Megalithic sites work. As with Stonehenge the stars are plotted through, what Enoch describes as, windows. (Stonehenge as a stone structure was not built then, but wooden post-holes of an original wooden structure are there). There is even a clear description of a visit to the Neolithic site of Newgrange on the Boyne Valley in Ireland.

THE MAGI LEAVE BRITAIN

In the ancient 'History of the British Kings' there is the story of Brutus, who it is said, named Britain. He set sail from Greece around 900 BC where he was told to travel:

> *'Beyond the setting of the sun, past the realms of Gaul, there lies an island in the sea, once occupied by Giants. Now it is empty.'*

After several adventures Brutus and his ships finally arrive:

> *'At that time the island of Britain was called Albion. It was uninhabited except for a few Giants. It was however, most attractive. When they explored the different districts, they drove the Giants whom they had discovered, to the caves in the mountains. Brutus called the land Britain after his name. Corineus, his General, called his region Cornwall. His son Kamber received Kambria, the region now called Wales and his other son, Albanactus took Albany, the area of Scotland.'*

THE MAGI TRAVEL SOUTH EAST

Where did the Giants go? Around 4000 BC a new race arrived in Mesopotamia. We call them the Sumerians. These mysterious Sumerians said they came from a land called Dilmun and they spoke a language unrelated to anything else. The explorer Thor Hyerdahl explains:

> *'From them we learn to write, from them we got the wheel, the art of forging metals, of building arches, of weaving cloth, of sowing seeds. They invented units of measure. They initiated real mathematics, made exact astronomical observations, kept track of time and devised a calendar system.'*

In the Book of Enoch the Watchers are accused of teaching men the secrets of Enchantment and Astronomy.

So we now have our Magi in Mesopotamia, where they are at the time of Christ: magicians who understood the secrets of enchantment and astronomy.

One other small point, some giant Magi went to one of the safest places on the planet, where they might be protected from a comet strike, Xinjiang Uigur in western China. A plateau encircled by the huge mountains of Tibet and Mongolia. Well believe it or not, there desiccated in the salty desert sands, wonderfully preserved, are our Giant Magi. For years Chinese archaeologists have been exhuming dozens of corpses from ritual burial sites, many over 4000 years old. They are extraordinary well preserved and as surprised archaeologist

Dr. Elizabeth Barber observed:

> *'The mummies were not Chinese, they had high-bridged noses, large eye sockets, dental overbite, blond or red hair, and many had full beards.'*

CHERCHIN MAN (see fig 2 for full colour)

The local archaeologists named them Cherchin Man and described them as 'giants of their time' as the men were 6' 6" tall and the women 6' 2".

Dr. Barber, an expert on ancient fabric and textiles, was astonished to find:

> *'They had excellent weaving skills, skills that had previously been assumed to have developed in Egypt. They also wove a kind of patterned band known mainly in Japan called kumihimo. The dominant weave of the Cherchin people was diagonal twill as in the material of a Scottish kilt.... Not only does it look like Scottish tartans but it also has the same weight, feel and initial thickness as kilt cloth.'*

Now hang on to your hats for her next bit:

> *'A female wore a terrifically tall conical hat, just like those we depict on witches riding broomsticks, or on medieval wizards intent on their magical spells. Our witches and wizards got their tall pointy hats from just where we also got the words magician and magic, namely Persia. Magus denotes a priest or sage of the Zoroastrian religion.'*

And remember the Welsh national costume has women with similar tall conical hats.

Dr. Barber then concludes – in HER WORDS not mine:

'Magi distinguished themselves with high hats, they also professed knowledge of astronomy, astrology and medicine, or how to control the weather by potent magic and how to contact the spirit world.'

Furthermore, the old Chinese word for a court magician was 'mag'. The Chinese symbol for a 'mag' is a cross with slightly splayed ends, identical to that used by the Knights Templar – (but that's another story).

This glimpse into Knight and Lomas' work has taken our story of the three Magi visiting Jesus over an impossible spread of distance and time and mind blowingness.

But before we complete that journey another small fact has to be confronted. In Spain Los Tres Reyes, (The three Kings) as they call them, are more important to children than the Nativity because they bring the kids presents. The day they arrive is the eve of Epiphany, which is the night of the 5th of January. What is this epiphany that is being celebrated? Strangely the eve of Epiphany is significant in many customs. Even in Britain, people sing the 12 days of Christmas and say it is custom not to take the Christmas decorations down before the 6th and unlucky to leave them up longer. Many English villages have odd customs that are carried out on the 6th January. What is the epiphany behind Epiphany? Well Jesus' birth date was traditionally celebrated on the eve of Epiphany and was moved to the 25th December, to fit in with Roman sun worshippers. So one is not celebrating Jesus' birth on the 25th December but the mid winter solstice.

Given all these oddities within the story of the Magi how does 'Life of Brian' treat the subject? Blasphemously? Not at all, the three wise men are shown in the Christian form: not coming from Persia but representing different areas of the world, one for instance being black. Of course there is one point in the dialogue that matches something of the real Magi; Brian's mother asks them,

"What star sign is he?"

"Capricorn," answers a Magi, truly being one of their known areas of expertise.

But is the icon of the Holy family at the end of the scene, blasphemous?

Again the film uses the very traditional Christian imagery because the gag demands that the audience quickly understand that these people in the next stable are Joseph, Mary and the infant Christ. We even play Holy majestic choirs and around their heads are mystical halos, so loved by Christian painters.

I should add though, that the halo is not originally a Christian image. In the medieval book, 'Christian Iconography' by the writer Didron, it describes three Byzantine miniatures of the tenth century, in which it is actually Satan who is depicted with a nimbus – a halo. This is because the halo was obviously the recognized sign of the 'Sun God' in Pagan times. The Christian authorities would later misappropriate the nimbus for Christ and the Saints just as they did with 25th December.

3

WHO'S WHO

Andre Jaquemin started doing Python soundtracks in a shed, lined with egg boxes, in his back garden. He and his partner Dave Howman are wonders at musical parodies. They were given the brief to create an intro that sounded like a Shirley Bassey type Bond song. They sat down at the piano and in ten minutes it was written. They wondered who could sing it and remembered a young 17 year old who had turned up at their studio with a demo tape. She was Welsh and Shirley Bassey is Welsh, and so without even an audition, Sonia Jones got the job. They did a demo recording, which Terry Gilliam liked, so they set up a professional recording session. Unfortunately Terry didn't think the professional track was as good as the demo, so that is what goes over the credits sequence. While these are running we should for later reference, credit the leading players in the history of the Israelites. The dates are approximations.

JOSEPH (1,700 BC)– sold by his brothers into Egypt.

12 TRIBES – arise from the brothers of Joseph who join him in Egypt.

MOSES (1,500 BC)- leads the 12 tribes out of Egypt into the desert.

JOSHUA – 40 years later Joshua conquers Canaan, kills the population and settles the 12 tribes into the area.

SAUL (1,200 BC) – from the tribe of Benjamin, becomes King.

DAVID – from the tribe of Judah, usurps the throne.

SOLOMON (1,000 BC) – David's son, builds the temple.

NEBUCHADNEZZAR (650 BC)– Ruler of Babylon, conquers Judea and destroys the Temple exiling many Jews to Babylon.

CYRUS (600 BC) – First Zoroastrian Persian Emperor; conquers Babylon and releases the Jews. Authorizes the rebuilding of the Temple.

ALEXANDER THE GREAT (350 BC) – Conquers the lot.

PTOLEMY (300 BC) – Alexander's general, became King of Egypt and Israel.

ANTIOCHUS (200 BC) – Conquers Israel and rules harshly.

JUDAS MACCABEE (150 BC) – revolts against Antiochus and makes himself
    King and Chief priest. Restores Jewish worship in the Temple.

HYRCANUS (60 BC) – invites Roman General Pompey in to help with his
    dispute with his brother. Pompey takes Israel for Rome.

PHARISEES, SADDUCEES & ESSENES. The main religious groups of the
    time. Pharisees gave rise to modern rabbinical Judaism. Sadducees were
    followers of a Priestly temple elite. Essenes were an ascetic group who
    had similar beliefs to Jesus.

HEROD THE GREAT (20 BC) – made King of Israel by the Romans. Renovates
    the Temple.

HEROD ANTIPAS (AD 10) – Son of Herod the Great who ruled Galilee at the
    time of Pilate.

TITUS (AD 70) – puts down the rebellion of the Israelites. And destroys the
    Temple.

HADRIAN (AD 140) – Puts down the last rebellion and expels the Jews from
    the area. Renames Jerusalem Aelia Capatolina and the land as Palestine.
    It remained so till 1947.

While we are crediting leading players, perhaps we should investigate the grandiose title given to Jesus, 'King of the Jews'. The first words attributed to our incredible Three Magi in the Bible are:

"Where is the one who has been born king of the Jews?"

'King of the Jews' is also used by Pilate, at the time of Jesus' death. Was He a King of the Jews in waiting? And is this why Herod would want to kill him?

    Although Herod brought stability and prosperity to Israel he was not considered to be a proper Jew as he was an Idumaean. To gain legitimacy as a King of Israel, Herod married a second wife Miriam who was a Princess from the Royal line. (You will enjoy the fact that Herod's first wife had the unlikely name of Doris). This second marriage didn't work out and he ended up killing her and his children by her, who were plotting to take over the throne. For this reason he is often said to be a monster but, in fact, this is par for the course in

Israel. Wise Solomon, it is said in the Bible, bumped off his brothers and any descendant of Saul who might threaten his position. And David had his rebellious son, Absalom, killed, producing that great image of Absalom trying to escape by horse when his hair gets caught in a tree and David's General rides up and lops off his head. So if Jesus had any legitimate claim to the throne it would make sense to 'leg it out' of Israel and go to live in Egypt. But what claim could he have on the throne. Perhaps as Luke and Matthew pronounce, he was from the line of David. Of course this blood link to the Davidic Royal family comes through his father Joseph, but after Luke and Matthew give Jesus' genealogy from King David, both say Mary was a virgin so he was the child of God! Which obviously does not make him Joseph's son and therefore gives him no claim to the throne of Israel. Given the contradictory statements by these two Gospels, we have a choice, either he was the Son of God and had no claim to the throne or he was the son of Joseph and did have a legitimate claim to the throne. We know that Jesus was not the Son of God for 300 years after his death, when at the Council of Niceae it was decided by a vote that he was in fact God's Son (say 43 for and 37 against). I don't buy this vote so for me he was the son of Joseph and therefore had a claim to the throne.

Let's follow the genealogy of Joseph as listed in the Bible. There is one in Matthew but I like the one in Luke (which differs substantially) and is a veritable 'who's who' of Biblical characters ending with Noah and Adam.

Luke 3:23
Now Jesus himself was about thirty years old when he began his ministry.
He was the son, so it was thought, of Joseph,
the son of Heli,
the son of Matthat,

There are then 40 unknown 'sons of' till you get to the interesting ones:

the son of Mattatha,
the son of Nathan,
the son of David,
the son of Jesse,
the son of Obed,
the son of Boaz,

the son of Salmon,
the son of Nahshon,
the son of Amminadab,
the son of Ram,
the son of Hezron,
the son of Perez,
the son of Judah,
the son of Jacob,
the son of Isaac,
the son of Abraham,
the son of Terah,
the son of Nahor,
the son of Serug,
the son of Reu,
the son of Peleg,
the son of Eber,
the son of Shelah,
the son of Cainan,
the son of Arphaxad,
the son of Shem,
the son of Noah,
the son of Lamech,
the son of Methuselah,
the son of Enoch,
the son of Jared,
the son of Mahalalel,
the son of Kenan,
the son of Enosh,
the son of Seth,
the son of Adam,
the son of God.

Some genealogy! The TV program 'Who do you think you are?' traces back the genealogy of celebrities, often finding embarrassingly, disreputable, ancestors. What about making Jesus our celebrity and checking to see if He has anyone embarrassing amongst His ancestors? Let's start with the father of the tribe of Judah, Judah himself.

'Judah met the daughter of a Canaanite man named Shua. He married her and lay with her; she became pregnant.'

So the tribe of Judah (from where the word Jew comes) are hardly Israelites but half Canaanite. And in fact in Jewish culture you are Jewish through your mother not your father, so one has to say the tribe of Judah are not Jewish at all. But even more surprising is David's great grandfather, Boaz. We find in Matthew's genealogy who the mother was.

'Salmon the father of Boaz, whose mother was Rahab,'

So Salmon was married to Rahab, a very interesting lady who has a rather chequered history.

'Then Joshua son of Nun secretly sent two spies from Shittim. "Go, look over the land," he said, "especially Jericho." So they went and entered the house of a prostitute named Rahab and stayed there.' (*Joshua 2:1*)

Yes this prostitute is our Rahab who helps the Israelites raid Jericho. This area lies beside the Great Rift Valley where the African Plate is splitting into two new separate plates. Not surprisingly Jericho was hit by an earthquake and left vulnerable to attack.

'When the trumpets sounded, the people shouted, and at the sound of the trumpet, when the people gave a loud shout, the wall collapsed; so every man charged straight in, and they took the city. They devoted the city to the Lord and destroyed with the sword every living thing in it—men and women, young and old, cattle, sheep and donkeys.' (*Joshua 6:20*)

Let's pause here to consider God's role in this mass murder of vulnerable people hit by an earthquake. Let me point you to Numbers 31:7 where God is complicit in another disgraceful mass murder. In my film, 'Chemical Wedding', Simon Callow, playing Aleister Crowley, quotes this, for which I took stick for daring to mention what is in the Bible. (Check Appendix 5 for an extraordinary experiment.) But continuing with Joshua 6:

THE LIFE OF ~~BRIAN~~ *JESUS*

'Joshua said to the two men who had spied out the land, "Go into the prostitute's house and bring her out and all who belong to her, in accordance with your oath to her." So the young men who had done the spying went in and brought out Rahab, her father and mother and brothers and all who belonged to her. They brought out her entire family and put them in a place outside the camp of Israel. Then they burned the whole city and everything in it, but they put the silver and gold and the articles of bronze and iron into the treasury of the Lord's house. But Joshua spared Rahab the prostitute, with her family and all who belonged to her, because she hid the men Joshua had sent as spies to Jericho—and she lives among the Israelites to this day.'

It clearly states in the Bible that David is a descendent of this prostitute and sneak who led the Israelites in, to murder all her neighbours.

Boaz, the father of Obed, whose mother was Ruth,
Obed the father of Jesse, and Jesse the father of King David.'

So, by implication, Jesus is also inauspiciously descended from this rather unpleasant prostitute! But also if Rahab lived in Jericho then she was probably not a Hebrew at all but like Judah's wife, Shua, a Canaanite. The Canaanites were also called Philistines, the word for 'sea people'; these are thought to be the Phoenicians.

Perhaps all this Philistine blood explains why David fought with the Philistines against the Israelites. Yes you read that right. You will probably be surprised to hear this hero of the Jewish people usurped the throne aided by 'the enemy'. All right, the one story you know is that David fought the Philistine giant, Goliath. Sorry, that is a story stolen from the battle of Gob.

'In another battle with the Philistines at Gob, Elhanan son of Jaare-Oregim the Bethlehemite killed Goliath the Gittite, who had a spear with a shaft like a weaver's rod.' (Samuel 21:19)

David is the son of Jesse so this appears to be another person killing Goliath. Something is very fishy here but there is no confusion about which side David is on in the battle of Jezreel.

'The Philistines gathered all their forces at Aphek, and Israel camped by the spring in Jezreel. As the Philistine rulers marched with their units of hundreds and thousands, David and his men were marching at the rear with Achish. The commanders of the Philistines asked, "What about these Hebrews?"

Achish replied, "Is this not David, who was an officer of Saul King of Israel? He has already been with me for over a year, and from the day he left Saul until now, I have found no fault in him." (Samuel 29)

It is also clear that both David and Solomon were not actual followers of the Jewish God, Yahweh.

'The high places that were east of Jerusalem on the south of the Hill of Corruption—the ones Solomon King of Israel had built for Ashtoreth the vile goddess of the Sidonians, for Chemosh the vile god of Moab, and for Molech the detestable god of the people of Ammon.'

So we have Jesus descended from a prostitute, a traitor and a believer in vile Gods. Interestingly, going back to the family tree from Rahab to David we have:

'Salmon, the father of Boaz, whose mother was Rahab,
Boaz the father of Obed, whose mother was Ruth,
Obed the father of Jesse, and
Jesse the father of King David.'

Obed's mother is Ruth, what do we know about Ruth?

'So Naomi returned from Moab accompanied by Ruth the Moabitess, the widow of her dead son.' (Ruth 1:18)

When they arrive back in Israel, Ruth gleans Boaz' fields with the rest of his servant girls, then one day there is a lovely romantic moment:

'When Boaz had finished eating and drinking and was in good

spirits, he went over to lie down at the far end of the grain pile. Ruth approached quietly, uncovered his feet and lay down. "Who are you?" he asked. "I am your servant Ruth," she said. "Spread the corner of your garment over me.'

So Boaz married Ruth a Moabitess. Moab is the historical name for a mountainous strip of land running along the eastern shore of the Dead Sea. The Moabites were a historical people, whose existence is attested to by numerous archaeological findings, most notably the Mesha Stele, which describes the Moabite victory over the son of King Omri of Israel. In fact the Moabites were often in conflict with their Israelite neighbours to the west. What about their origin? Sitting right on the Great Rift Valley, were the cities of Sodom and Gomorra, which were destroyed in what sounds like a 'Pompeii type' volcano explosion. One survivor was Abraham's nephew, Lot, and his two daughters, but unfortunately his wife never made it; she was turned into a pillar of salt.

'Lot and his two daughters left Zoar and settled in the mountains, for he was afraid to stay in Zoar. He and his two daughters lived in a cave. One day the older daughter said to the younger, "Our father is old, and there is no man around here to lie with us, as is the custom all over the earth. Let's get our father to drink wine and then lie with him and preserve our family line through our father." That night they got their father to drink wine, and the older daughter went in and lay with him. He was not aware of it when she lay down or when she got up... So both of Lot's daughters became pregnant by their father. The older daughter had a son, and she named him Moab; he is the father of the Moabites of today.' (Genesis 19:30)

Incest! The plot thickens. Back to our genealogy,

'David was the father of Solomon, whose mother had been Uriah's wife.'

Who was Uriah's wife?

'One evening David got up from his bed and walked around on the

roof of the palace. From the roof he saw a woman bathing. The woman was very beautiful, and David sent someone to find out about her. The man said, "Isn't this Bathsheba, the daughter of Eliam and the wife of Uriah the Hittite?" Then David sent messengers to get her. She came to him, and he slept with her…. The woman conceived and sent word to David, saying, "I am pregnant."' (2 Samuel 11:2)

This adds another questionable relative to Jesus. Now the notorious David rather sneakily 'does in' for Uriah.

'In the morning David wrote a letter to Joab and sent it with Uriah. In it he wrote, "Put Uriah in the front line where the fighting is fiercest. Then withdraw from him so he will be struck down and die." So while Joab had the city under siege, he put Uriah at a place where he knew the strongest defenders were. When the men of the city came out and fought against Joab, some of the men in David's army fell; moreover, Uriah the Hittite died.' (2 Samuel 11:14)

Why anyone would want to be related to this bastard David, is beyond me. And why any Jew should admire David when even his son Absalom rebelled against this awful despot is astonishing. It reminds me of the Northern Irish Protestants who have celebration marches for King William's victory at the battle of the Boyne. What they seem to forget is that non-conformist Protestants, like the Revered Ian Paisley, were persecuted by William of Orange and a quarter of a million of them left Ireland to go to America to escape his persecution. If Reverend Paisley had performed a marriage ceremony during the time of William of Orange he would have been jailed. Why don't people bother to read and learn from history? It could save a lot of problems, especially in Israel and Ireland?

Despite the fact that Jesus is related to some very questionable people he does still seem to have some claim to the throne. Of course to be King of the Jews you have to be anointed by a prophet or priest. Samuel anoints the first King of Israel, Saul.

'Then Samuel took a flask of oil and poured it on Saul's head and kissed him, saying, "Has not the Lord anointed you leader over his inheritance?"' (Samuel 10:1)

Nathaniel similarly anoints David and of course during the Coronation of British kings this ancient Jewish custom of anointing is also performed. I should add that traditionally the male British heirs to the throne are circumcised. Prince Charles was circumcised in Buckingham Palace by Rabbi Jacob Snowman, official Mohel of the London Jewish community.

So anointing is a major event in King making. This, in fact, is what 'the Messiah' means – the anointed one. And Christ is just the Greek form of 'the anointed one.' So if Jesus is the Christ, 'the 'anointed one', who could have anointed him?

> *'A woman came to him with an alabaster jar of very expensive perfume, which she poured on his head as he was reclining at the table.' (Matthew 26:7)*

And John tells us the name of this woman, who Matthew is so coy about. Although he now becomes quite coy about where she poured the perfumed oil.

> *'Jesus arrived at Bethany, where Lazarus lived, whom Jesus had raised from the dead. Here a dinner was given in Jesus' honour. Martha served, while Lazarus was among those reclining at the table with him. Then Mary took about a pint of pure nard, an expensive perfume, she poured it on Jesus' feet and wiped his feet with her hair. And the house was filled with the fragrance of the perfume.' (John 12)*

So the unbelievable answer to 'who anointed Jesus' is Mary Magdalene! And this is the only description of any sort of anointment anywhere, that makes Jesus be able to claim the title, 'Christ', the 'anointed one'.

Plenty has been written about this – that perhaps Mary was a high Priestess etc.. but I leave you to fathom out the incredible possibilities.

Again, as we will be dealing with occult imagery, paintings of Mary Magdalene show her with an alabaster jar for her perfumed oil. She is often dressed in red and green or red and gold with red hair as a scarlet woman, since the Roman Church decided to make her a prostitute.

One last point on this, the Gospel of Mark tells the same story.

> *'While he was in Bethany, reclining at the table in the home of a*

man known as Simon the Leper, a woman came with an alabaster
jar of very expensive perfume, made of pure nard. She broke the
jar and poured the perfume on his head.' (Mark 14:3)

This is followed by:

'Then Judas Iscariot, one of the Twelve, went to the chief priests
to betray Jesus to them. They were delighted to hear this and
promised to give him money. So he watched for an opportunity to
hand him over.' (Mark 14:10)

And then comes an account of the Last Supper. I believe the anointing
took place at the Last Supper, in Bethany (as almost every crucial event takes
place there). It was a replica of Psalm 23:

'Thou preparest a table before me in the presence of mine enemies:
thou anointest my head with oil; my cup runneth over.'

As quoted, this dinner was mentioned in John's Gospel with a clear
description of who is reclining at the table with Jesus.

'Jesus arrived at Bethany, where Lazarus lived, whom Jesus had
raised from the dead. Here a dinner was given in Jesus' honour.'
(John 12:2)

So either Jesus is having a lot of suppers in Bethany, or there is only one,
with a lot more people present than usual. There is a comedy sketch by the
Pythons of Michelangelo explaining to the Pope about his painting of the 'Last
Supper'.

POPE: I'm not happy about your painting of the last Supper.
MICHELANGELO: Oh, dear. It took me hours
POPE: Not happy at all.
MICHELANGELO: Is it the jello you don't like?
POPE: No.
MICHELANGELO: Oh, I know, you don't like the kangaroo?
POPE: What kangaroo?

JOHN AS POPE AND ERIC AS MICHELANGELO

MICHELANGELO: No problem, I'll paint him out.

POPE: I never saw a kangaroo!

MICHELANGELO: Uuh...he's right in the back. I'll paint him out! No sweat, I'll make him into a disciple.

POPE: Aah.

MICHELANGELO: All right?

POPE: That's the problem.

MICHELANGELO: What is?

POPE: The disciples.

MICHELANGELO: Are they too Jewish? I made Judas the most Jewish.

POPE: No, it's just that there are twenty-eight of them.

MICHELANGELO: Oh, well, another one will never matter, I'll make the kangaroo into another one.

POPE: No, that's not the point.

MICHELANGELO: All right. Well, I'll lose the kangaroo. Be honest, I wasn't perfectly happy with it.

POPE: That's not the point. There are twenty-eight disciples!

MICHELANGELO: Too many?

POPE: Well, of course it's too many!

MICHELANGELO: Yeah, I know that, but I wanted to give the impression of a real last supper. You know, not just any old last supper. Not like a last meal or a final snack. But you know, I wanted to give the impression of a real mother of a blow-out, you know?

POPE: There were only twelve disciples at the last supper.

MICHELANGELO: Well, maybe some of the others ones came along afterw...

POPE: *There were only twelve altogether.*

MICHELANGELO: *Well, maybe some of their friends came by, you know?*

POPE: *Look! There were just twelve disciples and our Lord at the last supper. The Bible clearly says so.*

MICHELANGELO: *No friends?*

POPE: *No friends.*

MICHELANGELO: *Waiters?*

POPE: *No.*

MICHELANGELO: *Cabaret?*

POPE: *No!*

MICHELANGELO: *You see, I like them, they help to flesh out the scene, I could lose a few, you know I could...*

POPE: *Look! There were only twelve disciples at...*

MICHELANGELO: *I've got it! I've got it! We'll call it "The Last But One Supper"!*

POPE: *What?*

MICHELANGELO: *Well there must have been one, if there was a last supper there must have been a one before that, so this, is the "Penultimate Supper"! The Bible doesn't say how many people were there now, does it?*

POPE: *No, but...*

MICHELANGELO: *Well there you are, then!*

POPE: *Look! The last supper is a significant event in the life of our Lord, the penultimate supper was not! Even if they had a conjurer and a mariachi band. Now, a last supper I commissioned from you, and a last supper I want! With twelve disciples and one Christ!*

MICHELANGELO: *One?!*

POPE: *Yes one! Now will you please tell me what in God's name possessed you to paint this with three Christs in it?*

MICHELANGELO: *It works, mate!*

POPE: *Works?*

MICHELANGELO: *Yeah! It looks great! The fat one balances the two skinny ones.*

POPE: *There was only one Redeemer!*

MICHELANGELO: *Ah, I know that, we all know that, what about a bit of artistic license.*

POPE: *Well one Messiah is what I want!*

MICHELANGELO: *I'll tell you what you want, mate! You want a bloody photographer! That's you want. Not a bloody creative artist to crease you up...*

POPE: *I'll tell you what I want! I want a last supper with one Christ, twelve disciples, no kangaroos, no trampoline acts, by Thursday lunch, or you don't get paid!*

MICHELANGELO: *Bloody fascist!*

Perhaps the supper from the Gospel of John (12:2) with Lazarus, Mary and Martha present, is from the 'Penultimate Supper' because, if it is not the penultimate supper, then Martha, Mary and Lazarus were at the 'Last Supper'. With maybe even three Jesuses! So you think three Jesuses is definitely not a possibility – just look at Appendix 2 where you will find nineteen Jesuses.

4

BLESSED ARE THE CHEESEMAKERS

One of our more grandiose images follows the credits, a crowd swarming up the mount at sunset to hear a sermon from Christ. Actually the shot wasn't planned and came about purely by accident. The crew had been shooting all day on a deserted hillside when at 4pm the extras suddenly disappeared. With most being local women, the excuse was that they had to go home and cook their husbands' dinners.

"But we haven't finished shooting!" yelled Terry Jones, sending his assistant director off to herd the largely unwilling crowd back up the hillside. Eric was beside Terry and tapped him on the shoulder. "It looks terrific," he said. "Turn the camera on them quick." Terry frantically spun round and reeled off as much footage as he could of this mass migration of people scrambling back up the mount and that's the shot we used.

There then follows the only shot of Jesus in the film. We could have had a lot of fun with this. Make him a black man, and upset all the racist Christians, or a fat man, and upset everybody.

The Pythons had sat down and watched most of the Biblical films while they were writing. 'King of Kings', 'Barabbas', 'The Greatest Story Ever Told'. Mike described the portrayal of the baddies as great but:

'The nearer you get to Jesus the more oppressive becomes the cloying tone of reverence. Everyone talks slower and slower and Jesus generally comes out of it all as the world's dullest man, with about as much charisma as a bollard.'

In fact the Pythons very respectfully cast one of Britain's most 'real actors', Ken Colley, as Jesus. Terry Gilliam had used Ken as a Fanatic in his first solo film, 'Jabberwocky' in 1977. In the film Ken is so wonderfully fanatical that he sets himself alight, and catapults himself over the battlements. So Terry Gilliam suggested Ken for the role and everyone agreed. I can't say he became famous for his wonderful portrayal of Jesus and is actually best known as Admiral Piett, in 'The Empire Strikes Back' and 'Return of the Jedi'.

For Jesus, Ken wears a brown wig, as he is short on follicles and Jesus is traditionally always shown with plenty of hair. So here again there can be no problem with the way the Pythons portray Jesus. But what exactly did the real Jesus look like?

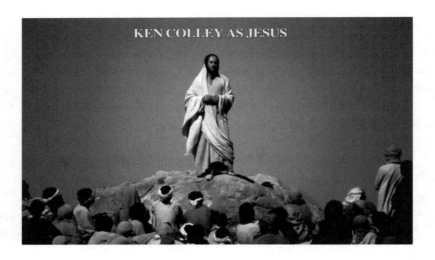

KEN COLLEY AS JESUS

Our brown wig was in no way as extreme as Jesus is shown in many Hollywood films with blond hair and blue eyes. We know very little about His mother's racial background but as a Jew she would obviously be dark haired with dark eyes.

His father, God, is always shown old, with grey hair, but perhaps in his youth he had blond hair and blue eyes; so Jesus as the Son of God, had picked up these traits. Although any of you who know about genetics know that blond hair is recessive to dark hair. Of course that is if God's genes act like normal human genes. Actually when I think about it, I suppose God's genes are probably always dominant.

There again if God created Jesus to do a specific job (to be humble etc.) then surely he should have made him ugly and deformed, which would be more useful for his message. If Jesus was beautiful then I think God made a really bad mistake.

I had to confront the nature of Jesus when I recently wrote a play about the philosopher, Friedrich Nietzsche, who was a friend of Wagner. Most of the dialogue came from their writings and one interchange concerned Nietzsche's autobiography, 'Ecce Homo'.

Wagner pulls a small book out of his pocket.
WAGNER: I have read your autobiography.
NIETZSCHE: 'Ecce Homo'. Behold the man.
WAGNER: Pilate's words when the flagellated Christ was brought before the
rabble. Do you come to redeem us as a Messiah?
NIETZSCHE: If I were a God I would hardly descend to earth to waste time
doing good acts and then nihilistically dying to redeem man's sins. Only
a madman could come up with such a ludicrous idea. No, I would come
down and do horrendous and sinful acts and in that way take on myself
man's guilt, a much more useful and less self-centered act.

It would only make sense to create Jesus as a beautiful person if he was going to function as Nietzsche suggests, but not the meek and mild version. If you think I am the only idiot who would come up with such an idea let me point you to the words of the biblical prophet, Isaiah.

> 'Who has believed our message and to whom has the arm of the Lord
> been revealed? He grew up before him like a tender shoot, and like a
> root out of dry ground. He had no beauty or majesty to attract us to
> him, nothing in his appearance that we should desire him. He was
> despised and rejected by men, a man of sorrows, and familiar with
> suffering. Like one from whom men hide their faces he was despised,
> and we esteemed him not. Surely he took up our infirmities and
> carried our sorrows, yet we considered him stricken by God, smitten
> by him, and afflicted. But he was pierced for our transgressions, he
> was crushed for our iniquities; the punishment that brought us peace
> was upon him, and by his wounds we are healed.' (Isaiah 53:2)

Isaiah is obviously suggesting that the coming messenger of the Lord would not be pretty.

But before we move away from the Hollywood blond, blue-eyed, Aryan, Jesus, we should mention Wagner here. Wagner's daughter married an Englishman called Houston Chamberlain who had written an autobiography of Wagner. Chamberlain also wrote a book, which was (like Wagner's music) to influence Hitler. It was published in 1899 and called '*The Foundations of the Nineteenth Century*'. In this well-respected book, at the time, he argued that:

> '*Certain anthropologists would fain teach us that all races are equally gifted; we point to history and answer: that is a lie! The races of mankind are markedly different in the nature and also in the extent of their gifts, and the Germanic races belong to the most highly gifted group, the group usually termed Aryan.*'

From this he concluded that Jesus was not a Jew but an Aryan.

> '*While Jesus may have been Jewish by religion, he was not Jewish by race. Otherwise, God must be a Jew.*'

His arguments from the Bible are interesting. In Kings 9:11 King Solomon sold Galilee to the king of Tyrus because the region was scarcely inhabited by Jews. And Jesus was born, not in Jewish Judaea, but in foreign Galilee, and Gelil haggoyim means 'district of heathens'. Chamberlain even quoted Jesus' words in the Bible, to prove that He himself denounced Jews:

> *Matthew 8:12 'but the children of the kingdom shall be cast out into outer darkness.'*
> *Matthew 23:33: 'Ye serpents, ye generation of vipers.'*

As mentioned before these are quotes from the later Gospels (not Mark) where Christianity is trying to separate itself from the Jews.

According to Chamberlain, Christianity developed into a murderous totalitarian system because of two factors. Firstly the Catholic Church's emergence from racial chaos after the fall of the Roman Empire; and secondly the laws of the Old Testament, which can be attributed to Jewish influence. He adds that, only after centuries of Roman Catholic terror did the Germanic forces, embodied by Francis of Assisi, Martin Luther and others turn Christianity into the religion that Jesus had envisioned. The Emperor Wilhelm

II was so convinced by these theories that he suggested that the Old Testament should be removed from the Bible to sever any remaining links between Christianity and Judaism.

Hitler, we know thought of Jews as a race rather than a religious group. He believed in an Aryan Jesus as he expressed several times later in his life. According to Hitler's mischling theory; as Jesus was fathered by a non-Jewish God, who never married, then Jesus was not Jewish. But however ridiculous you think an Aryan blue eyed, blond haired Jesus is: at noon on Saturday, 6th May 1938, a group of eminent Protestant theologians gathered at the historic Wartburg Castle, to celebrate the official opening of the Institute for the Study and Eradication of Jewish Influence on German Church Life. In the six years of its existence, as the Nazi regime carried out its genocide of the Jews, the Institute redefined Christianity as a Germanic religion whose founder, Jesus, was no Jew but rather had fought valiantly to destroy Judaism, falling as victim to that struggle. Germans were now called upon to be the victors in Jesus' own struggle against the Jews, who were said to be seeking Germany's destruction. The Institute achieved remarkable success, winning support from a host of church officials and theology professors who welcomed the removal of Jewish elements from Christian scripture and liturgy and the redefinition of Christianity as a Germanic, Aryan religion. Had Hitler won the war then it would now be blasphemy to mention that Jesus had anything to do with the people of the Old Testament.

Moving on from this rather unpleasant blue eyed, blond haired Jesus and assuming that his father was in fact Joseph from the bloodline of King David, what about the earliest images of him? Some think that the Turin Shroud has the image of the real Jesus. It is supposed to be the shroud that Jesus' body was wrapped in after the crucifixion and his image was printed onto the cloth. Unfortunately there are two problems here. Firstly that if you put paint on your face and wrap a cloth round it, when you unwrap it you would have a huge wide spread face with ears wide apart; it would look nothing like you. Secondly the shroud appeared just after the attack on the Knights Templar in France in 1307.

I think Knight and Lomas have made an interesting case in their book 'The Second Messiah' that this is a shroud used to wrap the live body of Jacques Demolay, the leader of the Knights Templar who was tortured before being burnt at the stake. It certainly looks like him and has his stature. They argue that because the Templars did not believe in the cross, Demolay was tortured by being nailed to a door; as the blood from one arm is not dribbling in the direction of an outstretched arm but a raised arm. He was then taken down alive and placed in the shroud used in the Masonic ritual of 'death and resurrection' that creates a Master Mason. The body in shock produced lactic acid, which made a photographic image on the cloth, not a printed image.

There is another ancient Holy relic with an image of Jesus on it. A non-biblical legend recounts that Veronica encountered Jesus along the Via Dolorosa on the way to Golgotha. When she paused to wipe the sweat off his face with her veil, his image was imprinted on the cloth. The event is commemorated by one of the Stations of the Cross. It was alleged the veil possessed miraculous properties, being able to quench thirst, cure blindness, and sometimes even raise the dead. According to some versions, Veronica later traveled to Rome to present the cloth to the Roman Emperor Tiberius. The story is not recorded until the Middle Ages and for this reason, is unlikely to be historical. Of course the name Veronica derives from the Latin 'vera' – true; and the Greek 'eikon' – image (as in Icon). So Veronica translates as 'true image,' what an extremely convenient name she has.

During the fourteenth century it became a central icon in the Roman Church and it was used to encourage Pilgrims to come to Rome instead of Santiago de Compostela. Many pilgrims returning from Rome had Veronica buttons which have been found over Europe. The Vatican deems that no one is allowed to inspect the image but the face is still displayed each year on Passion Sunday.

After Vespers there is a short procession within the basilica, then a bell rings and three canons carry the heavy frame out on the balcony below the statue of Angels with the Veronica. From this limited view no image is discernible and it is only possible to see the shape of the inner frame. A few who have seen it say that all that is left is a brown stain but we know the image because its origin is likely to be the image of Jesus associated with the Eastern Church, known as the Mandylion.

My hunch, for reasons I will explain later, is that the Mandylion is probably very close to the image of Jesus. The painting is dark skinned and has distinct points of the hair and beard, which have caused confusion about, which is beard and which is hair. Many early paintings do show something similar but try to beautify it. One feature that interests me is that the hair is parted in the middle.

There is a document, alleged to have been written by a Roman official, Publius Lentullus, in Jerusalem during Christ's lifetime. Although it is clearly a much later forgery, it has some interesting points:

'There has appeared in our city a man of great power named Jesus. The people call him a prophet and his disciples the Son of God. He is in stature a man of middle height and well proportioned, with a venerable face. His hair is the color of ripe chestnuts smooth almost to the ears, but above them wavy and curly with a slight bluish radiancy. And it flows over his shoulders. It is parted in the

*middle after the fashion of the people of Nazareth. His brow is
smooth and very calm with a face without a wrinkle or a blemish
lightly tinged with red. His nose and mouth are faultless. His beard
is luxuriant of the same color as his hair. His countenance is full
of simplicity and love. His eyes are expressive and brilliant. He is
terrible in reproof, sweet and gentle in admonition. His figure is
slender and erect.'*

Okay it is the usual flattering description except for one point. His hair
is parted in the middle after the 'fashion of the people of Nazareth'. What a
crazy idea! I'm sure the people of this village, Nazareth, did not have a particular
distinct fashion. So why did this author write it? I will investigate the fashion
conscious Nazarenes later, for now let's look at another story in the Bible which
might throw light on Jesus' appearance.

In Jericho, a rich tax collector named Zacchaeus climbs a tree to get a
good look at Jesus. It appears in Luke 19 and the wording of the story is
variously translated. The New International translation for instance reads:

*'He wanted to see who Jesus was, but being a short man he could
not, because of the crowd.'*

But this translation is trying to make clear something that is not clear in
more accurate translations. King James' version reads:

*'And he sought to see Jesus who he was; and could not for the
press, because he was of short stature. And he ran before, and
climbed up into a sycamore tree to see him.'*

Now suppose I write it this way,

'and he could not for the press, because He was short of stature.'

Now we get the idea that it is not Zacchaeus who is short of stature but
Jesus. You may think I'm plucking at straws here, finding just one reference in
the Bible and that one rather dubious.

But in the Slavonic copy of Josephus there is a description of a man
wanted by Pontius Pilate for claiming that he was the King of the Jews:

'A man of simple appearance, mature age, dark skin, small stature, three cubits high, hunchbacked with a long face, long nose, and meeting eyebrows… with scanty hair with a parting in the middle of his head, after the manner of the Nazirites, and with an undeveloped beard.'

Short, dark skinned, hunchback, long nose and meeting eyebrows – now your talking my kind of Jesus! Still not convinced; there is a scripture called Acts of Paul and Thecla in which this appears:

'a man small in size, bald-headed…with eyebrows meeting, rather hook-nosed.'

In the Acts of Peter, it quotes a prophet who described Jesus as:

'And we saw him and he had no beauty nor comeliness.'

The picture of Jesus as relatively unattractive comes from many other sources. In 'Acts of John', John says:

'And oft-times He would appear to me as a small man and uncomely.'

Justin Martyr in Trypho declared that Jesus was: *'made ugly by the sufferings and the humiliation that he endured.'*

Tertullian said: *'He would not have been spat upon by the Roman soldiers if his face had not been so ugly as to inspire spitting'*

I cannot prove that the language here is not harping back to the description I gave you in Isaiah, which was prominent among the early Christians, and these quotes might be an attempt to fit Him to the prophesy.

Dr. James Rendel Harris, an authority on biblical history and texts, quotes a Syriac document of the Eighth Century:

'Thy stature, O Christ, was smaller than that of the children of Jacob, who sinned against Thy Father who elected Thee, and who kindled the wrath of the Eternal Son who dwelt in Thee, and who angered the Holy Spirit who sanctified Thee.'

53

According to another record:

> *"Oft times He would appear to me as a small man and uncomely,*
> *and then again as one reaching unto Heaven. His head touched*
> *Heaven so that I was afraid and cried out, and He turning about*
> *appeared as a man of small stature."*

A description by St. Ephraem, the Syrian, says, '*God took human form*
and appeared with a stature of three human cubits while at the same time
assuming all things. He rose upon us little of stature.'

Okay, okay enough already about the little ugly Jesus, what about the
Python movie? In the TV debate, Malcolm Muggeridge said the film tried to
ridicule the sublime words of Jesus' 'Sermon on the Mount'. I think this misses
the point of the scene. Jesus' words may be wonderful but the crowd mishear
and misinterpret them. As I hope this book will show misinterpretations are
one of the main crimes of the Church. Here are the misinterpretations from the
scene.

JESUS: Blessed are the peacemakers.
TERRY GILLIAM: I think it was, "Blessed are the cheesemakers"!
CAROLE CLEAVLAND: What's so special about the cheesemakers?
TERRY BAYLER: Well, obviously it's not meant to be taken literally. It refers
*   to any manufacturers of dairy products.*
MIKE: What did he say?
CHARLES McKEOWN: Blessed are the Greek, I think.
TERRY BAYLER: What!
CHARLES McKEOWNN: Apparently he is going to inherit the earth.
TERRY BAYLER: Did anyone catch his name?

For future reference we had with us four actors who played other parts
around the Pythons. I will list them where possible. They are best known for:

TERRY BAYLER: 'I'm Brian and so is my wife.'
BERNARD McKENNA: 'Hands up all those who don't want to be crucified
        here.'
CHARLES McKEOWN: 'I was blind and now I can see! Ahhh!'
JOHN YOUNG: 'Crucifixion's a doddle.'

As someone who knows the Bible well I am still surprised by the amount of misinterpretation, or worse, when people claim to be followers then choose to ignore his teachings. Jesus is known to have spoken against hypocrites and the debating Bishop of Southwark certainly was guilty of that.

There is no question that the values that Jesus taught were fundamentaly Communist: against the accumulation of wealth, that property should be owned in common and declaring that the rich have no hope of getting to heaven. But how many Christians actually follow His beliefs, giving away their wealth? Like most people, they say that Communism will never work because of human nature. If that is the case then doesn't that mean that Christianity will never work either, so why bother? How does a supposedly dedicated Christian like ex-President Bush justify the power and wealth that his family have accumulated? (not to mention his war record).

Python's Sermon on the Mount certainly highlights a few fundamental problems for the followers of the Christian religion.

5

HALIBUT GOOD ENOUGH FOR JEHOVAH

There is an interesting group on 'Facebook' called 'Good Enough For Jehovah – Against Blasphemous Libel'; their objectives are stated as:

> *'This group is the official starting point for the "Good Enough For Jehovah" Anti-Blasphemous Libel Postcard Campaign. From here you will be able to download and print off the postcard. Simply sign it, stamp it and pop it in the post to let Dermot Ahern know that his Blasphemous libel law is not good for 21st century Ireland.'*

They continue.

> *'Taking our cue from the infamous Monty Python sketch from the Life of Brian whereby an old man is stoned to death for suggesting his supper was good enough for Jehovah. The postcard campaign aims to let the Minister for Justice know that his recent Blasphemous libel provisions are a joke worthy of the finest comedy brains of the last 50 years.'*

What more can I add? In this book about the blasphemous nature of 'Life of Brian', here is an actual sketch of the senseless and dangerous way blasphemy laws work. First, a rather silly expression is deemed to be blasphemous.

CLEESE: *Matthias, son of Deuteronomy of Gath.*

MATTHIAS: *(to Guard): Do I say, yes?*
GUARD: *Yes.*
MATTHIAS: *Yes.*
CLEESE: *You have been found guilty by the elders of the town of uttering the name of our Lord and so as a blasphemer you are to be stoned to death.*
MATTHIAS: *Look, I'd had a lovely supper and all I said to my wife was, 'That piece of halibut was good enough for Jehovah.'*
CLEESE: *Blasphemy! He's said it again.*

However absurd this may seem, it is accurate. Here is a modern day petition.

> 'A petition has been raised by the "Association for Jewish-Christian Friendship" of Rome and signed jointly by eminent Catholic and Jewish theologians and scholars. The petition requested that "publishing firms and the editorial staffs of newspapers and magazines" stop using the name "Jahweh" because it is "offensive to Jews, who consider the name of God to be unpronounceable." Their appeal, the Association says, is based on a "long-standing Jewish tradition" that "has been maintained without interruption" until today.'

Adding this to the fact that women were not allowed to go to stonings, we have the basis for the sketch. By the way, what is funny is that most of the women who are pretending to be men are actually men pretending to be women, pretending to be men! Get out of that one. *(See colour fig 3)*

But what I think is the funniest aspect of the sketch (and the most important) is the way these types of dogmatic accusations can get totally out of hand. In the film the religious official, John, thinks he can control the crowd… but…

JOHN: *Stop that! Stop it. Now look, no one is to stone anyone until I blow this whistle. Even…and I want to make this absolutely clear…even if they do say "Jehovah."*
Stones rain down and John goes down in a heap.

Here is the warning to all those who raise the cry blasphemy. Once the fanaticism is released there is no telling where it will end.

The blasphemy laws are contrary to the principle of free speech and are actually there to protect beliefs, not people. Mind you it is not only speech. One thing we never expected was that at the New York première of the film Eric describes how "A thousand Rabbi's turned up to complain. Why? Because John was wearing a headdress that was authentic." No one in the costume department could ever have imagined that in their attempt to get the costumes accurate for the period they would upset anyone.

In the film the actors obviously used polystyrene stones but when I had to put the real sound of 'stones hitting bone', I began thinking how much it hurt just being hit on the head with one stone thrown with force. I imagined what being stoned to death must have been like and I began to feel ill. It was probably a slow nasty process where the death would be caused by the final cracking of the skull. But what about the people performing such a violent act? The viciousness it must have released in them, to throw stones till the skull is totally smashed; a joint communal vigilante act of barbarism. As Jesus once said, 'Let him who is without guilt throw the first stone.'

6

STOP THINKING ABOUT SEX

"Stop thinking about sex," says Mandy to Brian as they head home after the stoning. "You're forty years old, now, you should have grown out of all that." Interestingly both Brian and Jesus' early years are absent and we come to them in early middle age. Officially it is said that Jesus was 30 when he began his ministry and died on the cross at 33. But there are calculations that make him forty. They go like this; Herod the Great completed his renovation of the Temple around 12 BC; Halley's comet passed over on 10th October 12 BC. Perhaps important Magi were attending the opening of the Temple when the comet passed by. This gives us Herod alive, the Magi and a star, satisfying many parts of Matthew's nativity story. All that is wrong is that it makes Jesus around 20 at the time of Quirinius and his census. But in the Slavonic Josephus, remember John the Baptist was also made an adult at the time of Quirinius. So perhaps the idea that Brian, and therefore Jesus, are both 40 years old when we take up their story is heavenly inspiration by the Pythons.

The gate of their hometown is that of Jerusalem; as Brian is shown later working at the Jerusalem Amphitheatre. But Jesus' hometown is alleged to have been Nazareth. I say alleged because there is no record of such a town or village existing at the time. Where in the Bible does it say they lived in Nazareth? Well to start with, after they escape Herod by going to Egypt the Bible says:

> 'After Herod died, an angel of the Lord appeared in a dream to
> Joseph in Egypt and said, "Get up, take the child and his mother
> and go to the land of Israel, for those who were trying to take the
> child's life are dead."
> So he got up, took the child and his mother and went to the land

of Israel. But when he heard that Archelaus was reigning in Judea in place of his father Herod, he was afraid to go there. Having been warned in a dream, he withdrew to the district of Galilee, and he went and lived in a town called Nazareth. So was fulfilled what was said through the prophets: "He will be called a Nazarene."

Jesus of Nazareth or Jesus the Nazarene? If we have no evidence that Nazareth, as a village, even existed at the time of Jesus why was this insignificant appellation added to Jesus' name. Thomas of York makes sense as York is a well-known town; or Alfred of Wessex after a known region but Erik of Ecclesfield makes no sense whatsoever, as nobody but the people of Ecclesfield (apologies to the villagers North of Sheffield) would have any clue what we are talking about. Jesus the Galilean might be more likely. We know of the rebel called Judas of Galilee and, as was mentioned, some believe he was in fact the template for Jesus who never existed. However even though I believe he probably did exist, I don't believe he was from Nazareth. I believe this is a cover up of the real title, Jesus the Nazarene.

Why does the prophet even say, *'he will be called a Nazarene'*? A Nazarene must have some meaning other than a person from a nonexistent town. What could it be? Numbers 6 tells us:

'The Lord said to Moses, "Speak to the Israelites and say to them: If a man or woman wants to make a special vow, a vow of separation to the Lord as a Nazirite, he must abstain from wine and other fermented drink and must not drink vinegar made from wine or from other fermented drink. He must not drink grape juice or eat grapes or raisins. As long as he is a Nazirite, he must not eat anything that comes from the grapevine, not even the seeds or skins. During the entire period of his vow of separation no razor may be used on his head. He must be holy until the period of his separation to the Lord is over; he must let the hair of his head grow long."'

A Nazirite then is someone dedicated to God. Samson for instance says to Delilah:

"No razor has ever been used on my head," said Samson, "because

I have been a Nazirite set apart to God since birth. If my head were shaved, my strength would leave me, and I would become as weak as any other man." (Judges 16:17)

If Jesus was not dedicated to God, not a Nazirite, it would be a bit of a surprise and as we mentioned the very earliest images of Jesus show him with long hair. Is there any other evidence that he was a Nazarene? You can rely on Mark's original Gospel, where, a servant girl spots Peter after the crucifixion:

'When she saw Peter warming himself, she looked closely at him. "You also were with that Nazarene, Jesus," she said. But he denied it.' (Mark 14:67)

This seems pretty conclusive but if you want more:

'As they entered the tomb, they saw a young man dressed in a white robe sitting on the right side, and they were alarmed. "Don't be alarmed," he said. "You are looking for Jesus the Nazarene, who was crucified. He has risen!' (Mark 16:4)

This is an angel telling us he is a Nazarene so if you believe in angels, then this is coming from the highest authority. Or maybe this angel is just one of the guys who nicked the body. You pays your money and you takes your choice.

But why has the appellation 'Jesus the Nazarene' been changed to 'Jesus of Nazareth'? The clue may come from the Bible itself. In 'Acts of the Apostles' Paul is brought before the Governor Felix for trial:

'And they brought their charges against Paul before the governor. When Paul was called in, Tertullus presented his case before Felix: "We have enjoyed a long period of peace under you, and your foresight has brought about reforms in this nation. Everywhere and in every way, most excellent Felix, we acknowledge this with profound gratitude. We have found this man to be a troublemaker, stirring up riots among the Jews all over the world. He is a ringleader of the Nazarene sect and even tried to desecrate the temple; so we seized him."' (Acts 24)

So it was known that Nazarenes were rebellious troublemakers out to overthrow the Roman occupation. To make Jesus palatable to a Roman audience the name Jesus the Nazarene was changed.

This quote also raises another important point. Note that it says Felix had been Governor for many years! Even Paul says it:

'When the governor motioned for him to speak, Paul replied: "I know that for a number of years you have been a judge over this nation; so I gladly make my defence."'

This may be important later as it throws a massive question mark over whether Pilate was in fact the Governor at the time of Christ's death.

To show how the Nazarene deception works, remember a quote written by a Roman official, Publius Lentullus in Jerusalem, which stated that the people of Nazareth had a particular fashion for parting their hair in the middle. I mentioned my scepticism at the time. Here is an older translation of the letter which is still as flattering but....

'A man of stature somewhat tall, and comely, with very reverent countenance, such as the beholders may both love and fear, his hair of the chestnut, full ripe, plain to His ears, whence downwards it is more orient and curling and wavering about His shoulders. In the midst of His head is a seam or partition in His hair, after the manner of the Nazarenes.'

Now we see how it worked, Nazarene was mistranslated as 'people from Nazareth', which is clearly ridiculous, suggesting that the people from one small village (if it even existed) had a particular hairstyle. Here it is clear that it was a devout religious sect who parted their hair in the middle. So the Nazarenes, like Samson, did not cut their hair but it also seems to be a feature that they parted it in the middle. This is one of the reasons I feel the Veronica is probably an accurate painting of Jesus in that it does have this central parting.

Also remember our Magi who visited Jesus, and their possible Giant ancestors who were found in China? There was a recent newspaper article, which recorded their name.

'According to ancient Chinese records, strangely tall, blond-red

hairy people were sufficiently well known in the area to have their own name, the Tokharians. At Quizil in the caves of a thousand Buddhas, you can see them on wall paintings. Blue eyed, bearded, hair characteristically centre-parted.'

Centre-parted! You tell me what this all means! While I return to the film.

As Mandy and Brian enter the Jerusalem city gate they are accosted by Michael Palin as an ex-leper. The idea was to shoot the scene in one take all the way from the gate to Mandy's house.

When I got the material back in the cutting rooms, of course, there was no editing I could do with it. Normally I might speed up or slow down pauses; lose lines which don't work etc. But here I was stuck with just one take from start to finish. I made a jump cut where I thought the dialogue had made the point and was slowing down the film. When we got back to London, Terry agreed with me and it was decided to re-shoot across the cut, at Shepperton studios. A set was built and we shot on what turned out to be a cloudy day. From this fact you can tell what is the London material because it is lit as opposed to being in natural sunshine.

I must say I think Mike really comes to the fore in 'Brian'. He is an incredible chameleon who just becomes different people. I was able to cut from him as Pilate, to him as a revolutionary because they were different people. John is always John and where John generally stole the TV shows, and Eric steals the stage shows, I think Mike is the one in 'Life of Brian'. If you watch a take of him as Pilate, his whole body is tight and his shoulders narrow. This is not Mike. When Terry calls cut, suddenly his body relaxes and it is Mike again. Even his wife didn't recognize it was Mike hanging in the Roman cell (Lucky Bastard). Now as the ex-leper he is healthy and muscular, as he skips around, although at rushes there was concern by Terry Gilliam that Mike just did not look period. As Mike remembers in his Diaries,

'I looked like a cross between Tarzan and Geronimo.'

In fact they re-shot the very end but I still used an original take where Mike skips away dancing round a patch of shit that he just notices at the last minute.

Everyone, make-up, wardrobe, etc, were all desperate to make the film look and feel authentic. In fact Mike mentions a moment of annoyance in his autobiography:

Mike begs for half a Dinari from Graham

'I find myself becoming very angry now whenever I see John wearing his tiny beard and moustache which was designed for him, when he complained about the discomfort of full beard. So the rest of the crowd look wonderful – absolutely convincing Biblical figures – and there, looming large on left of frame, is John looking like a sort of fourth rate Turkish illusionist advertising on the back of stage.'

I am a big fan of the Spanish surreal film director Luis Buñuel. He had a wicked, Pythonish sense of humour and made one film, 'Simon of the Desert', about the Christian ascetic saint who achieved fame because he lived for 39 years on top of a pillar near Aleppo in Syria. In the film Simon performs miracles, which the local population take very much for granted. I do believe there is a strong surreal comic connection between Buñuel and the Pythons and the ex-leper scene is exactly the sort of thing Buñuel could have done.

Talking of miracles, there is a vast collection of Jewish laws and traditions called the Talmud. They make interesting reading because they are infused with vigorous intellectual debate, humour and deep wisdom. The process of studying these sacred texts has been compared with the practice of Zen Buddhist Koan meditation. One text called the Toledot Yeshu is a very interesting Jewish version of the Jesus story.

'There was in the Temple a stone on which was engraved the Jehovah, [YHWH], that is to say, the Ineffable Name of God; this stone had been found by King David when the foundations of the Temple were being prepared and was deposited by him in the Holy of Holies. Jeschu, knowing this, came from Galilee and, penetrating into the Holy of Holies, read the Ineffable name, which he transcribed on to a piece of parchment and concealed in an incision under his skin. By this means he was able to work miracles and to persuade the people that he was the Son of God foretold by Isaiah. With the aid of Judas, the Sages of the Synagogue, succeeding in capturing Jeschu, who was then lead before the Great and Little Sanhedrin, by whom he was condemned to be stoned to death and his dead body was hung on a tree.'

This Jesus does not blaspheme by saying the name Jehovah but instead slips a parchment with it under his skin to give himself immaculate powers. Nice trick if you can do it.

7

NORTIUS MAXIMUS

Brian returns home to be confronted by an unpleasant truth. His father was not Mr. Cohen! No, it was a Roman centurion called Nortius Maximus, who after, 'sort of' raping Mandy. 'Voom! Like a rat out of an aqueduct'.

Refusing to accept the truth, Brian declares he is "Kosher, a Yid, a Red Sea Pedestrian and proud of it," and with that slams the door to his bedroom. Mandy turns to the waiting Roman soldier (Bernard McKenna) "Sex, sex, sex, that's all they think about," claps her hands and kneels at his feet. I asked Terry what he was doing and he said he didn't know about the clap but after it the Roman was about to get a blowjob.

So Brian has a Roman father; strangely there are some odd theories about Jesus' actual father, and one even suggests that like Brian, Jesus' father *was* a Roman. But not just any Roman, but the granddaddy of them all, Julius Caesar! Sounds ludicrous? Well, the argument goes like this. Julius Caesar had a child with Cleopatra called Caesarion. Cleopatra hoped that her son would eventually succeed his father as the head of the Roman Republic as well as Egypt. But on 15th March 44 BC Caesar was assassinated. Six months later, in Alexandria, Cleopatra named Caesarion as co-ruler of Egypt at the age of three. He was obviously only King in name, with Cleopatra keeping actual authority to herself. She then began an affair with Mark Anthony, who at that time shared control of the Republic in a triumvirate with Octavian and Lepidus. Anthony granted various eastern lands and titles to Caesarion and proclaimed him to be Caesar's true son and heir. These proclamations, known as the Donations of Alexandria, caused a fatal breach in Anthony's relations with Octavian, who used Roman resentment over the Donations to gain support for war against Anthony and Cleopatra. When Octavian invaded Egypt in 30 BC, Cleopatra sent Caesarion, then 17 years old, to the Red Sea port of Berenice for safety, with plans of an escape to India. When the battle was lost, Mark Anthony committed suicide prior to Octavian's entry into the capital. Cleopatra followed his example with the aid of an asp, although evidence does suggest that Octavian invented this story after bumping her off. Caesarion's guardians, including his tutor, either were themselves lured by false promises of mercy into returning the boy to Alexandria or perhaps even betrayed him; the records are unclear. Octavian had Caesarion executed there, with the words "Two Caesars is one too many." No details concerning his death have been documented; it is popularly thought that he was strangled. This lack of clarity has led people to suggest that Caesarion escaped to India where there are records of a possible Jesus. At the age of 30 he returned to Israel as the Jesus we know. The problem I have with this theory is that the time scale is out of kilter. If Caesarion was 17 around 30 BC and Pontius Pilate was procurator of Judea from AD 26-36, that means that if Caesarion returned from India to Israel during Pilate's time he would be at least 73. A very wise old man but unlikely to be the guy we know. Or to have him return in his thirties he would arrive in Israel before Herod had finished rebuilding the Temple. All a bit unsatisfactory.

Strangely there is yet another narrative that links Jesus' father with a Roman. It is not just one reference but there are several slight variations of this story and I think we can't totally dismiss them. This one comes again from the Jewish Talmud, quoted before about Jeschu having the name of God hidden in his skin. It relates Jeschu's origins:

> 'Miriam, a hairdresser of Bethlehem, affianced to a young man named Jochanan, was seduced by a libertine, Joseph Pandira, a Roman soldier, and gave birth to a son whom she named Jeschu. Jeschu was taken during his boyhood to Egypt, where he was initiated into the secret doctrines of the priests, and on his return to Palestine gave himself up to the practice of magic. On reaching manhood, Jeschu learnt the secret of his illegitimacy, on account of which he was driven out of the Synagogue and took refuge for a time in Galilee. ...(then comes the name of God under the skin and continues:) With the aid of Judas, the Sages of the Synagogue, succeed in capturing Jeschu, who was then lead before the Great and Little Sanhedrin, by whom he was condemned to be stoned to death and his dead body was hung on a tree.'

The father then is a Joseph; not the husband but a libertine Roman soldier (our Nortius Maximus). The other interesting point is that like the biblical Jesus he was taken to Egypt where he learnt the secret practices of the priest.

I wish I could tell you that I believe this legend which is so close to the story in 'Life of Brian'. I am afraid I don't think I can yet. My main worry is that it could well have been an attempt by Orthodox Judaism to discredit a man who claimed, heretically, to be the Son of God. But there is a niggle in my mind that maybe there is something in it. There is another more sympathetic version of the same story that comes from the Gnostic Christians and Johnnites (people who believe John the Baptist more important than Jesus).

> *'A young virgin of Nazareth, named Miriam, who had been betrothed to a youth of her tribe named Jochanan, was one day outraged by a certain man, Pandira, who introduced himself into her chamber in the garments, of her betrothed Jochanan. The latter being made acquainted with the misfortune quitted her without compromising her, she being in fact innocent.'*

The result was that she gives birth to a son who receives the name Yeshua, (or Jesus in Greek). This child is adopted by a Rabbi named Joseph, who carried him into Egypt, where he was initiated into the occult sciences, of the priests of Osiris. Yeshua and Joseph return to Judaea, where the knowledge of the youth soon attracts the attention of the priests, and excited their jealousy and hatred. At last, they publicly reproach him with the illegitimacy of his birth. Yeshua, who had been cared for by his adopted father Joseph, was informed by him of the crime of Pandira, and the misfortune of Miriam. His first impulse was to publicly deny her, saying to her in the midst of a marriage festival, *"Woman, what have I to do with thee?"* (This appears in the Bible.) But remembering that a poor woman should not be punished for having suffered what she could not prevent, he exclaimed: *"My mother has not sinned, she has not lost her innocence; she is immaculate, and yet she is a mother; be double honor therefore paid to her! As for myself, I have no father in this world. I am the Son of God and of humanity!"*

And thereupon he enters his mission. The Gnostic Christians were, in my mind much closer to the real beliefs of Jesus and the Jerusalem Church than the Roman Church, which is authoritarian, denying the personal experience. *'Don't think for yourselves, you're not all individuals.'* The Gnostics were strong in

Egypt and could well have been the priests who buried the Nag Hammadi Scrolls when their beliefs were termed heretical by the rising power of the Roman Church. Their influence stretched to the South of France where the Cathars seem to have held similar beliefs. They both had women Priests, and saw Mary Magdalene as a major religious teacher. (Of course, she was alleged to have actually travelled and died in the South of France). They also had a dualist view of the world like the Zoroastrians. They saw John the Baptist as the major character and Jesus to be secondary. The Gnostics do not take the stories of the Bible literally but as a method of initiation. I suspect they could have heard the Pandira story and then coloured it to explain Jesus' statement to his mother at the Wedding in Canaan.

The real question still is; how true is the original story? There are references to a Yeshua ben Pandira, which would be His name, if the story were true. I can give you an example from a Talmudic debate about the name Stada.

Shabbat 104b relates that a ben Stada brought magic from Egypt in incisions in his flesh. The debate then follows by asking if this tale was not about ben Pandira rather than ben Stada. This is refuted by the claim that it is both Pandira and Stada because his mother's husband was Stada but her lover was Pandira. And so it continues.

Unfortunately we cannot take this Midrashic story as necessarily true, as these types of tales are told as educational stories and are not necessarily factual. But even so, why debate about this name, ben Pandira, at all?

There is one source that makes me feel that the story may be true: it comes from the pen of Celsus, a Greek philosopher writing just a hundred years after the death of Christ. Celsus wrote, *'The True Discourse'*, the earliest anti-Christian polemic to reach us. The book is lost (probably destroyed) but we know what was in it because of the refutation by the Christian scholar, Origen. An interesting feature of Celsus' writing is that he always refers to Jesus' father by name as Panthera. It is taken by Celsus as given that Jesus was the illegitimate son of a Roman soldier of this name. Is he being sarcastic or is that the belief at the time before Matthew and Luke added their nativity stories? Strangely, there is a tomb of a Roman soldier named Pantera who was stationed in Israel around the time of Christ's birth. The tomb was found in Bad Kreuznach, in Germany.

Beside this very convincing detail I have yet another theory of my own. It does not make Jesus' father a Roman, but it raises the same issue of illegitimacy hinted at in the others. I advocated it in my occult film 'Chemical

Wedding', and it is based on the fact that there are several key mistranslations in the Bible.

You may not have considered that the word of God could have been mistranslated but translators are only human and mistranslations are common in the Bible. Some are insignificant. For example, Luke tells us that when Mary and Joseph arrived in Bethlehem, there was no room at the 'inn'. The Greek term translated as inn '*kataluma*' has multiple meanings. But when Luke uses the term again, at the Last Supper he clarifies his use. *Kataluma*, here, is not an inn but a large, upper room in a private house.

Other errors are more significant; God, for instance, does not part the Red Sea for the 'Red Sea Pedestrians'! No, that image of Charlton Heston waving his stick at the waters of the Red Sea causing them to part is just a mistranslation. It is now correctly translated in many Bibles as the 'Sea of Reeds'. This is important because, firstly the Red Sea is not in the path of the escaping Israelites as they leave their Northern Egyptian home town. But the 'Sea of Reeds' is on the Mediterranean coast of Egypt, which was in their path but also in the firing line for the Tsunami, caused by the explosion of the Santorini Volcano (original name Thera), which would cause the sea to suck out and return as a wall of water. The Thera volcano was probably responsible for all the other plagues of Egypt mentioned in the Bible. Egyptian records blame these chaotic conditions for the rioting and looting of Egypt's precious objects.

> '*The Israelites did as Moses instructed and asked the Egyptians for articles of silver and gold and for clothing. The Lord had made the Egyptians favourably disposed toward the people, and they gave them what they asked for; so they plundered the Egyptians.*' (*Exodus 12:35*)

I love the way the Egyptians were 'favourably disposed' to being plundered!

Another mistranslation is the term 'virgin'. But this one is by the original writer of Matthew himself. When he alleges Jesus was born of a virgin, he misquotes Isaiah 7:14: '*Behold, a 'virgin' shall be with child, and shall bring forth a son*', as a proof-text for the divine origin of Jesus. Jewish scholars assert that Matthew is in error, because Isaiah could not have meant virgin. The word *almah* just means *young woman*. It does not denote a virgin or sexual purity but age. A different Hebrew word, *bethulah*, is most commonly used for virgin even in modern Hebrew.

My key mistranslation concerning Jesus' father Joseph, is his job description, 'carpenter'. The Greek word thought to mean carpenter is 'ho tekton'. This is a well-known error, as even a modern Greek would translate Ho Tekton as a 'Master of the Craft'. Craft, that is, as in witchcraft or as a description of an expert in Masonic ritual which is also called 'the craft'.

You may think that the Bible clearly states that the young Jesus was brought up in his father's humble carpentry shop. We have the images in our minds and we know the stories. But no! These stories are not in the Bible. Just this mistranslation:

> *"Where did this man get this wisdom and these miraculous powers?" they asked. "Isn't this the ho tekton's (carpenter's) son? Isn't his mother's name Mary, and aren't his brothers James, Joseph, Simon and Judas? Aren't all his sisters with us?" (Matthew 13:55)*

And that's it in Matthew. No carpentry shop, just a mistranslation of the word 'ho tekton'. Luke is much the same as Matthew but the genealogy of Luke has a different father for our Joseph.

> *'Now Jesus himself was about thirty years old when he began his ministry. He was the son, so it was thought, of Joseph, the son of Heli. ' (Luke 3:23)*

So Joseph's name in Luke would be Joseph ben Heli but in Matthew he would be Joseph ben Jacob. He is either two different people or Jesus has two fathers; or this is just a silly mistake. As I like to say: you pays your money and takes your choice.

So Jesus was not born of a virgin, his father was not a carpenter, he didn't live in Nazareth and he was not even born in a stable.

So who was this mysterious Joseph who was a master of the craft? One thing we can say about him is that, in paintings, he is always shown as quite old. Also it must be obvious that if Joseph was from the Royal Line of David – the King line, he must have been an important person. Bloodline was considered extremely important in Israel, even the historian Josephus proudly begins his book with:

'The family from which I am derived is not an ignoble one, but hath descended all along from the priests.'

He then lists his family tree, which is almost as long as the one pertaining to Jesus himself.

My film 'Chemical Wedding' is about a man who believes he is the reincarnation of Aleister Crowley, the Edwardian Occultist. Crowley himself believed he was the reincarnation of the strange occultist Eliphas Levi, who died the same year Crowley was born. In my research for the film I found Eliphas Levi had made several rather startling statements. One I quote in the film is:

'Elders from the Line of David would impregnate a young maiden to preserve the blood-line.'

Lets just get our heads around this – an important, elderly man (Joseph?) would ritualistically have sex with young maidens to maintain the line of David. Did Eliphas Levi get this out of his weird imagination or did he have special knowledge giving a factual basis for such an allegation? Who was this occultist?

Eliphas Levi was the pseudonym of Alphonse Louis Constant, who was born in Paris 1810 and was the only son of a shoemaker. His father did not have the funds to privately educate his son so he sent Constant to St. Sulpice there to be educated as a priest (The oddness of the church of St Sulpice has become famous through Dan Brown's 'De Vinci Code').

While Constant was at St. Sulpice, he became intrigued by a lesson about animal magnetism, a vital energy of the human body which it was suggested was controlled by the 'Devil'. This sparked his curiosity and he began to study all that he could find about magic and the occult: producing his infamous conglomeratous sketch of the Sabbatic Goat.

He was ordained as a priest but later was thrown out of the Church and excommunicated for his left-wing political views and refusal to observe his vows of chastity. When writing, Constant took on the pen name 'Magus Eliphas Levi', which he arrived at by translating his first and second names to Hebrew. In 1861, he published his first and perhaps most important book, 'The Dogma and Ritual of High Magic'. His outrageous writings led to him serving three jail sentences. The introduction to 'The Dogma' begins:

'Behind the veil of all the hieratic and mystical allegories of ancient

doctrines, behind the darkness and strange ordeals of all initiations, under the seal of all sacred writings, in the ruins of Nineveh or Thebes, on the crumbling stones of old temples and on the blackened visage of the Assyrian or Egyptian sphinx, in the monstrous paintings which interpret to the faithful of India the inspired pages of the Vedas, in the cryptic emblems of our old books on alchemy, in the ceremonies practiced at reception by all secret societies, there are found indications of a common doctrine.'

Levi's Sabbatic Goat. The hermaphrodite with the pentagram and phallic caduceus and giving the sign of excommunication

So Levi's main belief was that there was a common doctrine behind everything from ancient Egypt to secret societies like the Knights Templar and modern Masonry. There are secret rituals in Masonry that indicate knowledge of the ancient past and of facts that we are only now discovering are true. I will mention these rituals where they prove relevant and you can decide for yourself their importance. One such arises in the Ancient Scottish Rite where in the 28th degree of the 'Knight of the Sun' it teaches the doctrine of 'the One True God', that there is just one God who appears under different names to different people. This is the opposite of Christianity, which claims theirs is the true God and the rest are false. This strikes me as very similar to Eliphas Levi's claim that there is fundamentally one doctrine behind every religion. Also in the 28th degree there is a lecture on truth delivered by nine leaders called the Thrice Perfect Fathers. They are named as the angels, Gabriel, Raphael, Michael, etc. It has been gleaned from the Dead Sea Scrolls that leading elders often took on the names of the angels. Could this mean that when the angel Gabriel visits the young Mary to tell her she will bear a child there is something more to this visit than just a message from God? Now think again about Levi's statement:

> *'Elders from the Line of David would impregnate a young maiden to preserve the blood-line.'*

This all makes me suspect that Levi was initiated into Masonic knowledge. Could he have studied this in the odd Parisian church of St. Sulpice, which is mentioned in the 'Holy Blood, Holy Grail' (and 'The Da Vinci Code') as a hotbed of strange occult teachings.

Where does this all take us? There is actually a Biblical Joseph who seems to fit the bill for Eliphas Levi's statement:

1. He is an important Elder from the line of David
2. He is a 'ho tekton'.
3. He is important enough to be a member of the Sanhedrin, the ruling Jewish Council under Roman occupation.
4. His associate, Nicodemus, also a member of the Sanhedrin, has secret meetings with Jesus.
5. He is described by John 19:38 to be a secret disciple of Jesus.
6. He is important enough to go and ask Pilate for permission to take the body of Jesus down from the cross.
7. He puts the body of Jesus in his family tomb.
8. And finally we are told in John 19:39:

> *'He (Joseph) was accompanied by Nicodemus, the man who earlier had visited Jesus at night. Nicodemus brought a mixture of myrrh*

and aloes, about seventy-five pounds. Taking Jesus' body, the two
of them wrapped it, with the spices, in strips of linen.'

Who would ask Pilate for the body of Jesus? A relative! Who would be allowed to prepare the body of Jesus? A relative!

Yes we are talking about Joseph of Aramathea, who might pass through the Gospels very briefly, but has enjoyed an incredible role in apocryphal books, occult stories and later legends.

Why does this man appear so frequently and importantly outside the Bible? And could he actually be Jesus' father? Well Joseph the father appears at Jesus' birth, then disappears. He never seems to die, or perhaps this is just an oversight in the Bible.

Importantly there is a synchronicity between Jesus and Joseph of Aramathea. After the nativity, Mary and a Joseph take Jesus to Egypt where they live for a while to escape Herod. Strangely, in legend, Joseph of Aramathea is also said to spend time in Egypt.

Hrabanus Maurus an early German monk, wrote that Joseph of Aramathea was a 'noblis decorium' and the Welsh monk Gildas equally describes him as a 'noble decurio'. A decurion was an overseer of mining estates and this is why it is thought that he derived his wealth from tin mines in Cornwall, which he visited from time to time. Astonishingly there is a persistent legend that Jesus as a teenager accompanied Joseph on one such visit. This is the background of the poem 'Jerusalem', by William Blake:

'And did those feet in ancient time walk upon England's mountains green?
And was the holy lamb of God on England's pleasant pastures seen?
And did the countenance divine shine forth upon our clouded hills?
And was Jerusalem builded here, among those dark satanic mills?'

Legend also has it that Joseph established a community of 12 believers in Glastonbury, where he was given 12 'hides of land' by King Arviragas and established there the first Christian Church. Legend? Well in the Doomsday book the 12 hides of land are listed and not taxed because of their religious significance.

It is difficult to establish the accuracy of whether a King Arviragas could have been in power at the time of Aramathea since Arviragus is thought to be a title not necessarily a person, just as Pendragon was. Let's look at the Kings of the Britons who might have ruled at the time. In the Triads, and some of the Welsh genealogies, Caractacus appears as the son of Bran. He is mentioned in the Triads as 'Bran the Blessed' following his acceptance of Christianity and his resignation of the crown in favour of his third son, Caractacus the Pendragon. Bran the Blessed became Arch Druid of Siluria in order to devote the remainder of his life to Christianity, into which Druidism was beginning to merge. Date-wise it would be Bran the Blessed who would have been in power when Jesus was a teenager and Caractcus' brother Arviragus (Gweirydd) would be King of the Siluria, where Glastonbury is sited, in the year AD 63 when it became a church. So possibly the visit of Jesus occurred before the establishment of the 12 hides, which happened just after the death of Jesus and suggests that the persecution and dispersal of Jews led Aramathea to Briton. Importantly, in the British Museum there is a manuscript, *'Genealogies of the Welsh Princes'* in which Bran is described as married to Enygeus (Anna) the daughter of Joseph of Aramathea who is referred to as a consabrina of Jesus' mother Mary. Whatever the truth is, there is little doubt that what must have impressed the Jews, and probably Jesus, about the Britons was that they had defeated Julius Caesar and were a free nation. There is also the distinct possibility that Jesus would be influenced by the ancient beliefs of the Druids such as the equality of the sexes. It would be nice to think that we British influenced Jesus! The possibility exists, since Elizabeth 1 cited Joseph's missionary work in England, when she told Roman Catholic bishops that the Church of England pre-dated the Roman Church. And evidence suggests that she was right.

The first appointed leader of the Church in Rome was in AD 58. And it was not Peter as the Roman Church claims (even though he died later in AD 64) but a Briton! And not just any old Briton, but Prince Linus, the son of Caratacus the Pendragon. So Rome's claim that the Popes have Apostolic decent from St. Peter is wrong; they have it from a Briton!

In his De Demonstratione Evangelii, Eusebius writes: 'the Apostles passed over the Ocean to the Islands known as Britain.' And Gildas states that the precepts of Christianity were carried to Britain in the last days of Tiberius,' who died in AD 37, twenty years before Prince Linus was made head of the Roman Church.

Okay, so there is evidence that suggests the possibility that Joseph came to Britain with the young Jesus, but what is more important is that he is mentioned in 'Monty Python and the Holy Grail' where, after killing the white rabbit with the Holy hand-grenade, the Knights find some writing on the wall of the rabbit's cave:

GALAHAD: *What language is that?*
BROTHER MAYNARD: *It's Aramaic!*
GALAHAD: *Of course! Joseph of Aramathea!*
LANCELOT: *Course!*
ARTHUR: *What does it say?*
MAYNARD: *It reads, 'Here may be found the last words of Joseph of Aramathea. He who is valiant and pure of spirit may find the Holy Grail in the Castle of aauugggh'.*
ARTHUR: *What?*
MAYNARD: *'... the Castle of aaugggh'.*
BEDEVIR: *What is that?*
MAYNARD: *He must have died while carving it.*
LANCELOT: *Oh, come on!*
MAYNARD: *Well, that's what it says.*
ARTHUR: *Look, if he was dying, he wouldn't bother to carve 'aaggggh'. He'd just say it!*
MAYNARD: *Well, that's what's carved in the rock!*
GALAHAD: *Perhaps he was dictating.*
ARTHUR: *Oh, shut up.*

The Pythons are not the only ones to link Joseph of Aramathea with the Grail. He is there right from the beginning of the Grail legend. Another little point that arises from this quote, Aramathea is often spelt Arimathea to try to say Joseph came from a small town called Harimathea, which is thought unlikely. There are several other suggestions, like he is named after Ramah in Dan. My own hunch is that he should be spelt Aramathea and, like 'The Holy Grail' hints, Joseph is from where the language Aramaic came from, Mesopotamia. They are an ancient people who worshipped the storm God El, as do the Israelites as shown by their names Michael, Israel, Emmanuel etc. Today, some Syriac Christians are descendants of the Arameans. But this is just a theory.

The stories of the Holy Grail appear at the same time as the Knights Templar 1000 years after the destruction of the Jerusalem Temple. Here I will not deal with the evidence. I will just state (as sensationally as I can) their probable history.

The first rebellion of the Jews in AD 66 led the Romans to destroy the Jerusalem Temple, kill thousands and scattered many Jews around the world.

Christian pilgrims visited Santiago de Compostela in Northern Spain, because James died there. Santiago is Spanish for James and the probable etymology of the word Compostela is from the local Vulgar Latin, Composita Tella, meaning 'burial ground'. Mary Magdalene went to the South of France where there was a large Jewish community. The Mandaeans, followers of John the Baptist, went to Iraq. Important blood-line Jews married into the Royal families of Europe. These Rex Deus (God King) families were instrumental in forming the Crusade to retake the Holy Land from the Seljuk Turks. Their conquest of Jerusalem seemed to confirm to the Crusaders the Biblical Book of Revelations:

> '*The Angel laid hold on the dragon, that old serpent, which is Satan, and bound him a thousand years, and cast him into the bottomless pit, and shut him up, that he should deceive the nations no more, till the thousand years should be fulfilled.... And when the thousand years are expired, Satan shall be loosed out of his prison, and shall go out to deceive the nations which are in the four quarters of the earth, Gog, and Magog, to gather them together to battle.' (Revelations 20)*

Once Jerusalem was conquered, nine Knights related to these Rex Deus families formed the Knights Templar in 1119. Actually in Masonry it says there were in fact eleven Knights and as usual Masonic information seems to be more reliable and research shows that Hugh of Champaign and Falk of Anjou were extras to the usual nine quoted. They swore an oath of secrecy and a pledge to hold in common anything they own, or more importantly, find, because they set out tunnelling below the ruins of the Jerusalem Temple. The excavations took some 6 or 7 years and during that time the Knights were totally inconspicuous. Then suddenly in 1129 they are in Europe, taking on initiates and becoming the most powerful and rich organization in Europe. They had a massive navy; they invented international banking and owned huge tracts of land, evidenced by the place name Temple in so many countries of Europe. What did they find under the Temple that stimulated this flourishing? In 1945 the Dead Sea Scrolls were discovered and amongst them the distinctive Copper Scrolls, a list of the treasures and books of knowledge, which had been hidden from the invading Romans.

At the same time as the Knights Temple were formed, romantic tales began to appear by writers associated with the Rex Deus families that built on the idea of an ancient lineage connecting Jesus with Medieval Europe. In each romance the Grail is kept by the family of Percival, the direct descendent of Joseph of Aramathea. The authors go to considerable length to explain this lineage and its significance. Even in Eric's musical, Spamalot, the leading singer is the 'Lady of the Lake' who in Grail romances, not only 'lies in ponds distributing scimitars', but also nurtures Lancelot du Lac. She is thought to relate to Eleanor of Aquitaine, because the writer, Chrétien de Troyes composed his story for Eleanor's daughter, Countess Marie de Champagne who is thought to be bloodline.

Strangely Arthurian legend says that although Arthur's mother was married, she had become pregnant to another man without any disgrace because she had accepted him under the influence of a magician. Arthur gathers 12 knights round him and leads his people till he is mortally wounded and his body is taken to the west, where there is a romantic land, called Avalon.

Ponder that, while we continue to investigate the nature of the Grail, which Joseph of Aramathea brings from the Holy Land. When Gawain sees it, it appears to be a series of images or visions. The first is a crowned king, crucified. The second is a child. The third is a man wearing a crown of thorns. The fourth is a non specific manifestation and the fifth is a chalice. Each vision is accompanied by a specific aroma and a glowing light.

In 'Monty Python and the Holy Grail', the original script had an ending where Arthur and his army attack the Grail castle, everybody is killed and the only survivors, Arthur and Bedavir enter the castle. There, in the Chapel on the Altar, is the glowing Grail Chalice. They sink to their knees to holy music and the Grail floats gently up into the air and disappears through the roof on its way to heaven. Cut to Arthur and Bedavir leaving the castle and walking past the dead bodies saying:

ARTHUR: *That was a nice Grail.*
BEDAVIR: *Yes it was, a really nice Grail.*
ARTHUR: *Best Grail I've ever seen.*

We pull out to reveal the thousands of dead bodies around them as they walk away.

BEDAVIR: *Yes, the way it glowed was great.*
ARTHUR: *And floated up.*
BEDAVIR: *And disappeared…*

ARTHUR: Fantastic, just fantastic....

Their voices fade out slowly.

Unfortunately we couldn't afford the helicopter and the amount of extras needed so the ending was changed to me dressed as a Policeman bringing the film abruptly to an end by putting my hand over the lens. Much cheaper!

Me bringing 'Holy Grail' to an end

Most of the mythical stories we have quoted, like the Pandira one, all seem to say that Yeshua learnt his magic and mysticism from the priests of Egypt. It suggests to me that Jesus lived in Egypt, till the time came for him to return to Israel and begin his mission.

When Joseph took Jesus to Egypt as a child, the place they would most likely have settled, the place where there was a large Jewish community, was Alexandria. At that very time in Alexandria there was a charismatic sage called Timotheus who fused Osiris and Dionysus to produce a new God for the city called Serapis. Like all the mystery religions at the time, the features of this God were:

1.   A God made flesh.

2. His father is God his mother a mortal virgin.
3. He is born in a humble cave on 25th December.
4. He offers his followers a chance to be born again through the rites of baptism.
5. He miraculously turns water into wine at a wedding.
6. He rides triumphantly on a donkey while people wave palms in his honour.
7. He dies at Easter-time as a sacrifice for the sins of the world.
8. After his death he descends to hell, then on the third day he rises and ascends in triumph.
9. His followers await his return during the last days when he will judge mankind.
10. His death and resurrection are celebrated by a ritual meal of bread and wine – symbolizing the body and blood.

Sounds familiar? What about the philosophy of the Mystery religions?

1. Be pure of thought and deed.
2. Have a personal loving relationship with God.
3. Love your neighbour.
4. Love your enemies.
5. Embrace poverty and humility.
6. Believe in one God.
7. Attack idolatry.
8. The Son of God is the embodiment of the logos.
9. Conceived of God as a Holy Trinity.

What more can I say? Just to repeat Eliphas Levi's statement:

'Elders from the line of David would impregnate a young girl to preserve the bloodline.'

Crazy idea from this 17th century occultist? Not if I add something that the historian Josephus says about a major religious sect of the time of Christ, the Essenes:

'They do not marry out of pleasure but for the sake of posterity.'

8

OTTER'S NOSES

Jerusalem Coliseum, Children's Matinee, Brian is selling Roman snacks. I cannot find any record of a Coliseum or Amphitheatre in Jerusalem other than a modern one in the University. There were Amphitheatres in Israel but they seemed to have been placed in the Romanized towns. Caesarea has a large Amphitheatre with its very own vomitarium and being, the Roman Capital of Israel, it would be the place where the Roman Governor Pilate would have lived. The other Roman town was Tiberius (now modern Tveria) where recently a Roman Amphitheatre has also been discovered.

We shot the scene in the impressive Roman coliseum, in the city of El Jem, Northern Tunisia, a sleepy place without much character. But the coliseum is great, almost as big as the one in Rome, and in better condition.

Interestingly, the Coliseum in Rome was built by Titus after his return to Rome from the Jewish Wars. It is therefore thought that it was mainly Jewish slaves brought back from Israel who built the impressive structure

In amongst the sparse crowd at the Children's Matinee are a group of Jewish revolutionaries, called the 'Peoples Front of Judea' or is it 'The Judean People's Front' or is it the 'Popular Front'? No that's right, the 'Popular Front' is sitting over to the left, 'SPLITTER!'

Anyway they want to clear the Romans out of Israel. First thing to notice is that their female member, Judith, is treated as an equal. In fact, it is she who sorts out Stan's problem:

JUDITH: *Why do you want to be Loretta, Stan?*
ERIC: *I want to have babies.*
JOHN: *You want to have babies?!*

The crew picture taken at the amphitheatre
The author is centre front in a vest. Find all six Pythons for a prize and bonus
points if you can spot the 'splitter'.

ERIC: *It's every man's right to have babies if he wants them.*
JOHN: *But... you can't have babies.*
ERIC: *Don't you oppress me.*
JOHN: *I'm not oppressing you, Stan. You haven't got a womb! Where's the*
foetus going to gestate? You going to keep it in a box?
ERIC: *crying*
JUDITH: *Here! I've got an idea. Suppose you agree that he can't actually have*
babies, not having a womb, which is nobody's fault, not even the Romans,
but that he can have the right to have babies.
MIKE: *Good idea, Judith. We shall fight the oppressors for your right to have*
babies, brother. Sister. Sorry.

You may think that egalitarianism between men and women would be
strange for those days. And perhaps it was, but not amongst Jesus' group. The
Roman Church may have tried to hide the egalitarian nature of the Nazarenes
but it is clear Mary Magdalene is a major player in the group. It is she who

anoints Jesus; she is at the Cross and it is she who finds the body missing, the first witness of the resurrection.

The best surviving document of the Gnostics, who are clearly closer to the real Nazarenes than the Roman Church, is called the Pistis Sophia. It presents a long dialogue in the form of questions from the disciples and Jesus giving the answers. Of the 64 questions, 39 are presented by Mary Magdalene. And Jesus says of Mary:

> *"Mary, thou blessed one, whom I will perfect in all mysteries of those of the height, discourse in openness, thou, whose heart is raised to the kingdom of heaven more than all thy brethren."*

Interestingly the Roman Church forgets her intellectual ability and the egalitarian nature of her position and instead presents her as a prostitute. Here is the relevant passage from the Bible, which they use as evidence:

> *'and also some women who had been cured of evil spirits and diseases: Mary called Magdalene from whom seven demons had come out.' (Luke 8:2)*

From this, the Roman Church blackened her name. The Eastern Orthodox Church never conspired in this character assassination and she was made a Saint with no reference to prostitution.

The Nag Hammadi Gnostic Gospel of Mary Magdalene also describes tensions and jealousy between Mary Magdalene and Peter:

> *'Then Mary wept and said to Peter, "My brother Peter, what do you think? Do you think that I have thought this up myself in my heart, or that I am lying about the Saviour?" Levi answered and said, "Peter you have always been hot tempered. Now I see you contending against the woman like the adversaries. But if the Saviour made her worthy, who are you indeed to reject her? Surely the Saviour knows her very well."'*

How appropriate this is, when it is claimed that Peter was founder of the misogynous Roman Church.

When Brian approaches the group of revolutionaries because he fancies

Judith, he confuses the name. John was supposed to go into a huge swearing tirade.

BRIAN: *Are you the Judean People's Front?*
JOHN: *Fuck off!*
BRIAN: *What?*
JOHN: *Judean fucking People's fucking Front. We're the People's Front of*
    Judea! Judean Fucking People's fucking Front. Cant!

We shot it two ways and in the end used the milder version. The rhythm of the original is still there but John finishes 'Judean's Peoples Front, Cawk! And later the same.

JOHN: *Listen. The only people we hate more than the Romans are the fucking*
    Judean People's Front.
P.F.J.: *Yeah...*
JUDITH: *Splitters.*
P.F.J.: *Splitters...*
MIKE: *And the Judean Popular People's Front.*
P.F.J.: *Yeah. Splitters. Splitters...*
ERIC: *And the People's Front of Judea.*
P.F.J.: *Yeah. Splitters. Splitters...*
JOHN *What?*
ERIC: *The People's Front of Judea. Splitters.*
JOHN: *We're the People's Front of Judea!*
ERIC: *Oh. I thought we were the Popular Front.*
JOHN: *People's Front! C-huh.???*
MIKE: *Whatever happened to the Popular Front, Reg?*
JOHN: *He's over there.*
P.F.J.: *SPLITTER!*

The names of the groups come from modern left wing politics, but there were in fact many conflicting Jewish groups, but their divisions were based on religious differences. Like Catholics and Protestants; or Sunni and Shiite. As with these groups there was often raw hostility between the factions.

Josephus tells us something about the three main groups. The Pharisees, the Sadducees and the Essenes. The Pharisees are the spiritual fathers of modern

Rabbinic Judaism. The Sadducees were elitists who wanted to maintain the priestly caste. The main focus of Sadducee life was rituals associated with the Temple, including animal sacrifice. The Sadducees disappeared in AD 70 after the destruction of the Temple. None of the writings of the Sadducees survived, so the little we know about them comes from their Pharisaic opponents.

The key difference between the warring factions lies between those who wanted to accept Greek philosophies, which had dominated Mediterranean thinking after Alexander's conquest (modernist), and those who wanted to maintain their ancient tribal rules.

These two "parties" served in the Great Sanhedrin, a kind of Jewish Supreme Court made up of 71 members whose responsibility it was to interpret civil and religious laws.

The Essenes appear to be an ascetic sect that emerged out of disgust with the other two. They were more in line with the heretical Greek thinking of the Mystery religions. This sect believed the others had corrupted the city and the Temple. Many moved out of Jerusalem and lived a monastic life in the desert, adopting strict dietary laws and some remained celibate. The Essenes are believed to be an offshoot of the monastic group that lived in Qumran, near the Dead Sea, and it is from their scribes that we get the Dead Sea Scrolls. Their leader was called the 'Teacher of Righteousness' who some believe was a term used for Jesus' brother James.

Besides these three there were subgroups, splinters, racial groups and politicos who were against Roman Rule.

1. Sacarri
2. Zealots
3. Nazarenes
4. Mandeans
5. Samarians

Surprisingly, the actual arrival of the Romans into Israel was due to infighting between two brothers who represented two different religious factions.

After the death of King Alexander of Israel in 76 BC, his widow, Salome, succeeded to the throne and installed her elder son Hyrcanus as High Priest (a woman could not hold the position). Before her death in 67 BC, she named Hyrcanus as successor to the Kingship as well. Hyrcanus shared his mother's religious views, sympathetic to the Pharisees. His younger brother, Alexander who like his father, supported the Sadducees, rose in rebellion. A civil war broke out. This brotherly dispute was to prove fatal to the fortunes of the dynasty and for Israel, for waiting in the wings was Hyrcanus' General, a man called Antipater, the father of Herod the Great.

The brothers competed to bribe the Roman General Pompey, who was stationed in Syria, to aid them. Pompey marched to Jerusalem, ostensibly in support of Hyrcanus but in fact took control of Israel. He allowed Hyrcanus to remain High Priest but not King. This success led to Pompey's nomination for the First Triumvirate with Julius Caesar.

Unfortunately the brothers, and as such, the Sadducees and Pharisees, could not stop fighting and at one point Hyrcanus was captured and his ears were sliced off because a mutilated man could not become High Priest. So not only is the infighting in Brian accurate but people are up to the craziest things, like cutting off ears for religious purposes (could make a very silly sketch).

So the Romans took control of Israel because of divisional infighting. Antipater, through General Pompey, became more and more powerful. Unfortunately, Julius Caesar defeated Pompey, so Antipater lost his benefactor and offered financial support to those who murdered Caesar. For this he was promptly poisoned. After the battle of Philippi where Caesar's murderers were defeated, Herod somehow convinced Mark Anthony and Octavian that his father had been forced to help Caesar's murderers, so when Anthony marched into Asia, in 43 BC, he made Herod King of Israel, and this was the setting for the birth of Jesus and Brian.

Notice that in the list of sects, I have mentioned the Nazarenes again. This sect were followers of Jesus, who were tolerated as a minor sect prior to the rebellion against Rome. Unfortunately, these Judeo-Christians interpreted the destruction of the Temple by the Romans as divine retribution, converting many Jews to their ideas and obviously antagonizing even the most liberal rabbinic opinion. To expose and isolate dangerous elements within the Jewish camp, Rabbi Samuel ha-Katan then enlarged and adapted the Birkat Hamazon, the 'grace after meal', that Jewish Law prescribes to follow a meal that includes bread. The revised text reads as follows:

> *For apostates who have rejected Your Torah let there be no hope, and may the Nazarenes and heretics perish in an instant.'*

Now this is a malediction, which no sectarian could recite aloud in the synagogue and to which they could not possibly respond 'amen'. It thus effectively barred the Nazarenes from public worship and severed their ties with the Jewish people.

9

LATIN FOR BEGINNERS

As a task to join the Peoples Front of Judea, Brian is to write 'Romans Go Home' on the Palace wall. Unfortunately Brian's Latin is not so good and is corrected by John as the Roman Centurion. What is interesting here is what language did people speak at the time and, by inference, what language did Jesus speak?

Though Israelites had once spoken Hebrew as their primary language, this changed when Israel was colonized, first by the Assyrians and then by the Babylonians in the sixth-century BC. Their language, Aramaic, was an ancient Semitic language related to Hebrew much as French is related to Spanish or as Cantonese is related to Mandarin. It appears to have been the common language of Israel during the time of Jesus.

We find direct evidence for Aramaic from the New Testament gospels. Though these gospels were written originally in Greek, at several points Jesus' words are given in Aramaic, for example: Mark 5:41 "Talitha koum" – "Little girl, get up!" Or Mark 15:34 "Eloi, Eloi, lema sabachtani?" – "My God, my God, why have you forsaken me?" The fact that the actual Aramaic words were written, even by Greek speaking Christians make it almost certain that they were originally spoken in Aramaic. Final evidence of the current languages in use comes from Acts of the Apostles where it says:

'When they heard Paul speak to them in Aramaic, they became very quiet.'

It seems from this that he was speaking in Greek, his hometown language (Tarsus) but then switched to the local language, Aramaic, which therefore makes it virtually certain that the locals spoke Aramaic.

After the conquests of Alexander the Great, Greek became the common language of the Empire. In fact Josephus wrote his histories in Greek even though they were for Romans. Educated Israelites would have also spoken Greek, as educated Indians speak English after the British colonial period. If Jesus was from Galilee he would have spoken Aramaic with a very specific accent and had he been a carpenter's son in a small village he would probably not speak Greek but several times throughout the New Testament Jesus converses with someone who spoke only Greek. For example, the dialogue with the Roman centurion in Matthew 8:5-13 and of course the interchange between Jesus and Pilate, who was hardly the sort of gracious governor who would have made the effort to learn the tongue of his subject people.

In 'Life of Brian' it makes sense that Brian would try to write in Latin, the home language of the oppressors, but would make a hash of it. I would suggest that had he written in the common language, Greek, he would have done a better job.

This writing on the wall presents us with a serious Biblical issue. If, as suggested, Jesus could speak Greek, then the big question is: could he read and write in Greek as well? If he could, then ask yourself what did he read? Probably the most influential Greek books of the time were those written by the Greek philosophers, especially Plato. Can we recognize any influence of Greek philosophy in the teachings of Jesus?

> *'This is the Philosopher's way, to be flogged like an ass and to love those who beat him, to be father and brother of all humanity'* (Epictetus)

Sound like a Christian idea to you? What about:

> *'It is never right to do wrong and never right to take revenge, nor is it right to give evil, or in the case of one who has suffered some injury, to attempt to get even.'* (Socrates dialogue by Plato)

And how about this, which might remind you of a camel trying to get through the eye of a needle:

> *'It is impossible for an exceptionally good man to be exceptionally rich.'* (Plato)

90

Actually he did not have to be able to read to hear the philosophy of Cynicism. These ascetics travelled around the Empire in rough cloaks carrying begging bags and thorn sticks, preaching their philosophy, that the purpose of life was to live a life of virtue in agreement with Nature. This meant rejecting all conventional desires for wealth, power, health, and fame, and living a simple life free from all possessions. I like the founder Diogenes who lived his life in a tub on the streets of Athens.

They called their philosophy 'the way' and suggested that as reasoning creatures, people could gain happiness by rigorous training. They believed that the world belonged equally to everyone, and that suffering was caused by false judgments of what was valuable. Many of these thoughts were later absorbed into Stoicism from which one can recognize the life style of John the Baptist.

I'm afraid there is hardly an idea from Jesus that does not come from the Greek philosophers. And why not? If he read these great works, why would he not be influenced by them?

Love thy neighbour, love thy enemy, be pure in thought, believe in the ever-living soul, heaven and hell etc. These are all in the writings of the Greek philosophers. In fact, early Christians dealt with this problem in several different ways. Either as the Christian father, Clement of Alexander who thought that:

The Gospels were 'Perfect Platonism' and Socrates and other Greek philosophers were 'Christians before Christ'.

Or this torturous explanation by Justin Martyr:

'Not because the teachings of Plato are different from those of Christ, but because they are not in all respects similar, as neither are those of the Stoics, poets and historians.'

Or by complete hostility:

'If Platonists have said aught that is true and in harmony with the faith, we are not to shrink from it, but to claim it for our own use from those who have unlawful possession of it.' (St. Augustine)

No wonder the Church tried to destroy the works of Plato and the other philosophers. The few books we have were saved by the Caliph of Baghdad who had them translated into Arabic and all our surviving copies are translations back from the Arabic. Unfortunately many books we know of didn't make it through this Christian persecution. But if Jesus was brought up in Egypt where the Jews of Alexandria had totally abandoned Hebrew he would not only speak Greek but probably read and write it too. Mind you, if he was the Son of God, then presumably he could read and write any language he cared to, so he must have read Greek philosophy or my name isn't Brian Cohen.

Okay, that's not funny, but in a comedy film you can usually predict where your laughs are going to be. However after Brian has written, 'Romans Go Home' all over the palace wall and the guard says, 'Now don't do it again," there was a laugh I hadn't predicted and I am still a bit surprised by it. The line is funny, but not funny enough to get more than a smile. Perhaps it is the way Charles McKeown says it, or my strong belief is that when we pull out to show the whole palace painted – the statement gives a point for the laugh – what I call the release point. By the way we never painted on the walls of the ancient fort in Tunisia. A false wall was built near Brian and then the other writing was superimposed at a later date.

10

WHAT HAVE THE ROMANS EVER DONE FOR US?

In fact it was not the Romans who brought a degree of peace and prosperity to Israel, it was Herod the Great. Not only did he bring peace but he carried out some amazing building projects, which are tourist attractions even to this day. He built the town of Caesarea where he excavated a deep-sea port. The incredible fortress at Masada perched high on the mountaintop. He supported the financially strapped Olympic Games and ensured its future. I must just divert here to tell you that in AD 66 the emperor Nero visited Greece and performed at the Olympic Games, despite the rules against non-Greek participation. He was of course honoured with a victory in every single contest. Mind you, two years later he lost the contest for Emperor and cut his own throat. Back to Herod's achievements: I can make a reasonable case that it was because of Herod the Great that Judaism survives to this day. It is too complicated an argument to make here but just remember the powerful Ancient British religion and culture of Druidism was totally wiped out by the Romans and hardly a trace of it survives to this day. Perhaps the Welsh Eisteddfod festival of bardic poetry and song is the final vestige.

The most important act of Herod was that he rebuilt Solomon's Temple. With all this, the Israelites still did not like him. Even today, he gets a bad press from both Christians and Jews and, I am ashamed to say, historians. If I hear another historian say that Herod was a ruthless despot I am seriously going to damage their noses. We know the victors write history so why do modern historians buy into this propaganda. Herod was no more despotic than any of the others, David, Solomon and if you want a real despot look no further than the Emperor Constantine who is so beloved by Christians for forcing his brand of 'orthodox' Christianity onto the Roman Empire and ultimately down our throats. Ever heard a historian say he was a murdering despot? Of course not! He is even a Saint. But in Croatia in 326, Constantine had his eldest son, Crispus, seized and put to death by 'cold poison'. He then had his wife, the Empress Fausta, killed at the behest of his mother. Fausta was left to die in an over-heated bath. Their names were wiped from the face of many inscriptions and reference to them in the literary records was erased. That great Christian writer Eusebius, edited 'Praise of Crispus' out of later copies of his 'Historia Ecclesiastica' and his 'Vita Constantini' contains no mention of Fausta or Crispus at all. So don't be surprised if his 'orthodox' histories of Christianity are a pack of lies from start to finish.

Now I've got that off my chest, let me try to explain why the Jews did not like Herod. The problem was that he was not an Israelite but an Edomite (Latin: Idumaen). The Edomites were a Semitic tribe who lived near the Dead Sea and were mythically thought to arise from Jacob's elder brother Esau who, in a rather peculiar biblical story lost his birthright, when his younger brother Jacob pretended to be hairy like Esau, and was left everything by his blind father. So you can imagine relations between the Edomites and Israelites from then on were pretty tumultuous. The Edomites were defeated by King Saul of Israel in the late 1000s BC and then by King David forty years later in the 'Valley of Salt' (Dead Sea). The Edomite prince, Hadad escaped and fled to Egypt, and after David's death returned and tried to start a rebellion, but failed and escaped to Syria. From that time Edom remained a vassal of Israel. But when Nebuchadnezzar invaded Israel, the Edomites saw their chance and joined Nebuchadnezzar's troops, helping him plunder Jerusalem. For this reason the Prophets denounced Edom violently, hence the Book of Psalms gives this lovely saying,

"Moab is my washpot: over Edom will I cast out my shoe."

I suppose this is like throwing your shoe at President Bush but adds a chamber pot emptied on his head. This hatred of the Edomites extends to the Torah, which advocates that the congregation must not receive descendants of a marriage between an Israelite and an Edomite until the fourth generation. I must admit my sympathies go to the Edomites because they lost their birthright to Jacob's trick of donning a sheep's skin to fool his blind father by pretending to be hairy. Had this hairy trick not succeeded then the land of Israel would now be called Edom.

Rome generally let the actual Kings rule their tributary states as this created stability but because the two warring brothers caused so much havoc they were forced to appoint Herod as their King of Israel. It was Herod's father's association with Mark Anthony and Julius Caesar, which had sowed the seeds of his power. His loyalty to Mark Anthony gave him enough power to prevent Cleopatra's claims on large areas of Israel. With all this – still nobody likes him to this day though the Israelites go and 'wail' at his wall but refuse to credit it by calling it Herod's Temple.

After Herod the Great died in 4 BC it all went terribly wrong, the kingdom was split into two. Herod's son Herod Antipas ruled Galilee and his brother, Archelaus, ruled Judea. If you remember Matthew mentions him on the return of Joseph and Jesus from Egypt:

'But when he heard that Archelaus was reigning in Judea in place of his father Herod, he was afraid to go there. Having been warned in a dream, he withdrew to the district of Galilee.'

A damn smart dream because Archelaus was an extremely ruthless leader, as Josephus tells:

'He quelled a Pharisee sedition with the utmost cruelty slaying nearly three thousand of them'.

After direct complaints to Rome, Archelaus was deposed in the year AD 6 and banished to Vienne in Gaul. Galilee remained under the Kingship of Herod Antipas but Samaria, Judea and Idumea became the Roman province of Judaea ruled by a Roman procurator. Enter Pontius Pilate.

But what have the Romans ever done for us? They built the aqueduct! Yes one of Pontius Pilate's projects was to build an aqueduct, but do you think the Judeans were grateful? Not according to Josephus:

'In an attempt to bring Judea into the Roman system Pilate began the construction of an aqueduct using money from the sacred treasure known as Corbonas; the water was brought from a distance of seventy kilometres. Indignant at this proceeding, the populace formed a ring round the tribunal of Pilate, then on a visit to Jerusalem, and besieged him with angry clamour. He, foreseeing the tumult, had interspersed among the crowd a troop of his soldiers, armed but disguised in civilian dress, with orders not to use their swords, but to beat any rioters with cudgels. When the Jews were in full torrent of abuse, from his tribunal, he gave the agreed signal. Large numbers of the Jews perished, some from the blows, which they received, others trodden to death by their companions in the ensuing flight. Cowed by the fate of the victims, the multitude was reduced to silence.'

Again 'Life of Brian' seems to reflect the actual situation in Jerusalem. But I would like to make one point here. History is written by the victors and there is no question that any successful conqueror, is ruthless. Take this episode from Josephus.

> *'The governor was not amused when some Jewish jokers passed the hat round for 'our poor procurator Florus'. He demanded their punishment, but when his policemen could not find the mockers, he had some passersby arrested and crucified.'*

This shows, not only a lack of a sense of humour, but a ruthless pompousness. Think how we view reprisals by Hitler's generals in occupied lands. And of course, had Hitler won the war we would now be praising him for managing to get the trains to run on time. The educated Greeks saw the Romans as ruthless primitives unable to understand the humanity of the philosophers. Vespasian and other emperors showed their hand when they issued edicts against 'mathematicians'. The director of 'Brian', Terry Jones, also offers us the chance to see the Romans from a non-Roman perspective. In his TV series 'The Barbarians', he revealed that most of those written off by the Romans as uncivilized, savage and barbarians were in fact organized, motivated and intelligent groups of people. This original and fascinating study reverses the propaganda and opens our eyes to who really established the civilized world. If you thought that highly developed religious philosophy and legal systems based on respect were Roman inventions, then think again. Far from civilizing the societies they conquered, the Romans destroyed much of what they found. In Gaul, perhaps 2 million fell victim to the conquest either killed or enslaved. And from then the population began a steady decline as they were kept well under the subsistence level. Terry quotes the Roman historian Tacitus who put a savage condemnation of the conquest into the mouth of a Celtic leader:

> *'If you want to rule the whole world does it follow that everyone else welcomes enslavement? To robbery, slaughter, plunder, they give the lying name freedom. They make a wilderness and call it peace.'*

Where have I heard that before? Terry Jones corrects the impression given in Brian and answers the question *'what did the Romans do for us?'* With: *'they murdered our population and destroyed our culture.'*

So Brian 'who is to be called Brian' is accepted as a member of the People's Front of Judea (the PFJ) for his daring painting job. Every one of these heroic revolutionaries is prepared to fight to the death to rid Israel of the Romans.

'I'm not!' Oh yes, except one. But they have an audacious plan; to raid Pilate's Palace and kidnap Pilate's wife, hold her for ransom and make demands:

JOHN: We're giving Pilate two days to dismantle the entire apparatus of the Roman Imperialist State, and if he doesn't agree immediately, we execute her.

MATTHIAS: Cut her head off?

MIKE: Cut all her bits off. Send 'em back on the hour every hour. Show them we're not to be trifled with.

JOHN: Also, we're demanding a ten foot mahogany statue of the Emperor Julius Caesar with his dock hangin' out.

ERIC: What? They'll never agree to that, Reg.

JOHN: No. That's just a bargaining counter.

I don't know why that last bit was never filmed, I think it would have got a laugh, even though it is very silly.

11

THE RAID

Obviously Pilate's Palace would not be in Jerusalem but in the Roman capital Caesarea; if he had a residence in Jerusalem it would be Herod's Palace. But garrison soldiers would certainly have barracks in Jerusalem for, as Josephus says, soldiers were present at all the major Jewish festivals to prevent trouble. One event that Josephus recounts, could almost have been written by the Pythons, and gives us several clues. It occurred when Cumanus was Procurator, a few years after the time of Christ.

> *'The people had assembled in Jerusalem for the feast of Unleavened Bread, and the Roman cohort stood on guard over the Temple colonnade, armed men always being on duty at feasts to forestall any rioting by the vast crowd. One of the soldiers pulled up his garment and bent over indecently, turning his backside towards the Jews and making a noise as indecent as his attitude. This infuriated the whole crowd, who noisily appealed to Cumanus to punish the soldier, while the less restrained of the young men and the naturally tumultuous section of the people rushed into battle, and snatching up stones hurled them at the soldiers. Cumanus, fearing that the whole population would rush at him, sent for more heavy infantry. When these poured into the colonnades, the Jews were seized with uncontrollable panic, turned tail and fled from the Temple into the City. So violently did the dense mass struggle to escape that they trod on each other, and more than 30,000 were crushed to death. Thus the Feast ended in distress to the whole nation and bereavement to every household.'*

I'm sure if I told you Mike Palin wrote this and that it was a scene we cut from 'Life of Brian', you would have believed me. Although the figure of 30,000 deaths from the fart is probably an exaggeration, we do get the fact that the Procurator was in Jerusalem during the Festivals and so probably had some sort of residence there, but it definitely would not be his main residence for a raid. And his wife would certainly live in Caesarea. By the way a wife does get a brief mention in the Bible. She has a dream that Jesus is innocent and pops in to tell Pilate. In Josephus (in the obviously forged bit), she actually gets to meet Jesus.

> 'And he [Pilate] had that wonder-doer brought up. And when he had instituted a trial concerning him, he perceived that he is a doer of good... and set him free. He had, you should know, healed his dying wife.'

Wow, Jesus had dropped into the Roman Procurator's Palace and performed a miracle on his dying wife. How did the Bible miss this crucial miracle?

For having this wondrous dream, she has been made a Saint in the Orthodox Church, St. Procula. Around the 15th Century she got a first name, Claudia Procula. I can't tell you where these names came from all I know is that we cut her out of the film.

We made two cuts in the raid. The first occurs as the PFJ are creeping along the corridors and they nearly bump into some Romans who are playing hide and seek. Secondly when the PFJ arrive at Pilate's wife's door they come face to face with another group of revolutionaries, The Campaign For Free Galilee, who for some reason John does with a Welsh accent. (Not a bad choice, as the Galileans were known to speak Aramaic with a strong accent.) In the script, the encounter is much longer, resulting in the actual appearance of Pilate's wife.

DEADLY DIRK: Campaign for Free Galilee.
MIKE: Oh. Uh, People's Front of Judea. Officials.
DEADLY DIRK: Oh.
MIKE: What's your group doing here?
DEADLY DIRK: We're going to kidnap Pilate's wife, take her back, issue demands.
MIKE: So are we.
DEADLY DIRK: What?
MIKE: That's our plan!
DEADLY DIRK: We were here first!

MIKE: *What do you mean?*
DEADLY DIRK: *We thought of it first!*
WARRIS: *Oh, yeah?*
DEADLY DIRK: *Yes, a couple of years ago!*
P.F.J.: *Ha. Heh. Ha ha.*
DEADLY DIRK: *We did!*
MIKE: *Okay, come on. You got all your demands worked out, then?*
DEADLY DIRK: *'Course we have.*
MIKE: *What are they?*
DEADLY DIRK: *Well, I'm not telling you.*
MIKE: *Oh, come on. Pull the other one.*
DEADLY DIRK: *That's not the point! We thought of it before you!*
MIKE: *You didn't.*
C.F.G.: *We bloody did!*
DEADLY DIRK: *You bastards! We've been planning this for months.*
MIKE: *Well, tough titty for you, Fish Face.*

Deadly Dirk pokes Mike in the eye and the groups begin to fight.

BRIAN: *Brothers! Brothers! We should be struggling together!*
MIKE: *We are! Ohh.*
BRIAN: *We mustn't fight each other! Surely we should be united against the common enemy!*
EVERYONE: *The Judean People's Front!*
BRIAN: *No, no! The Romans!*
EVERYONE: *Oh, yeah. Yeah. Yeah. Yes.*
MIKE: *Yeah. He's right. Let's go in, get her out, and we can argue afterwards.*
DEADLY DIRK: *All right.*
RANDOM: *Yeah.*
DEADLY DIRK: *Solidarity!*
MIKE: *Oh yeah, solidarity.*
RANDOM: *Let's go get her.*

There is suspenseful music as they approach the door and creep into the bedroom and jump on the sleeping figure in the bed. There is a scuffle but slowly the figure of PILATE'S WIFE rises — and rises — and rises. She is enormous; the revolutionaries are hanging on desperately.

100

PILATE'S GIGANTIC WIFE ESCAPES WITH
REVOLUTIONARIES HANGING ON FOR DEAR LIFE

MIKE: I got her. I got her. Quick. I got her! I— I— Uhm. She got me. Help! She
   got me. She g—
   They chase her round the corridors. Twice round and back she runs into
   the bedroom.
MIKE: Get the door! The door! Get the door!

The door slams and the bolts are shot closed.

DEADLY DIRK: Shit!
MIKE: You stupid—
DEADLY DIRK: I don't believe it.
MIKE: You stupid bastard.
   Deadly Dirk cracks him in the face and another fight breaks out. Two
   Roman soldiers pass by and watch the fighting in amazement. Brian tries
   to pull the Revolutionaries apart.
BRIAN: Brothers! Brothers!

Too late they have knocked each other out. Brian sees the Roman soldiers and
gets ready for a fight. The doors of the bedroom open behind him and the
Gigantic figure of Pilate's wife, raises a fist and brings down a hammer blow
that flattens Brian.

The massive Pilate's wife was played by a large man, you can see him in the haggling scene where he comes up behind Brian, forcing him to haggle with Eric. But as Pilate's wife, he just didn't look believable so it didn't work in the context of the film.

The factionist infighting between different groups, which is a major theme of the 'Life of Brian', is never shown in other Biblical films, yet it is absolutely key to understanding Israel at the time.

As mentioned before, even the entry of the Romans into Israel, in the first place, was caused by infighting between the Sadducees and the Pharisees. But worse was to follow, which would result in disaster for the Jews with repercussions to this very day.

Thirty years after the time of Christ a revolt occurred. In AD 66, the Roman emperor Nero needed money, and ordered his representative in Judaea, Gessius Florus, to confiscate it from the Temple treasure. Remember Josephus wrote the section about passing the hat round.

'The governor was not amused when some Jewish jokers passed the hat round for 'our poor procurator Florus'. He demanded their punishment, but when his policemen could not find the mockers, he had some passersby arrested and crucified.'

Of course this was tactless and brutal, but it would not have led to the war if there had not been other deeper causes, mainly the religious tension between the Jewish populace and the Roman government. As mentioned, I keep coming across links between Britain and Israel, and I have a theory that one of the stimulants for the AD 66 rebellion of the Jews was the uprising 4 years earlier by Boadicea, Queen of the Brittonic Iceni. This rebellion must have been an inspiration for those wishing to take on the Romans. In Israel, concern about a potential uprising led Jewish liberals to send an envoy to plead with Nero, but too late; one of the Roman garrisons in Jerusalem was annihilated. Urgently Cestius Gallus, the legate of Syria marched his legions into Israel to help restore order. Then occurred something that shocked the Roman world. An ambush by the Israelites at Beth Heron defeated the Romans and freed Israel. This may have been a Jewish success, but it was clear that the Romans would return with a larger army, and many people fled, leaving Israel in the hands of the radicals.

The shock in Rome over the defeat at the battle of Beth Heron led Nero to order General Vespasian to march his legions from the now subdued Britain, to Israel to suppress the rebellion. But by the time Vespasian arrived, Rome was in turmoil. Nero's failure in Israel, followed by his increasing erratic behaviour lost him all support. When the senate declared him an enemy of the people, he fled Rome and ended by thrusting a dagger into his throat. The newly installed Emperor Galba, was soon murdered by a rival which triggered a civil war in what became the 'Year of the Four Emperors'.

In Israel, in AD 69 Vespasian succeeded in quelling Northern Israel and was subsequently hailed emperor by the legions under his command. He decided to return to Rome to claim the throne from Vitellius. This led to delays in the Roman advance, as Vespasian's son Titus took over conduct of the war.

The leaders of the collapsed Northern revolt, John of Giscala and Simon Bar Giora, managed to escape to Jerusalem. Then began the craziest events that are tragically mirrored in the fighting between the 'PFJ' and the 'Campaign For Free Galilee' in 'Life of Brian'. With the Romans at the door a brutal civil war erupted between the Israelites! The Zealots and the fanatical Sicarii executed anyone advocating surrender, and by AD 69 the entire leadership of the southern revolt was dead, killed by Jewish hands in the infighting.

Finally Titus arrived at the fortified city walls of Jerusalem, but if you think this would have united the defending forces, you have another think coming. Extraordinarily the infighting continued within the sieged city. Zealots under Eleazar Ben Simon held the Temple; Sicarii led by Simon Bar Giora held the upper city. A stockpiled supply of food was intentionally burned by Jewish leaders, to induce the defenders to fight against the siege, instead of negotiating peace. As a result, many city dwellers and soldiers died of starvation. By now the Romans were not prepared to negotiate. The soldiers were counting the potential spoils that awaited them, so any Judeans who attempted to escape from the divided city were crucified, with as many as five hundred crucifixions occurring in one day.

The siege continued till AD 70 and the two Zealot leaders only ceased hostilities and joined forces to defend the city when the Romans began to construct ramparts for the final attack. When the Romans broke through, what followed was possibly a tragic accident: a mixture of happenstance or narrowly cynical political calculation, which depressingly foreshadows George W. Bush and Tony Blair stumbling into the Iraq catastrophe.

According to Josephus, Titus just wanted to put down the rebellion but by the time they broke through on 29th July AD 70, random indiscipline by marauding soldiers burnt down the Jerusalem Temple. Titus decided to brazen out the destruction of this famous ancient shrine and to make a feature of it. He proclaimed the victory not just over Judea but the religion and the culture called Judaism. Titus' triumphal parade in Rome featured the scrolls of the Jewish law, together with other temple regalia, which were later depicted in carvings on his triumphal arch. Certainly, Vespasian based his shaky claim to rule on his victory over the Jews, and his successors saw no need to challenge that handy justification for their imperial power. Here begins the specific persecution of the Jews.

The Israelites believed in one God and had just one Temple to house him. All the different Jewish sects, worshipped there. Sadducees, Pharisees, Sacarii, Nazareans, all believing in the coming Davidic Messiah. Some gentiles in the Roman Empire converted to Judaism and allowed themselves to be circumcised. One small group of Jews believed the Messiah had already come and this man, Jesus Kristos, had predicted the destruction of the Temple, which would initiate 'the End of Days'. Jews all over the Empire had sent regular donations to the Temple, but after Vespasian's victory, he introduced a tax on Jews to prevent the rebuilding of the Temple. To avoid this tax and general persecution aimed at Jews, the followers of Jesus separated themselves and became specifically Christians.

There followed several events that caused this sect to expand and believe the 'End of Days' had begun. Firstly, as mentioned, the destruction of the Temple as predicted. Secondly the appearance of Halley's Comet in AD 70. Thirdly the eruption of Vesuvius in AD 79 and the destruction of Pompeii, which must have appeared like an 'End of Days' event. And finally the rising sun moving into the star sign Pisces, signifying a new age. The original symbol for Kristos followers was the fish.

The taxation and persecution of the Jews led to further revolts and finally Hadrian wiped out resistance, ploughed Jerusalem with a yoke of oxen and Jews were transported to Egypt or sold into slavery. Jerusalem was turned into a pagan city called Aelia Capitolina, the name being a combination of Hadrian's own name and that of the Roman God Capitolinus (Jupiter). Two large statues were placed on the site of the Temple, obviously a sacrilege. The Jews were forbidden to live there but were permitted to enter only on the 9th of Av to mourn their losses in the revolt. The Romans renamed Israel, Palestine, a name that derives from the previous occupants of the land: the Philistines!

Christian emperors continued the persecution and refused to allow the Temple to be rebuilt, as it was a symbol of Christ's victory over the Jews. One last hope arrived in the form of my namesake, the Emperor Julian. He was the last non-Christian ruler of the Roman Empire who aspired to return the empire to its ancient Roman values. He purged the top-heavy state bureaucracy and rejected Christianity in favour of Neo-Platonist paganism. He is therefore titled Julian the Apostate by the Church. Julian proposed to allow the Jews to rebuild their Temple and regain their homeland. Unfortunately, he was killed in a war against Persia before this could be undertaken, and all hope of preventing the disaster, which befell the Jews in the 20th Century disappeared.

Well there was one glimmer of hope in 1918, and that revolved around Laurence of Arabia. In June 1916, there was an Arab revolt against the Turks. Laurence became liaison officer to the leader Faisal forming a strong friendship. Laurence's over-riding aim was to produce a military success for the Arabs that would help to win them a claim to self-government. After victory, Lawrence immediately began to press the case for Arab independence and joined Emir Faisal at the Paris Peace Conference. Now astonishingly, Faisal exchanged letters of agreement with Chaim Weizmann head of the World Zionist organization. I leave you to read the correspondence and wonder what type of world would have been created had Britain and France not reneged on the deal.

> From Faisal – *'The two main branches of the Semitic family, Arabs and Jews, understand one another, and I hope that as a result of interchange of ideas at the Peace Conference, which will be guided by ideals of self-determination and nationality, each nation will make definite progress towards the realization of its aspirations. Arabs are not jealous of Zionist Jews, and intend to give them fair play and the Zionist Jews have assured the Nationalist Arabs of their intention to see that they too have fair play in their respective areas. Turkish intrigue in Palestine has raised jealousy between the Jewish colonists and the local peasants, but the mutual understanding of the aims of Arabs and Jews will at once clear away the last trace of this former bitterness, which, indeed, had already practically disappeared before the war by the work of the Arab Secret Revolutionary Committee, which in Syria and elsewhere laid the foundation of the Arab military successes of the past two years.'*

The areas discussed were detailed in a letter from Faisal to the President of the Zionist Organization of America:

> *"The Arabs, especially the educated among us, look with the*

King Faisal and Zionist leader Chaim Weizmann wearing Arab costume as a sign of friendship

deepest sympathy on the Zionist movement. Our deputation here in Paris is fully acquainted with the proposals submitted yesterday by the Zionist Organization to the Peace Conference, and we regard them as moderate and proper."

The proposals submitted by the Zionist Organization to the Peace Conference were:

"The boundaries of Palestine shall follow the general lines set out below: Starting on the North at a point on the Mediterranean Sea in the vicinity South of Sidon and following the watersheds of the foothills of the Lebanon as far as Jisr el Karaon, thence to El Bire following the dividing line between the two basins of the Wadi El Korn and the Wadi Et Teim thence in a southerly direction following the dividing line between the Eastern and Western slopes of the Hermon, to the vicinity West of Beit Jenn. In the East a line close to and West of the Hedjaz Railway terminating in the Gulf of Akaba. In the South a frontier to be agreed upon with the Egyptian Government. In the West the Mediterranean Sea. The

details of the delimitations, or any necessary adjustments of detail, shall be settled by a Special Commission on which there shall be Jewish representation."

I'm sorry if this failure of the British and French to relinquish their colonies thereby scuppering this agreement leaves you as depressed as it does me. And remember poor Laurence who must also have been depressed and disappeared for many years, reappearing as an aircraftman in the RAF under the name John Hume Ross.

12
BIGGUS DICKUS

Brian is captured and thrown into jail with a hanging man who considers Brian to be a *'lucky, lucky bastard'*. Thanks to Mike Palin's amazing ability to just become different people I was able to cut from the end of the scene; from Mike saying, "Terrific race the Romans," directly to Mike as Pilate without the slightest disruption for the audience.

The fun of the scene is based on the premise that you say a silly name, in this case, Biggus Dickus, and if anybody laughs they get thrown to the lions. And on top of this you have Pilate with a silly speech impediment. It's the perfect setup to get the audience into hysterics.

There is one gag, that made me laugh in the script, but does not work in the film. With Pilate's speech impediment he cannot say his R's. So we get statements in the script like:

PILATE: *So, you dare to waid us.*
BRIAN: *To what, sir?*
PILATE: *Stwike him, Centuwion, vewy woughly!*
    Slap
BRIAN: *Aaah!*
CENTURION: *And, throw him to the floor, sir?*
PILATE: *What?*
CENTURION: *Thwow him to the floor again, sir?*
PILATE: *Oh, yes. Thwow him to the floor, please.*
    Brian is thrown to the floor again.
PILATE: *Now, Jewish wapscallion*
BRIAN: *I'm not Jewish. I'm a Roman.*
PILATE: *A Woman?*

BRIAN: *No, no. Roman.*
    Slap
BRIAN: *Aah!*

So in the script you see that he is saying Woman for Roman – but of course when Mike actually says it, it comes out as Wowman not our actual pronunciation, which is more like Wuman.

I hope you spotted that after denying his Roman blood and insisting he is a '*Kike! A Yid! A Hebe! A Hook-nose! A Red Sea Pedestrian, and proud of it!*' Now when Brian is brought before Pilate he suddenly pleads that he is Roman and as such should be treated differently. What a turnabout, you may think, and you would be right, but in fact this is exactly what happens with Paul of Tarsus in the Bible. Paul starts by telling the Jews:

> "*I am a Jew, born in Tarsus of Cilicia, but brought up in this city. I studied under Gamaliel and was thoroughly trained in the law of our ancestors. I was just as zealous for God as any of you are.*"

Fine but then after a rumpus in Jerusalem, Paul is dragged before the Roman commander:

> '*The commander ordered that Paul be taken into the barracks. He directed that he be flogged and interrogated in order to find out why the people were shouting at him. As they stretched him out to flog him, Paul said to the centurion standing there, "Is it legal for you to flog a Roman citizen who hasn't even been found guilty?"*
>
> *When the centurion heard this, he went to the commander and reported it. "What are you going to do?" he asked. "This man is a Roman citizen."*
>
> *The commander went to Paul and asked, "Tell me, are you a Roman citizen?"*
>
> *"Yes, I am," he answered.*
>
> *Then the commander said, "I had to pay a lot of money for my citizenship."*
>
> *Paul replied, "I was born a citizen."*'

Like Brian, Paul never mentions his Roman citizenship until he is arrested and about to be flogged then suddenly; hang on guys, I'm a Roman!

This actually rings true because as a Roman citizen he could appeal direct to the Emperor.

PILATE: So, your father was a Woman. Who was he?
BRIAN: Nartius Maximus.

John slaps Brian quite a bit in this scene. If you look at the slaps you will see I have pinched a couple of frames of film to make the hits have more impact. There is one hit that I couldn't doctor because Pilate is walking across the screen after he warns one of the guards. If I pinched frames here, Pilate would jump across the screen, so you will see how poor the original hits look.

After much merriment at the expense of Biggus Dickus, the first Guard, Charles McKeown is dragged off by John to go and fight *'Wabid wild animals within a week'*. John thought the scene should end there as it just becomes too silly. Pilate suddenly drops out of character and starts teasing the soldiers with.

> *'Anybody else feel like a little giggle when I mention my fwiend Biggus Dickus?'*

John is probably right in theory, but that's the fun of doing comedy, every now and then something works that is unexpected. It is probably just that the audience is enjoying the scene so much that they are happy to see it carry on, even though Mike is (if you look carefully) corpsing.

PILATE: What about you? Do you find it wisible when I say the name 'Biggus'. (Mike corpses here)
GUARD : chuckle
PILATE: ...'Dickus'?
> *The Guard purses his lips closed. But the two near Brian giggle. Pilate turns and moves behind them.*
PILATE: He has a wife, you know. You know what she's called?
> *They shake their heads in fear.*

On each take Mike would say a different name for the wife to make the

Guards actually laugh. In the cutting room I had to decide which was the funniest. They were all so good that it was hard to choose.

PILATE: *She's called... 'Incontinentia'. 'Incontinentia Buttocks'.*
The Guards burst out in uncontrollable laughter.
PILATE: *Stop it! I've had enough of this wowdy webel sniggewing behaviour. Silence! Call yourselves Pwaetowian guards?*
Brian makes a run for it.
PILATE: *Seize him! Seize him! Blow your noses and seize him!*

That last line is ad-libbed, it comes from the fact that Bernard had a bad cold; every time Mike went behind them to say a different name, Bernard would burst out laughing and his nose would run.

Mike's Pontius Pilate is funny but also quick to castigate his soldiers and crucify his subjects. The Biblical Pilate, though, is an okay guy, washing his hands of Christ's crucifixion, which is blamed on the Jews. Let's try to sort out who the real Pilate was and which interpretation is the most accurate.

Pilate was the Roman governor of Judea, not all Israel, as Herod Antipas ruled Galilee. He arrived in Caesarea, which was the Roman Capital in AD 26. Josephus writes about him:

'Pilate, being sent by Tiberius as Prefect to Judaea, introduced into Jerusalem, by night, Military Standards with the effigy of Caesar. When day broke, the Jews were in consternation, considering their law against craven images in the Holy City had been trampled on. It was for this reason that the previous prefects, when they entered Jerusalem, used standards that had no such ornaments. Pilate was the first to bring standards into Jerusalem. The indignation of the townspeople stirred the country folk, who flocked together in crowds. Hastening to Caesarea, the Jews implored Pilate to remove the standards from Jerusalem and to uphold the laws of their ancestors. When Pilate refused, they fell prostrate around his palace and for five whole days and nights remained motionless in that position. On the sixth day he secretly armed and placed his troops in position in the great stadium. Pilate took his seat on his tribunal and summoned the multitude, with the apparent intention of answering them. Once in he gave the arranged signal to his armed

*soldiers to surround the Jews. Finding themselves in a ring of
troops, three deep, the Jews were struck dumb. Pilate, threatening
to cut them down, if they refused to admit Caesar's images,
signalled to the soldiers to draw their swords. Thereupon the Jews,
as by concerted action, flung themselves in a body on the ground,
extended their necks, and exclaimed that they were ready to die
rather than to transgress the law. Overcome with astonishment at
such intense religious zeal, Pilate gave orders for the immediate
removal of the standards from Jerusalem and to return them to
Caesarea.'*

It is clear from this that Pilate's Palace was in Caesarea. But before we
continue to examine the historical Pilate, let's look at the Biblical one.

*'Then Pilate announced to the chief priests and the crowd, "I find
no basis for a charge against this man."*
  *But they insisted, "He stirs up the people all over Judea by his
teaching. He started in Galilee and has come all the way here."*
  *On hearing this, Pilate asked if the man was a Galilean. When
he learned that Jesus was under Herod's jurisdiction, he sent him
to Herod, who was also in Jerusalem at that time. When Herod
saw Jesus, he was greatly pleased, he hoped to see him perform
some miracle. He plied him with many questions, but Jesus gave
him no answer. Then Herod and his soldiers ridiculed and mocked
him. Dressing him in an elegant robe, they sent him back to Pilate.
That day Herod and Pilate became friends—before this they had
been enemies.' (Luke 23)*

That last statement is interesting. Herod and Pilate had been enemies, a
fact that is confirmed by Philo of Alexandria, who was related to the Herodian
dynasty and probably had the same antagonism towards Pilate. See how this
influences his version of Josephus' story about the military shields.

*'Pilate was an official who had been appointed prefect of Judaea.
With the intention of annoying the Jews rather than of honouring
Tiberius, he set up gilded shields in Herod's palace in the Holy
City.'*

Philo here is accusing Pilate of purposefully annoying the Jews.

> 'But when the Jews at large learnt of this action, which was indeed already widely known, they chose as their spokesmen the king's [Herod the Great] four sons, who enjoyed prestige and rank equal to that of kings, and besought Pilate to undo his innovation in the shape of the shields, and not to violate their native customs, which had hitherto been invariably preserved inviolate by kings and emperors alike.'

As Philo is related to Herod, he sympathetically suggests Herod was involved in trying to preserve the Jewish customs. Then follows a tirade that probably reflects the Herodian family's hatred of Pilate.

> 'When Pilate, who was a man of inflexible, stubborn and cruel disposition, obstinately refused, they shouted: 'Do not cause a revolt! Do not cause a war! Do not break the peace! Disrespect done to our ancient laws brings no honour to the emperor. Do not make Tiberius an excuse for insulting our nation. He does not want any of our traditions done away with. If you say that he does, show us some decree or letter or something of the sort, so that we may cease troubling you and appeal to our master by means of an embassy.'

Now instead of Pilate being moved by the passion of the Jews, a totally different explanation follows for why Pilate removed the Standards:

> 'This last remark exasperated Pilate most of all, for he was afraid that if they really sent an embassy, they would bring accusations against the rest of his administration as well, specifying in detail his venality, his violence, his thefts, his assaults, his abusive behaviour, his frequent executions of untried prisoners, and his endless savage ferocity.'

So he was worried that Jewish and mainly Herodian representation to Tiberius may reveal his ruthlessness and mismanagement.

> 'So, as he was a spiteful and angry person, he was in a serious

dilemma; for he had neither the courage to remove what he had once set up, nor the desire to do anything which would please his subjects, but at the same time he was well aware of Tiberius' firmness on these matters. When the Jewish officials saw this, and realized that Pilate was regretting what he had done, although he did not wish to show it, they wrote a letter to Tiberius, pleading their case as forcibly as they could.

What words, what threats Tiberius uttered against Pilate when he read it! It would be superfluous to describe his anger, although he was not easily moved to anger, since his reaction speaks for itself. For immediately, without even waiting until the next day, he wrote to Pilate, reproaching and rebuking him a thousand times for his new-fangled audacity and telling him to remove the shields at once and have them taken from the capital to the coastal city of Caesarea, to be dedicated in the temple of Augustus. This was duly done. In this way both the honour of the emperor and the traditional policy regarding Jerusalem were preserved.'

I cannot believe this last part about Tiberius' involvement because it sounds like they are communicating by email. Letters to and from Rome would have taken months yet from start to finish the events only took a week. Philo lived in Alexandria and must have heard the story much later than the real event. Philo shows that the Bible is right in that there was hostility between Herod and Pilate, but while he may have been ruthless, it is unlikely that Pilate deliberately provoked the Jews. The Romans could be harsh masters, but they were not stupid. There are coins designed and minted during Pilate's time and if he wanted to provoke the Jews he could have put the Emperors head on them or an eagle. Instead he uses neutral motifs, which the Jews were long accustomed to seeing on their money.

While we are talking about coins, remember the story of Jesus throwing over the tables of the Money Changers. I have often wondered what these Money Changers were doing outside the Temple? My theory is that Jews were arriving from all over the Empire to visit the Temple, often with coins that would have 'graven images' on them like the Emperor's head. These would not be allowed in the Temple so would have to be changed for local inoffensive coins. Well, it's a theory.

What does all this tell us about Pilate? He was obviously disliked by the

Coins of the years 30 (top) and 32 (bottom)

Herodian family, Philo of Alexander really seems to have hated him and Josephus suggests he was at least, insensitive. So nobody outside the Bible has a good word to say about him.

'Life of Brian's' Pilate is closer to the real person than the Christian version since the Church of Rome, in an attempt to exonerate the Romans made the crucifixion a result of Jewish pressure. And boy are they a bunch of pressurizing bastards in Mel Gibson's 'Passion'. One has to feel so sorry for Gibson's poor old Pilate. Another typical example of this comes from the apocryphal Gospel of Peter, which absolves Pilate of responsibility for the crucifixion of Jesus, placing it instead on Herod and the Jews, who unlike Pilate refuse to "wash their hands." Peter even follows this with Pilate having intimate knowledge of the resurrection when he writes, soldiers saw three men and a cross miraculously walking out of the tomb and reported it to Pilate who reiterates his innocence,

"I am pure from the blood of the Son of God."

He then commands the soldiers not to tell anyone what they have seen so that they would not *"fall into the hands of the people of the Jews and be stoned."*

Those of you still pondering on the 'twins' might be interested in the possible origin of our Procurator's name. Pilatus was a hat worn by the devotees of the Castorian cult who lived in Dacia (modern Romania) and Pileatus was used as a cognomen by the descendants of the ruler Burebista of Dacia, whose descendants are known to have been soldiers stationed in Judea, Britain and Spain. In their cult, Castor and Pollux were Twins who shared the same mother but had different fathers, one being a God, which meant that Pollux was immortal and Castor was mortal. That the twins were popular at the time can be found in the Bible. When St. Paul was shipwrecked on the Island of Malta it tells how:

> '*After three months we put out to sea in a ship that had wintered in the island. It was an Alexandrain ship with the figurehead of the twin gods Castor and Pollux.*' (Acts 28:11)

If Pilate was in fact a follower of the twins Castor and Pollux, there may be important implications, which I will deal with later.

13

CHARIOT OF THE GODS

Chased up the winding stairs, escape for Brian seems hopeless. When suddenly he falls from the tall tower and drops into a passing Alien spaceship, 'The jammy bastard'. Okay you believe this has nothing to do with the real Jesus story but you are wrong. There is one logical explanation for the movement of the star over Bethlehem, not mentioned previously: that it was a UFO. There are UFO worshippers who meet on hilltops at night and pray to communicate with those very spacemen they believe descended that night on Bethlehem. They came from an advanced planet, bringing an Alien, Jesus with superior knowledge to help mankind on their journey to peace. And that is why a UFO happens to be passing by at this very moment in Brian's life.

TERRY DIRECTS GRAHAM TO JUMP (onto a matress)

I remember going to the cinema with Terry Gilliam to see 'Star Wars' when it first came out. We were both knocked out by the very opening shot. Terry wanted to have a go at doing a miniature 'Star Wars' sequence and so was born the spaceship scene.

We shot the whole sequence in a small, room-sized studio in Neals Yard in London. There is a blue plaque on the wall there, that says it was the Monty Python office. This is wrong. Mike Palin, Terry Gilliam and myself rented it. Mike helped Andre Jaquemin (writer of the 'Brian Song') build a recording studio there and in the basement Terry started Peerless Camera Company which would do the optical effects for us (put the stars onto our model spaceship). Terry and I had cutting rooms and a small studio in the upper part. I shot many miniatures in that studio. Those of you who know 'Timebandits' will remember the sequence where the Bandits swing out of hanging cages. Surprisingly, some of this I shot in our tiny studio. When the spaceship crashes and Brian steps out unscathed, the guy who says 'You jammy bastard' is Charles Knode who was the costume designer. He got the part after he did a great performance in 'Holy Grail'. At the Wedding Castle, which Lancelot attacks, there are two entrance guards. Lancelot slays one, who is Tommy the Props man and rushes past the other who is Charles. He turns and says, "Hey!" That brilliant delivery got him the part in 'Brian'.

Actually the line was changed to "You lucky bastard," because it was thought *'jammy bastard'* would not be understood by Americans.

CHARLES SAYS 'JAMMY BASTARD'   CHARLES SAYS 'HEY'

Chased by Roman soldiers, Brian runs through the market place where Prophets harangue the populace. Terry Gilliam is covered in mud and yelling vociferously, the next is Charles McKeown doing a Rev Paisley and finally Mike Palin, as what we called the Boring Prophet.

Prophets were major characters in Israel's history. Somehow their presence is missed in other Biblical films. In Israel, a prophet was seen as a person who spoke as a representative of God, and the intention of the message was always to effect a social change to conform to God's desired standards. Oddly in Hebrew, the word that traditionally translates as prophet is Navi, which means 'spokesperson'. (In Britain a navi is an unskilled railway worker.)

> 'The Lord your God said… "I will raise up for them a prophet like you from among their brothers; I will put my words in his mouth, and he will tell them everything I command him. If anyone does not listen to my words that the prophet speaks in my name, I myself will call him to account.' (Deuteronomy 18)

Thus, the navi was thought to be the "mouth" of God. But then the problems begin, and Deuteronomy itself raises them.

> "A prophet who presumes to speak in my name anything I have not commanded him to say… must be put to death."

Okay watch out if you dare to speak for God and you don't have a direct line to the Almighty. But…

> 'You may say to yourselves, "How can we know when a message has not been spoken by the Lord?"
> If what a prophet proclaims in the name of the Lord does not take place or come true, that is a message the Lord has not spoken. That prophet has spoken presumptuously. Do not be afraid of him.'

Afraid of him? Why would we be afraid of him, we have just 'put him to death'?

The other prophets were scripted but Mike did five takes of his Boring Prophet, which he felt compelled to make different each time and recalls, in his autobiography, feeling quite exhilarated by the experience. As a 'stream of consciousness', Mike's boring words are more likely to be the actual words of God! So perhaps God is a bit boring, which is a lot nicer than the Hail and Brimstone God that most prophets of Israel spoke as His mouthpiece.

Still pursued by the Roman soldiers, Brian stops at the beard sellers to grab a disguise but is stuck haggling. Editing-wise there is an interesting story here for film students. After shooting each day we would send the film back to London to be processed and the rushes were sent back to us in Tunisia. After my assistant, Rodney Glenn, had sunk the sound to the picture we would show rushes to the crew and actors in a large room in the Hotel.

The haggling scene consisted of three shots:

Shot 1 a wide two shot of Brian and Eric.
Shot 2 a single close up of Brian.
Shot 3 a single close up of Eric.

The first thing that came up in rushes was shot 1 – the two shot. There were 3 takes of this. The crew rolled around laughing – it was very funny watching the interaction between Graham and Eric. Probably the biggest laughter ever at rushes. After the wide shot, came Eric's close up. Now this take, with just Eric on his own, didn't get much laughter; nor did Graham's close up, which followed. At the end of rushes both Graham and Eric, separately, came up to me and said, don't use the close ups, the two shot works on its own, just like the 'Prince in the Tower' scene in Holy Grail. For those who don't remember this, it is Terry Jones in his most magnificent performance as the soppy Prince in the tower, who is refusing to marry the Princess. His father is Mike.

TERRY: *But I don't like her.*
MIKE: *Don't like her? What's wrong with her? She's beautiful, she's rich, she's got huge... tracts of land.*
TERRY: *I know, but I want the girl that I marry to have... a certain... special... [music] ...something...*
MIKE: *Cut that out, cut that out. Look, you're marryin' Princess Lucky, so you'd better get used to the idea. [smack]*

Now follows the scene which is all shot in one wide shot of the two Guards at the door, Eric and Graham, in which Graham says nothing but just hiccups.

MIKE: *Guards! Make sure the Prince doesn't leave this room until I come and get 'im.*
ERIC: *Not to leave the room even if you come and get him.*
GRAHAM: *Hic* MIKE: *No, no. Until I come and get him.*

MIKE INSTRUCTS GUARDS, ERIC AND GRAHAM

ERIC: *Until you come and get him, we're not to enter the room.*

MIKE: *No, no, no. You stay in the room and make sure 'e doesn't leave.*

ERIC: *And you'll come and get him.*

GRAHAM: *Hic!*

MIKE: *Right.*

ERIC: *We don't need to do anything, apart from just stop him entering the room.*

MIKE: *No, no. Leaving the room.*

ERIC: *Leaving the room, yes.*

MIKE: *All right?*

ERIC: *Right. Oh, if-if-if, uh, if-if-if, uh, if-if-if we...*

MIKE: *Yes, what is it?*

ERIC: *Oh, if-if, oh—*

MIKE: *Look, it's quite simple. You just stay here, and make sure 'e doesn't leave the room. All right?*

GRAHAM: *Hic!*

MIKE: *Right.*

ERIC: *Oh, I remember. Uh, can he leave the room with us?*

MIKE: *N- No no no. You just keep him in here, and make sure—*

ERIC: *Oh, yes, we'll keep him in here, obviously. But if he had to leave and we were—*

MIKE: *No, no, just keep him in here—*

ERIC: *Until you, or anyone else,—*
MIKE: *No, not anyone else, just me—*
ERIC: *Just you.*
GRAHAM: *Hic!*
MIKE: *Get back.*
ERIC: *Get back.*
MIKE: *Right?*
ERIC: *Right, we'll stay here until you get back.*
MIKE: *And, uh, make sure he doesn't leave.*
ERIC: *What?*
MIKE: *Make sure 'e doesn't leave.*
ERIC: *The Prince?*
MIKE: *Yes, make sure 'e doesn't leave.*
ERIC: *Oh, yes, of course. I thought you meant him. Y'know, it seemed a bit daft, me having to guard him when he's a guard.*
MIKE: *Is that clear?*
GRAHAM: *Hic!*
ERIC: *Oh, quite clear, no problems.*
MIKE: *Right.*

He starts to leave, the Guards follow.

MIKE: *Where are you going?*
ERIC: *We're coming with you.*
MIKE: *No no, I want you to stay here and make sure 'e doesn't leave.*
ERIC: *Oh, I see. Right.*

And that's it! A massive 1 minute 33 seconds, which is long in a film because if you stay on a single shot that long you end up in real time.

A common error made by comedians is that the only way to do film comedy is in the wide, two shot, so that the original comedic timing between the comedians is maintained. The Prince in the Tower scene seems to reinforce this. But it is not true, and what happened with the Haggling scene is a good example of why.

After Graham and Eric had both said I had to use the two shot, who was I to argue? I put the two shot in the film and ordered a second copy of the two shot from London. I did an edit of this with the close ups and put it in a tin for later. We finished filming and returned to London. I had been assembling the film while on location so I was ready to show a rough cut after just a week. I ran it to the Pythons in a Soho screening room. The film worked great and they laughed throughout. But after the screening there was one problem – surprisingly the Haggling scene didn't work! The scene that got the most laughs in rushes just seemed to peter out. It started okay but then the laughs just dried up. It was decided that John would come to my Neals Yard cutting room and see if he could solve the problem. Next morning I took the two shot out of the film and inserted my edit in to the film. John came round, took one look and said, "Oh that seems to work." And that was it.

So why did the funniest scene in rushes, not work in the film, and what was the difference with this and the Prince in the tower?

The answer is, as I hinted before, all to do with film time and real time. Films are like H.G. Wells time machine. We can speed up time for instance, 'Gone With the Wind' tells the story of the American Civil War, which lasted four years, in just two hours. Alternatively if Hitchcock has a bomb in a bag and the bag on the bus, with a 5 minute fuse, those five minutes are stretched to ten. So in editing we can cut from a man heading towards his street door, to him getting in his car and lose the boring stuff. Or alternatively we can cut from a watch showing 5 minutes to midnight, then to the army preparing to attack, on to the wives talking as they wait for news on the radio, on to the enemy unaware of the danger; to a guard suddenly thinking he hears something but finds out it is a cat; then back to the clock which now shows 4 minutes to midnight even though we have been away 3 minutes. But, here is the crux, if you cover a scene in one shot, with no editing, then obviously you are in real time.

I remember in film school how all the students wanted to do a great take all in one, which I always found crazy. The magic of film is editing and when I wanted to do something in one shot, I wrote a theatre play, 'Twilight of the Gods' which required a different discipline.

It is not that a single long take cannot work. Let us look at the most famous real time sequence in Orson Wells', 'Touch of Evil'. It is the opening shot of the film and lasts 3 minutes 20 seconds. It starts with a close up of a timer on a bomb being set and then the bomb is put in the back of a car. It ends with the bomb going off. Here is the typical type of eulogy for the shot:

'In the opening shot of Touch of Evil, Orson Welles is able to create tension and suspense by effectively using the off frame aspect of the mise-en-scene. By allowing the scene to move outside the

*focus of action, at particularly untimely moments, Welles places
the audience in short but effective moments of unresolved tension
and suspense, effectively luring the spectator psychologically
further into the opening shot and the rest of the film.'*

I however think this is bunk. For a start, when you watch the film you
don't pay attention to the fact that this is one take, because you don't know it
is going to be that unless you have been told. If you become aware that it is one
shot, then the film is not gripping you, you are outside of the film's 'mise-en-
scene'. (if that term means anything at all – it means the sum total of actors,
lighting, sets, costumes, makeup, camera angles etc. which convey that moment
of the story.)

The logistics of the Welles' shot make it great fun to watch, and knowing
that the border guard kept fluffing his lines, nearly driving Welles mad, adds to
the enjoyment. But the scene has no tension mainly because we are not yet
involved with the people. Is the bomb going to blow up a good father of three
or a fascist police Chief? What are we to think about it?

If this appeared in the middle of the film when we do know the people,
it would still work okay because this is the sort of situation where you don't
want to condense time but in fact, as per the Hitchcock example, to expand it.
Even so, with a few cutaways of the bomb in the car and a bit of ticking on the
sound track, I could easily add more tension.

So why does the Holy Grail Guards work as one shot but the Haggling
doesn't, even though both were hilarious in rushes? Holy Grail is an episodic
film; one adventure follows another with different characters and goals, which
have to be established. In Grail, we have episodes like the Tale of Sir Robin, who
confronts the three headed knight or Galahad, tempted in Castle Anthrax by,
*'eightscore young blondes and brunettes, all between sixteen and nineteen-and-
a-half'*.

Lancelot's episode begins with a shot of swamp castle. (Bodium Castle,
which I shot on my own, setting light to a bit of newspaper with wet leaves in
the foreground to give the idea of mist coming up from the swamp. Well we
didn't have much money!) This is followed by Mike and Terry (father and son)
establishing the plot of the episode, which is that the son is going to be kept in
the Tower (guarded) till he marries the Princess; which will lead to Lancelot's
attempt to rescue him (thinking he is a her).

So the Guards are part of the set up and as such able to be leisurely. The haggling however is the exact opposite. It is in the body of the film, with the characters and situations established and worse of all it is in the middle of a chase. Chase scenes are usually cut the fastest to maintain energy. As a two shot the haggling worked in rushes but when cut into the film, because of the urgency of the situation, it appeared to get slower and slower. What I did was let the two shot run for a while and then I cut to the close ups, speeding up the space between their deliveries. When Terry Jones saw it working, he realized why, and how we had to increase the pressure on Brian, so he even added a cut away of the soldiers searching for Brian. If I had told Eric and Graham that there was going to be a cut away in the middle in Tunisia, they would have fired me there and then.

Now you can see why the theory, that the wide two shot is the only way to do comedy in film is wrong. Firstly, it all depends on where we are in the film, as to whether you can go to real time. Just for an example, I knew an editor who took the comedians two shot, marked where each person spoke and cut in the close ups, trying to preserve the original comedians timing. This does not work either, because when you switch from one angle to another, time changes, the mind has to readjust to the new shot, so you have to find a new timing. And then it just boils down to whether the editor has any feel for comic timing. So in one respect, the comedians are right, wanting their scene left on the two shot does mean that the editor can't totally f... it up. I change all the timings in my cuts: John Cleese often has a natural pause after being asked a question. I stretch it to see if it is funnier, and sometimes it is. Or I will bring a line in quicker, as with the Haggling.

'ERIC: No, no you go to 14 now.
BRIAN: All right I'll give you 14.
ERIC: 14, are you joking!'

So it is funnier to rush in Eric's *'14, are you joking!'* to take Brian by surprise.

By the way, if you are an editor, don't ever tell the actors you are doing this; just ask them if they are happy with their performance. Terry Jones, for instance, loves the pause in the scene where Judith comes out naked and makes a speech in front of Mandy and Brian. Mandy appears so shell shocked that after Judith finishes, she takes an age to say *'Who's that!?'* I don't think I have ever told Terry I created it in the cutting rooms. The thing is however much you can add as an editor, the talent is still the writers and performers and we are just enhancing that, so it would be arrogant to tell them.

Enough of this haggling let's get on with the chase. Brian makes it to the PFJ's headquarters where he gets harangued by John for bringing the Romans.

BRIAN: *I'm sorry, Reg.*

JOHN: *Oh, it's all right, siblings. He's sorry. He's sorry he led the fifth legion straight to our official headquarters. Well, that's all right then, Brian. Sit down. Have a scone. Make yourself at home. YOU KLUTZ!!! You stupid, bird-brained, flat-headed... (There is a knocking at the door. Everyone scarpers.)*

Klutz was obviously 'Cant', which was like 'Caesar's dock hanging out' used as a bargaining ploy to get the British censors to give us a more lenient AA certificate.

At a very late stage, Terry, speeded up the soldiers, entering the PFJ's headquarters, to search for revolutionaries, so we had no footsteps for them. Footsteps, are done by 'footsteps artists', who watch the film and walk around, the recording studio, with different shoes on different surfaces. The footsteps we had were the slow version. So Terry got us to empty our keys and loose change in to a film can and he shook it to the speed of the soldiers. A nice bit of improvising. I must admit to two favourite lines in this scene outside the door: *'Crucifixion's a doddle'* and *'Found this spoon, Sir'*. Don't know why they just make me laugh and by the way Matthias who says *'Crucifixion's a doddle'* and is also the man being stoned, is John Young, who we met in Scotland on Holy Grail. He played the Historian who gets killed, which is also quite a nice quiz question. Where is there a horse in Holy Grail? Even Terry Jones couldn't remember when I quizzed him. Answer, it was the killing of the Historian.

The final gag of the scene is one of those silly moments that step outside the reality of the film, the last bang on the door and demand by John:

JOHN: *Open up!*

MATTHIAS: *You haven't given us time to hide!*

I cut sharp on that, to Brian falling on to the Boring Prophet, so as not to linger on the fact that we stepped outside the logic of the film, which can turn the film from a proper movie to a bit of light entertainment.

14
CONSIDER THE LILIES

Once Brian falls on the Boring Prophet, I found it difficult to explain in the edit what exactly was going on. I did show my original edit to Terry and it was decided to re-shoot some bits. You can tell what is the re-shoot material because the woman in the original was Gwen Taylor (Don't you call my husband bignose), but she wasn't available for the re-shoot so Carol Cleavland took her place. The re-shoots did improve things, but I am still not sure it is totally clear. In the original script it says, after knocking the Boring Prophet off the platform and into the pot, Brian spots a Roman soldier standing guard. The soldier glances round suspiciously, making Brian feel he has to start speaking, as if he is one of the prophets. He begins with his parable about the birds and the lilies. A man sleeping on the platform wakes and takes a fancy to Brian's gourd. Half way through John with his troops come by and Brian panics into:

BRIAN: *Ooh! Eh, uh, b— b— now— now hear this! Blessed are they who convert their neighbour's ox, for they shall inhibit their girth,..*
MAN: *Rubbish!*
BRIAN: *...and to them only shall be given...*

At this point John's troop pass by and pick up the waiting soldier and march away, so Brian trails off to:

BRIAN: *..to them only... shall... be... given...*

And now he is free to come off the platform but the crowd are suddenly curious about what he was about to say.

Now I have that off my chest, I'd just like to point out one of the things

127

that make 'Life of Brian' a proper film. It is the use of themes that appear from one scene to another. When Brian begins preaching, the man (Terry Bayler) starts haggling for his gourd, thereby reprising the haggling scene; which in itself is a reprise of the stoning scene because he is haggling for a beard to disguise himself. Things like 'Big Nose' or Terry Bayler and his wife always together, the way crucifixion begins to enter the film, starting with the 'Crucifixion's a doddle' conversation. If you can remember Jack Lemon in the 'Apartment' tells a story about shooting himself in the leg. At the end of the film we see him packing and notice the handgun. Then at the end as Shirley MacLaine runs up his stairs we hear a bang, fear the worse and then Lemon opens the door with a bottle of champagne. I have noticed in some Bergman films that have this devise where the seeds of the end drama are laid in the middle. Not to mention Shakespeare constantly referring to eyes and the way we see, only to have a protagonist have his eyes gouged out: 'Out vile jellies!'

The gourd given to Brian at the haggling is then passed to Terry Bayler and then later becomes an item of veneration to the crowd. If you know Buñuel's 'Viridiana', a skipping rope moves through the film from a girl skipping to a man hanging himself, to a tramp tying up his trousers, to tying Viridiana's hands before she is about to be raped. Even Biggus Dickus makes a re-entry when he appears in person at the end. It is partly for these reasons that, I believe, 'Life of Brian' is a proper film.

But what makes it a great film is that it deals with fundamental human failures, which have led to the religious fundamentalism that plagues our planet today, from the misunderstandings of the teachings of great people, to silly tendencies to interpret banal incidents as "signs from God", and the factions and infighting that can emerge from this. When Brian loses his shoe, some of his over-zealous followers declare it to be a sign but they can't agree on what it means, and nearly come to blows. Another follower instructs them to "Cast off the shoe. Follow the gourd!" Suddenly the gourd is seen as significant and important when in truth the gourd is actually a cheap, unwanted gift.

In Antonioni's film, 'Blow Up', there is a moment when David Hemmings goes into a club where a band is playing. The guitarist smashes up his guitar and throws it into the audience. There is an almighty struggle for it and David Hemmings manages to grab it and escape into the street. Once in the street he looks at it. It is a broken guitar, with no apparent value. He throws it away. A great film about reality and illusion, which begins with a man in a pauper's doss house, who comes out and gets into a Rolls Royce.

When the crowd chase off, we are left with Spike Milligan demanding, "Let us pray." So let us pause for a moment in prayer for the great man himself. All the Pythons will admit to having been totally influenced by Spike. He was an exceptional person, a unique moralist, a revolutionary, surrealist comedian, and as a student of Nietzsche, I myself recognize him as a great philosopher. He could be extremely silly while being exceptionally perceptive, wonderfully human and brilliantly intelligent. When my other hero, the surrealist film director Buñuel, died I felt really sad because I had not had a chance to meet him, although I had met Spike, I felt a dreadful loss at his death because his like will not be seen on this planet for a long time.

I tried to emulate him in my film 'Chemical Wedding' and be extremely silly while dealing with Quantum Physics, the complexity of time and occultism. It didn't work, half the critics didn't get it, but the reviews were fun. From those who were embarrassed about liking it, *'My guilty pleasure of the year'*, to *'Simon Callow is playing to a gallery somewhere near the planet Venus.'* And *'thoroughly entertaining although at times you wonder if the filmmakers haven't lost their senses.'* But unfortunately a common one by the so-called intellectual press was, *'It was funny but wasn't meant to be!'* Oh dear, how could they get it so wrong. When we were filming one scene, I had to be locked off the set because I couldn't stop laughing at what Simon and Jud were doing.

Talking about reviews, the Pythons don't have much luck with them. 'Holy Grail' hardly got a nod from the critics with things like *'Pythons do their stuff again.'* After the critics viewing, there were drinks and snacks and I remember the critics just sat around, nibbling and talking to each other about what hotel they were going to stay in at Cannes. Not one even asked *'How the hell did you do this costume epic for £200,000?'* I had proved that my method of production could produce quality for a price afforded by Britain, a possible formula for the British film industry. They missed it. Terry Gilliam's 'Jabberwocky' was almost totally ignored, but Ridley Scott took our costume designer for 'Blade Runner' and Stanley Kubrick wanted our cameraman Terry Bedford for 'Barry Lyndon'. They spotted what was going on with Terry's visually exciting work. The critics? – Forget it. They were talking about it not being as funny as a normal Python film. Terry's classics, 'Timebandits' and 'Brazil', were equally missed by the British critics but at least on 'Life of Brian' they admitted it was very funny; although one of my favourite films I did with Terry Jones directing, 'Wind in the Willows', was also ignored. Oh dear, Python films have become classics in spite of them.

Back to the chase! So Brian suddenly has unwanted followers who pursue him out of the gates and up into the desert. Notice by the way, in one shot, a stationary shepherd watching the throng rush past. This is Chuck the electrician who donned a costume to stand in front of a telegraph pole to conceal it.

15

I WAS BLIND
AND NOW I CAN SEE

Leaping down a hole to hide, Brian lands on the director's foot. Yes, Terry is directing the film in the nude, as he puts in another wonderful performance, as Simon the Hermit.

The Holy Man in the desert is very much a thing of the time of Christ. The Judean Desert is close to Jerusalem, just past Bethlehem and is bordered by the Mountains of Judea to the West and by the Dead Sea to the East. It is known for its rugged landscape and mountain caves, which have provided a refuge and hiding place for rebels and zealots throughout history, as well as solitude and isolation to monks and hermits. But perhaps there is more to this Hermit than just a brilliant performance. Could this scene offer us a complete understanding, not only of Jesus, but of the entire history of religion? Let's go on a wander through space and time.

The Judean desert is where the Dead Sea Scrolls were found and where are located the ruins of Qumran, thought to have been inhabited by Essenes. Certainly Pliny, geographer and explorer, located them in the desert near the north-western shore of the Dead Sea.

Who were these Essenes? Josephus tells us that there were Essenes throughout Israel, but Qumran was probably their communal centre, where they practiced their beliefs in piety, renouncing personal property and sharing their possessions with the community. Philo of Alexandria adds that they lived by agriculture and handicrafts, rejecting slavery. They abstained from the animal sacrifices of the Temple and their meals were solemn community affairs. Essenes followed a solar, 364-day calendar as opposed to official Judaism, which used a lunar one. They ritually immersed in water, which suggested to many scholars a link with John the Baptist. They forbade the expression of anger; they ate together after prayer; devoted themselves to charity and benevolence, studied the books of the elders, and were very mindful of the names of the angels kept in their sacred writings. They believed in the immortality of the soul. It is said they preserved secrets and it took 3 years of preparation to be initiated into the community. Transgressors were excluded from the sect.

There is obviously a great similarity between Essene thought and the beliefs assigned to Jesus. Kingdom of God, baptism, sacred meals, immortality of the soul, the position of a central Teacher of Righteousness, and rejection of private property and slavery, all suggest a close kinship between them. The writers of the Dead Sea Scrolls even believed themselves to be the true remnant of Israel living in the last days (The End of Days) and they eagerly awaited the appearance of both a political messiah and an eschatological high priest.

This is all too close for comfort, especially as we know the main expansion of Christianity came about through the belief in the 'End of Days' concept and also spread amongst the slaves, holding out a potential release from bondage. But where did these Essene concepts come from? Were they just a product of the mood of the times or have they an historical origin?

Perhaps, over the next 10 pages, I can take you on a strange journey I made at the beginning of my film career. I got a job to film the 500th anniversary celebration of a hospital, which turned out to be Bethlam Royal Hospital, a mental institution. When I arrived in the hospital grounds just outside London, I thought, 500th anniversary, has this place been going since the time of Shakespeare? Then I started filming the arrival of the dignitaries, the Bishop of London, the Lord Mayor of the City of London. It was all a bit weird. After filming the speeches, I met up with the archivist, Patricia Alderidge and she explained this was the infamous Bedlam, which had considerable wealth having been left money and property over the ages. Bethlam Hospital owned the site of South Africa House in Trafalgar Square, the Cumberland Hotel, and much more. I had got interested in the Masons and my suspicions were aroused by the nature of the dignitaries. The old city trade organisations were administered by committees, many of whom where Masons. I had filmed in quite an ornate hall in the city, called the Tallow Chandlers Hall. Tallow Chandlers were candle makers, a once important trade but now obviously irrelevant. But they still had to have a committee to administer their property and monies. I may be totally wrong about the Masonic nature of these old city trades, so I stand to be corrected.

Anyway Patricia, the archivist, told me that the old Bedlam was in the

building which now houses the Imperial War Museum and that an important Victorian painter, Richard Dadd, was incarcerated there for a crime that shocked the world. His story was so remarkable that I thought I would write a film script. First I went to the Imperial War Museum, with plans that Patricia gave me of its layout when it was an asylum. It seemed weirdly appropriate that the building was full of weapons and I could just imagine the ghosts of the lunatics wandering around this crazy arsenal of destruction. Taking my plans, I went down to where the padded cells were. It was now a canteen, I could see from the plans that the alcoves you sat in were the padded cells. (It has now been revamped). Richard Dadd spent 30 years locked up in the building where he continued painting. His most famous painting from his time in Bedlam is the 'Fairy Feller's Masterstroke', a view between grass blades of a peopled world of fairy folk. It is nothing like any other of the Victorian paintings that surround it in the Tate Gallery.

In 1863 the criminal lunatics were moved to Broadmoor, so I followed the trail there to photograph Dadd's paintings and screens, which are still in the asylum amongst the criminal lunatics.

Born in Chatham in 1817, Dadd came to London and enrolled in the Academy Schools. Richard was a friend of all the famous Victorian artists of the time, Frith (of Derby Day), Augustus Egg and Charles Dickens who, like Dadd had been brought up in Chatham. But Dadd's story really begins in Newport in 1839 when a Chartist demonstration, (Chartists were demonstrating for one man one vote), was ambushed by troops under the leadership of the

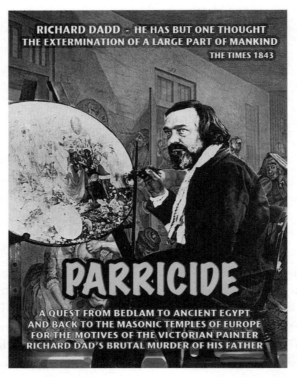

Richard Dadd painting in Bedlam (the poster for the film)

mayor of Newport, one Thomas Phillips. Twenty marchers were killed and Phillips was subsequently knighted by Queen Victoria, while the leaders of the Chartists were found guilty of 'High Treason against the Queen' and sentenced to be hung, drawn and quartered.

Sir Thomas decided to leave England and venture on what was called the 'grand tour'. This was before the advent of cameras, so he looked around for a painter. Richard Dadd was recommended to him by the famous travelling painter, David Roberts, to record the journey. Phillips and Dadd were away for a year, travelling by boat, diligence and horseback through Italy and Greece to Constantinople and on to Cairo. Here in Egypt Richard Dadd's whole world began to crumble, as he was forced to question the basis of his every belief. He wrote in a letter from Luxor:

'...*here among the monuments of Egypt we find ourselves*

conversing with a People, highly civilized and acquainted with the Arts and Sciences to a degree that puts to shame our puerile notions of them and at so early a date in our chronology as to make us laugh at the extreme youth of our race. These Egyptians were a mighty generation to have built the Pyramids of Ghiza and other things so extremely curious and so terribly astounding that they call upon our faith. Sometimes I have lain down at night with my imagination so full of wild vagaries that I have really and truly doubted of my own sanity.'

By the time the travellers returned to England, Richard Dadd had taken to the worship of the Egyptian God, Osiris. These opinions and his strange violent outbursts were to convince his friends that he had returned home mad and soon the whole country would know of this madness, for on the 1st September 1843 the newspapers broke the story of a crime which was to revolt the nation!

'PARRICIDE – One of the most appalling murders, involving the dreadful crime of parricide; the victim an affectionate parent; and the murderer an artist of acknowledged genius, was committed in the peaceful village of Cobham. From the respectability of the parties and the absence of all possible motive to the commission of the horrible deed, the occurrence has excited the most intense interest. The name of the deceased is William Dadd, and that of his son, Richard Dadd, a young painter of great ability who returned last June from a tour through the Middle East where he had been travelling under the patronage of Sir Thomas Phillips, the Mayor of Newport, knighted for his part in quelling the Chartist uprising. He has carried off several prizes at the Royal Academy, but it was discovered on his return from Egypt that his intellect was affected. He became flighty in manner and expressed much dislike towards his patron.'
(THE TIMES Friday 1st September 1843)

It was assumed Richard had committed suicide after the dreadful deed but in fact he had escaped to France where he attempted another murder before being arrested and investigated in the Claremont Asylum.

'He relates with the greatest coolness that in the park of Lord Darnly, he was seized, being with him who said to be his father, with a divine inspiration, which commanded him to sacrifice him; he immediately plunged his knife into his breast, and as death came not fast enough, he made deep wounds in his neck with a razor. When asked by Dr. Leblanc, what he thought of such an action, he replied that he considered it a good one, since he had destroyed an enemy of God. After committing this crime, Richard Dadd proceeded to the nearest port, embarked to France and in a diligence passing through Fontainebleau at night, was taken, says he, with another inspiration from the star Osiris to attack a fellow passenger. He considers this also a good action and has but one thought, the extermination of a large part of mankind.'
(ILLUSTRATED LONDON NEWS 16 Sept 1843)

Right up to his death in Broadmoor, Richard maintained his belief that 'Osiris was the true God and Christ was a poor copy', which he repeated when interviewed on Boxing Day 1877.

'He is an old man with a long and flowing snow white beard, with mild blue eyes that beam benignly through spectacles when he conversed. His manner is unassuming but impressive, an accomplished old man – scholar, musician, poet, painter, sage. He says his views and those of society are at variance; that is all. His convictions differ from those of other men; they will not make allowances for him as he would for them; they do not recognize in all its intensity that which has become to him an ever-present and abiding law – the will of mighty Osiris. He bears no malice but he feels he is misunderstood, and therefore somewhat aggrieved.'
(THE WORLD 26 Dec 1877)

To write the script I needed to understand Dadd and see why he advocated such weird beliefs. I had never heard of Osiris so I first went to the British Museum and grabbing a load of books, headed off to Egypt. My ancient history was limited, I knew the Roman Empire was around the time of Christ and the Greek civilization about 300 years before that. I assumed that the Egyptian Empire had just preceded this, so my first surprise was to discover how ancient the culture was. The Greek historian Herodotus in 350 BC visited Egypt and the Pyramids, which were even then, an ancient tourist site whose builders had long been forgotten in the mists of time. We go back 2,000 years to Christ but you have to go back another 2,500 years to get to the time of these amazing builders. Inside the Great Pyramid of Cheops, as I rose up the impressive gallery to the Kings Chamber, I began to think, that perhaps Dadd was right, if you believe in a God, you should believe in the original one, not one invented thousands of years later. There is a prayer in the ancient Pyramid Text that sounds exactly like the Lord's Prayer and of course Jesus spent time in Egypt where, according to many quotes I have given, he learnt his magic from the Egyptian priests.

I travelled down to the Temples of Luxor and as I began to understand the Zen nature of the ancient Egyptian religion, I also realized that there was more to Richard Dadd's argument, with astonishing similarities between the ancient Egyptian God, Osiris, and the Jesus story.

Osiris, Isis and their son Horus, form a Holy Trinity, similar to the Christian trinity, but keeping to the antifeminist nature of Christianity the mother goddess is switched to the Holy Ghost. The birth of Horus comes about when Osiris is murdered by Seth and his body cut into 15 pieces. Isis finds the pieces and using her magic she fuses them together in resurrection, but she is missing the phallus. She pleads with Thoth the Lord of Measures, and he gives her his measuring reed as a substitute phallus. She then has a non-carnal union with Osiris to produce the son, Horus. A virgin birth! The resurrected Osiris then abides in the West, where the souls of the dead go to be judged by him. Superficially this is a death and resurrection story but we know the Egyptian priests were like scientists, so is there a mystery meaning behind the story? Why is the Lord of Measures involved and as Dadd knew Osiris was the constellation we call Orion, which appears in winter and disappears over summer – it dies and resurrects.

The ancients were influenced by the movement of the stars and told stories, which held information for the initiates. Sirius the Dog Star, associated with Isis is the brightest star in the sky (not counting the planets). It can be found by following Orion's belt downwards. The line up of the pyramids transcribe Orion's belt from the sky to the earth. 'As above so below'. To build them, they must have had incredible mathematical knowledge. What happened to it?

This thought led me from Dadd to a man I knew a little about from my maths class at school. About 500 years before Christ, Pythagoras invented a mathematical method to produce a right angle triangle. Or did he, because to build the Pyramids the ancient Egyptians must have known how to generate an accurate right angle triangle 2,000 years before the time of Pythagoras. I noticed that Pythagoras had come to Egypt to study the Egyptian mysteries under the Priests of Memphis, so I assumed that this was one of the mysteries taught to him by the priests. But Pythagoras turns out to be much more important than a man who might have generated a theorem. He was the first person to be called a Philosopher (lover of knowledge) and was the subject of elaborate legends surrounding his historic persona. Aristotle described him as a wonder-worker and somewhat of a supernatural figure, attributing to him such aspects as a golden thigh, which was a sign of divinity. According to Aristotle, some ancients believed that he had the ability to travel through space and time, and to communicate with animals and plants. He was also thought to be the Son of God (Apollo) and born of a virgin. Plato declared that above all, Pythagoras was famous for leaving behind him a 'way of life'.

Returning to Greece, he set up an organization, which was in some ways a school, in some ways a brotherhood, and in some ways a monastery. Although very secretive, it becomes clear that it was based upon the mysticism of numbers (mathematics) and a dying and resurrecting God based on Osiris but switched in the story to a minor Greek God, called Dionysius. Pythagoras was credited with devising the tetractys, the triangular figure of four rows, which add up to the perfect number, ten. As a mystical symbol, it was very important to the worship of the Pythagoreans, and Iamblichus suggests they even swore oaths by it:

'And the inventions were so admirable, and so divinized, by those who understood them, that the members used them as forms of oath: "By him who handed to our generation the tetractys, source of the roots of ever-flowing nature."' (Iamblichus)

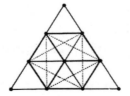

TERRY JONES DIRECTING 'LIFE OF BRIAN'

CHERCHIN MAN

FRONT LEFT: A WOMAN, MIKE, GWEN TAYLOR THEN ERIC. BEHIND MIKE
IS TERRY BAYLOR CHARLES McKEOWN AND TERRY GILLIAM

JOHN, GEORGE HARRISON AND ERIC

BERNARD McKENNA WITH NOSE COLD, MIKE
AND ANDREW MacLACHLAN

LEFT: CHARLES McKEOWN, TERRY GILLIAM
MIKE, A TUNISIAN AND JOHN YOUNG

CHRIST CROWNED WITH THORNS BY HIERONYMUS BOSCH

TERRY STEALS THE SHOW WITH
'HE'S NOT THE MESSIAH HE'S A VERY NAUGHTY BOY'

GRAHAM DOUBLES UP AS BIGGUS DICKUS

MIKE PALIN ALMOST UNRECOGNISABLE AS A LUCKY BASTARD

SPIKE MILLIGAN ON HOLIDAY IN TUNISIA

BRIAN HAGGLES ERIC FOR A BEARD

THE AMOLFINI MARRIAGE BY JAN VAN EYKE

T CROSSES AND MAGDALENE'S RED HAIR IN VAN EYKE'S
'CRUCIFIXION & THE LAST JUDGMENT'

ERIC AND TERRY GILLIAM HELP TO SLOW DOWN THE PACE

BRIAN HANGS READY TO KICK THE BORING PROPHET INTO THE POT

REMOVING NAILS FROM CRUCIFIED BODIES

MIKE'S STATUE HEADS TO TOWN WITH SKELETAL BODIES IN
FOREGROUND LEFT UP TO ROT

THE CRUCIFIXION PARTY CARRYING SMALL CROSSES LIKE ALL FILMS

TERRY HELPS CONDEMNED MAN ONLY
TO BE CAUGHT BY BERNARD WITH CROSS

ERIC WITH HIS SUICIDE SQUAD ARRIVE AT THE CRUCIFIXION SITE

AUTHOR JULIAN DOYLE ARRESTS
DIRCTOR TERRY JONES IN 'HOLY GRAIL'

JOHN RECEIVES DIRECTION FROM A BEARDED TERRY JONES
ON THE FIRST DAY OF FILMING

From the tetractys you can generate many important geometrical structures. Connecting the ten dots forms nine triangles. Six of these are involved in the forming of the cube. The same triangles, when lines are drawn between them, also reveal a six pointed star with a dot in the centre. Only seven dots are used in forming the cube and the star. Qabbalistically, the three unused corner dots represent the threefold, invisible causal universe.

The Pythagoreans appear to have put all their property into a common stock. There were many women among the adherents, who were treated equally having taken the same vows. They functioned in total secrecy and Porphyry stated that, candidates had to pass through a period of probation, in which their powers of maintaining silence were especially tested, as well as their general temper and mental capacity. There were also gradations among the members themselves. It was an old Pythagorean maxim that *every thing was not to be told to every body*. Thus the Pythagoreans were divided into an inner circle called the mathematikoi (learners) and an outer circle called the akousmatikoi (listeners). Porphyry wrote, 'the mathematikoi learned the more detailed and exactly elaborated version of this knowledge, the akousmatikoi were those who had heard only the summary headings of his writings, without the more exact exposition.' They had common meals, at which they met in companies of ten. Considerable importance was attached to music and gymnastics in the daily exercises of the disciples, encouraging a lofty serenity and self-possession. The members showed a devoted attachment to each other, to the exclusion of those who did not belong. There were even secret symbols and handshakes, by which members of the sect could recognize each other, even if they had never met before.

My research was making me feel there was a direct relationship between the ancient wisdom of Egypt through the Pythagoreans to the Knights Templar who concealed this knowledge during the 'dark ages' when the church suppressed such knowledge. And then on to modern masonry which uses Egyptian symbols, like the Pyramid on the dollar bill. You can see more of these symbols in my film 'Chemical Wedding', which shows a Masonic initiation around the chequered carpet.

On my return to London, I went to the central Masonic Temple in Great Queen Street. There, Grand Lodge suggests that Masonry began officially in the 18th Century with no previous connection but this I found was a deception. By the way, just as you enter the Temple there is a huge portrait of George Washington wearing his Masonic apron. Masonry was the main guiding influence on Washington's life, but I watched 13 episodes of a TV series about him, yet not once did he enter a Masonic lodge or even mention Masonry. Why all the big secrecy?

Only esoterikoi, who know the secret handshake, should carry on reading this chapter. In fact, I would really like this section to be written in hidden ink so that only mathematikoi could read it, and all exoterikoi should skip to the next chapter. Because as Pythagoras said, '*every thing is not to be told to every body*'

Okay esoterikoi, here is a fishy story from the Bible with hidden secrets embedded within, for your investigation. John chapter 21:1-10 reads:

> *After these things Jesus appeared again to his disciples, by the Sea of Tiberias. It happened this way: Simon Peter; Thomas, called Didymus; Nathanael from Cana in Galilee; the sons of Zebedee, and two other disciples were together. "I'm going out to fish," Simon Peter told them, and they said, "We will go with you." So they got into the boat, but that night they caught nothing.*
>
> *Next morning, Jesus stood on the shore, but the disciples did not realize it was him. He called out to them, "Friends, have you any fish?"*
>
> *"No," they answered.*
>
> *He said, "Throw your net on the right side of the boat and you will find some."*
>
> *When they did, they were unable to haul the net in because of the multitude of fishes. Then the disciple whom Jesus loved said to Peter, "It is the Lord!"*
>
> *As soon as Simon Peter heard him say, "It is the Lord," he wrapped his outer garment around him, for he was naked, and jumped into the water. The other disciples followed in the boat, towing the net full of fish, for they were just 200 cubits from the shore. When they landed, they saw a fire of burning coals there with fish on it, and some bread. Jesus said to them, "Bring some of the fish you have caught." Simon Peter climbed aboard and dragged the net ashore. It was full of great fish, 153 of them.*

The akousmatikoi (listeners) would read this story as men going out to fish who see the risen Christ on the shore. This is how Christians would also see it. But what would initiated esoterikoi (learners) make of it? Or for that matter Gnostic Christians who believed the Bible was not literal but full of esoteric knowledge? Let's bring all our knowledge past and present (and mathematical) to bear on it.

> *After these things Jesus appeared again to his disciples, by the Sea of Tiberias.*

Who and when, would someone call the Sea of Galilee, the Sea of Tiberius? Tiberius only came to the throne in AD 14 (when Jesus was around 14) and Herod Antipas built the city of Tiberius on the Sea of Galilee when Jesus was over 20. I leave that one for you to ponder.

> *Simon Peter; Thomas, called Didymus; Nathanael from Cana in Galilee; the sons of Zebedee, and two other disciples were together.*
> *"I'm going out to fish," said Simon Peter.*

Counting the disciples, there are 7.

1. Simon called Peter. Translated into modern language this is Simon called 'Rock' who therefore sounds to me like a bodyguard. Consider Peter's actions as Jesus is arrested in the Garden of Gethsemane. Our Rocky draws a sword and lobs off the ear of an official, which Jesus glues back on. So how come this meek and mild Jesus, is accompanied by a man with a sword, if he is not the bodyguard?
2. Thomas called Dydimus. As initiates you already know that Thomas called Didymus is nonsense because it translates as 'Twin called Twin' who is actually Judas Thomas. (Judas the Twin)
3. Nathanael from Cana. This disciple seems extremely gullible because when Jesus first meets him he says:
   "Here is a true Israelite, with nothing false."
   "How do you know me?" Nathanael asked.
   "I saw you while you were still under the fig tree before Philip called you," Jesus answered.
   Then Nathanael declared, "Rabbi, you are the Son of God; you are the King of Israel."
   Jesus said, "You believe because I told you I saw you under the fig tree. You shall see greater things than that."
   Make what you will of that.

4 and 5. The sons of Zebadee are James and John, who in Mark's Gospel, Jesus calls Boenerges, from the Hebrew ben reghesh 'Sons of Thunder'. This could make their father, Zebadee, the thunderer, perhaps a tub-thumping preacher with a loud voice. Maybe James himself followed in his father's footsteps for he found his way to Spain where he was known as a preacher. His final resting place was the main European pilgrimage site of Santiago de Compostela in Spain. But let's take you to a deeper level of understanding. The term 'Sons of Thunder' is not new to Jesus. It was the name given to Castor and Pollux, twin Gods from Greece, who were popular in Rome. The twins shared the same mother but had different fathers, which meant that Pollux was immortal and Castor was mortal. When Castor died, Pollux asked Zeus to let him share his own immortality with his twin to keep them together, as one had gone to Hades and the other to Heaven. On alternate days, one twin would be alive and the other dead. They represented the higher and lower self, which cannot both be alive at the same time. This was the origin of a common image of the Roman God Mithras with two torchbearers on either side; one with his torch upwards and the other downwards. In the Bible the two criminals being crucified either side of Christ, one going to heaven and the other to hell, are thought to come from our Greco-Roman twins. Castor and Pollux are also the names of the twin stars of the constellation of Gemini.

6 and 7 are suddenly unnamed, except that we get that someone on the boat is the 'disciple who Jesus loved'! Perhaps it is one of the unnamed 6 and 7. The name of 'the disciple Jesus loved' has been removed, as it has in all his Biblical appearances. We will work out who he is later but certainly here, like elsewhere in the Bible, he seems to know more than the others.

Then the disciple whom Jesus loved said to Peter, "It is the Lord!"
As soon as Simon Peter heard him say, it is the Lord, he wrapped his outer garment around him, for he was naked, and jumped into the water.

Odd one this, you usually take your clothes off to jump into the water! Not put them on.

…for they were just 200 cubits from the shore.

Bit of arithmetic seems to be rearing its ugly head, but more follows.

> *Simon Peter climbed aboard and dragged the net ashore. It was full of great fish, 153 of them.*

Too many numbers for me, there must be something the mathematikoi could make of this. Well, there is a fable recorded 350 years before Christ, about Pythagoras, in which he was watching fishermen bring in their catch.

"If I can guess the exact number of fish you caught" said Pythagoras, "Then you must give me the catch."

Pythagoras being a vegetarian believed that no animal should be killed. The fishermen agreed, and Pythagoras states the number as 153! Which was correct, and so he demanded the fishermen, return the fish to the sea.

Coincidence? Or did the biblical writer know about Pythagoras and steal the story? Well it wouldn't be the first time. Besides being a miraculous healer, it was written by Iamblichus, that Pythagoras tranquillized the waters of the sea in order for his disciples to pass over them more easily.

Not convinced yet? Then let us look at it with the eye of the initiated mathematikoi. Take the number 153 and see what it has to do with fishes. The Pythagoreans regarded the number 153 as a 'sacred number'. It is used in a mathematical ratio that Archimedes called the 'measure of the fish' to produce the mystical symbol of the vesica piscis, or 'sign of the fish'.

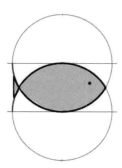

This shape is created by the intersection of two circles with the same radius, intersecting in such a way that the centre of each circle lies on the circumference of the other. Where they cross they form the shape of a fish. The mystic ratio of the vesica piscis is 153:265. Besides being crucial for generating many geometrical shapes, what esoteric and astrological information can we make of this image? Because there is a wobble on the earth's axis, every 2000 years the sun rises in a different astrological sign. This is called the 'precession of the equinoxes' and the full cycle, called the Platonic year, takes 265,765 years to complete. 10,000 years ago the sun rose in the constellation of Leo, that is why some people believe that the Sphinx, which points to Leo, was built then. 8,000 years ago it moved into the sign of Taurus, so the Bull became a sacred symbol for the ancient Egyptians. Then 2,000 years later it moved into Aries. At that time Alexander the Great conquered Egypt and was initiated into this knowledge by the priests at Memphis. He then portrayed himself on coins, with ram's horns as the chosen one of his age. At the time of Christ the sun was moving into the constellation of Pisces and so Christians equated Jesus with the fish and used it as the symbol for Christianity. We are now in *'the dawning of the age'* of Aquarius so watch out for water signs.

Talking of water, the cover of the Chalice Well in Glastonbury depicts a version of the vesica piscis design.

GLASTONBURY WELL   **MASONIC SEAL**

The vesica piscis has been the subject of mystical speculation at several periods of history, and is viewed as important in the Kabala and Freemasonry where it is used in the shapes of the collars worn by officiants of the Masonic rituals. It is also considered the proper shape for the enclosure of the seals of Masonic lodges.

Would Jesus have this secret knowledge and known of the mystical number significance of the story or was it the writers who put them in? Here is a letter written by Saint Clement of Alexandria just 100 years after Christ and 200 years before the Bible was edited into its present form. It concerns the Gospel of Mark.

'During Peter's stay in Rome he [Mark] wrote [an account of] the Lord's doings, not, however, declaring all, nor yet hinting at the secret ones, but selecting those he thought useful for increasing the faith of those who were being instructed. But when Peter died as a martyr, Mark came over to Alexandria, bringing both his own notes and those of Peter, from which he transferred to his former book the things suitable to whatever makes for progress toward Gnosis. He composed a more spiritual Gospel for the use of those being perfected. Nevertheless, he yet did not divulge the things not to be uttered, nor did he write down the Hierophantic teaching of the Lord. Dying, he left his composition to the church in Alexandria, where it even yet is most carefully guarded, being read only to those who are being initiated into the great mysteries.'

There were obviously some secrets that were for initiates only, but what about sacred numbers? If the Bible is true then Jesus clearly knew all this. Take a look at the feeding of the 5,000 with 5 loaves and 2 fishes. What does Jesus say about this in Mark 8:18?

"Do ye not remember? When I break the 5 loaves among 5,000, how many baskets full of fragments took ye up?"
   They said unto him," 12"
   "And when the 7 among 4,000, how many baskets full of fragments took ye up?"
   And they said, "7"
   And He said unto them, <u>"How is it that ye do not understand?"</u>

Because they are not Mathematikoi! Unfortunately the Bible either cut out the rest or Jesus never told us because it goes straight on to:

Then they came to Bethsaida, and some people brought a blind man and begged Jesus to touch him. He took the blind man by the hand and led him outside the village. When he had spit on the man's eyes and put his hands on him, Jesus asked, "Do you see anything?" He looked up and said –
"I was blind and now I can see!"

Well he doesn't quite say that but I have to say that in the film, Charles McKeown, after saying this line, made the most wonderful fall into the hole, flat on his face! My problem was that to see the fall properly you had to be on the wide shot; but the dialogue is best on close up. If I cut to the wide shot, showing the hole as he steps forward, the audience will get what is about to happen. So I had to conceal that cut somehow. If you watch it you will see that, as Charles steps forward and says, "I was blind and now I can see," he throws his white stick away. I cut out with the stick as if the cut is to watch the stick, not reveal the hole. So before the audience register the hole, he has fallen in it.

From the Pythagoreans there was a direct relationship to Socrates, the Skeptics and the Stoics and on to groups like the Therapeutae. Christian Bishop Eusebius read Philo's wonderful description of Therapeutae and assumed they were a Christian community and in fact Christian readers still believed this until the end of the 18th century, when it became clear that it was impossible because Philo wrote his 'On the Contemplative Life' when Jesus was 10. So it was impossible for Therapeutae to be Christians but not impossible for Christians to be Therapeutae.

What did Philo write that convinced Bishop Eusebius that these were Christians?

> 'These men abandon their property without being influenced by any predominant attraction, and flee without even turning their heads back again.'

He adds that they lived in solitude during the six days of the week and gathered together on Saturday for the common prayer and meal. They ritually fasted, and kept alive the memory of God in continuous prayer. They meditated and studied arcane writings, including formulae for numerological and allegorical interpretations. Once in seven weeks they would meet for a night-long vigil after a banquet where they served one another.

> 'For they are not waited on by slaves, because they deem any possession of servants whatever to be contrary to nature.'

It is no wonder they were thought to be Christians imitating the 'last supper' followed by a vigil just like that in the garden of Gethsemane. There is a theory that Pythagoras even influenced Buddhism and Buddhism returned to influence the creation of the Therapeutae, (see Appendix 3)

A few more numbers for you. Jesus surrounds himself with 12 disciples, thought to represent the 12 tribes of Israel, but in the Mithras religion, 12 disciples surround the Godman dressed up to represent the 12 signs of the zodiac. The circle of 12 around a central one derives from the sacred geometry of Pythagoras: if a sphere is surrounded by others of exactly the same dimensions, then exactly 12 will be able to fit round the central one with all in contact. No more no less.

Some of you must be getting fed up with all this maths so let's switch disciplines and give you a chance to test your new found knowledge, in art. Look at this painting by Bosch, 'Christ Crowned with Thorns'. *(See colour plate fig 7.)*

The man with the thorns has an iron arm and an arrow through his hat. Another has his hand on Jesus shoulder like he's befriending him, as is one who seems to be holding his hands. And the fourth has him gripped by the collar. What could these rather odd features mean?

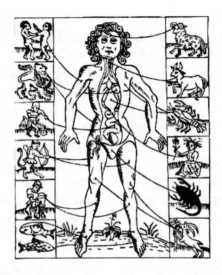

There are four distinct types each representing the four elements, air, fire, earth and water. The Fire type, the choleric is at the top. His armoured hand signifies not only the violence of the choleric type but in astrological tradition, iron is the metal of Mars, the planet that rules over zodiacal Aries, which in turn rules over the head of man. That is why it is he who is placing the crown of thorns on Christ's head. The Air type, the sanguine, is also at the top of the picture and is resting his hand on the shoulder – a gesture, which has double significance.

Firstly in astrology the shoulders are ruled by the air sign Gemini. It also appears that this sanguine type is befriending Christ and is about to speak to him. Speech is obviously carried through the medium of air and the sanguine type is associated with all forms of speech from the high drama to the chatter of imbeciles. But the oak leaves in the hat and his staff remind us that Christ will be thrust into the Air on a cross which was thought in medieval times to have been made of Oak. The lower figure to the left, Water, the phlegmatic type is making a lewd gesture towards Christ's hands, which are over his private parts. This links the phlegmatic with the Zodiacal Scorpio, the water sign that rules over the sexual organs. The moon symbol on his headdress is also associated in occult tradition with the sexual organs and with the lunar demons who have through the sexual organs direct access to man. The gesture of the Water type is to man's weakest point. See his wooden stave forms a cross with the stave held by the Air type. Then the Earth type, the melancholic, reaches up from his low earthly position and will drag the body down to its final resting place. I was blind and now I can see. Oh this is fun!

In the Pythagorean Mystery religions people were baptized in three of the elements, air, fire and water. A winnowing fan is used for air and lo and behold, it appears in the Bible, where John the Baptist says:

> "I indeed baptize you with water unto repentance, but He who is coming after me is mightier than I . . . He will baptize you with the Holy Breath and fire. His winnowing fan is in His hand."

Now John the Baptist is our archetypal hermit, not naked like Terry's hermit but dressed in animal skins and living the ascetic life, like a solo Essene. Josephus mentioned him and his death but unfortunately without the great details of 7 veils and heads on platters. But there appear to be other details about John that make him and Jesus rather mystical. As Joseph Cambell writes:

> 'The rite of Baptism comes from Sumeria and was part of the celebration of the water God Ea. 'God of the House of Water'. In the Hellenistic period, Ea was called Aonnes, which is in Greek Ionnes, Latin Johannes and English, John. Several scholars have suggested that there was never a Jesus and John but just a Water God and a Sun God.'

Jesus begins his mission by being baptized by John. John is born from an old infertile woman on the summer solstice when the sun begins to wane; while Jesus is born six months later, of an unfertilized maiden, at the winter solstice when the sun begins to wax again. And doesn't John say about Jesus, 'He must grow greater while I must grow less'!

John is born in the astrological sign of Cancer, a water sign, which represented the gate of the souls into incarnation, while Jesus is born in Capricorn, which represented the gate of souls out of incarnation into immortality. John baptizes in water, Jesus in air and fire.

And the real John? He seems to have been close to the Essenes and Therapeutae with his water cleansing ritual and vows of poverty. Josephus tells us he had a big following which is why Herod Antipas had him killed. Only after his death did Jesus begin teaching and attempting in some way to assume his mantle.

Mandaeans baptizing and performing secret Masonic handshake

Perhaps the best picture comes from an ancient ethnic people, still living today, who are followers of John the Baptist. They speak Aramaic, their places of worship are near rivers so that they can perform regular baptisms. These are the Mandaeans who maintain great secrecy upon initiates; full explanation being reserved for those considered able to understand and preserve the gnosis.

They believe Jesus is a false prophet who betrayed John's mystic teaching and made them available to the uninitiated. Like Masons they have secret handshakes of identification and like Gnostics, Zoroastrians and our Magi, they are dualists, believing in a cosmic Father and Mother, Light and Darkness, similar to yin and yang. Planets and stars influence fate and human beings, and good souls reside in a land over the western ocean below a star called 'Merica'. Nice to note here that Knight and Lomas suggest this name goes back to Egypt and forward to the Knights Templar who, when outlawed, sailed ships out of La Rochelle in France to La Merica or as we know it today, America. This certainly is a far more convincing explanation for the name America than the norm given in text books. Those amongst the community of Mandaeans who possess secret knowledge are called Nazuraiia or Nazoreans. At the same time the uninitiated laity are called 'Mandaeans', from the term manda—'gnosis'. Most of the present day Mandaeans live in Iraq. Although they see John the Baptist as a prophet, they in fact trace their ideology back to Pythagoras and Egypt. They believe that they once lived in Egypt and this sounds possible since their God of Darkness is called Ptahil, similar to the Egyptian God Ptah.

Probably during the turmoil caused by the Thera Volcano, they left at the same time as the Israelites, migrating into the land of Canaan. At the time of the Roman destruction of Israel, they moved to Mesopotamia.

In 1290 the Mandaeans were discovered in Iraq by a Dominican Catholic. However the Catholic Church suppressed his writings, and others who encountered them, until 1940. What were they so worried about? Perhaps it is because of the belief by the Mandaeans that Jesus was a 'false messiah', who perverted the secret teachings entrusted to him by John.

There are quite a few others who are of a similar opinion. They are called Johnites and you can locate them by their reverence to John the Baptist. The mass of churches in the South of France indicate that he was important to the population there. The Knights Templar who were alleged to spit on the cross also held him in esteem. And what about that strange Parisian Church from the 'Da Vinci Code', St Sulpice. Although the church is said to be to St. Peter, for some reason nobody seems to mention what is round to the right side of St. Sulpice. There, imposingly, is a huge statue of John the Baptist with, importantly, his index finger raised. Either it points to heaven, which could be a feature of any religious statue, or perhaps it is a statue proclaiming that John the Baptist is number one! 'Number one' means that Jesus was not number one.

Okay you think this is a bit farfetched? Let me show you some more pointing fingers in Leonardo Da Vinci paintings and then look back at this statue and tell me what you make of it. Consider the Leonardo painting of The Virgin of the Rocks.

There are of course two versions, one in the Paris Louvre and the other

The Virgin of the Rocks – Louvre version (left) and London version (right)

in the National Gallery, London. In the Louvre version, it is hard to tell which of the two children is Jesus and which is John the Baptist, so who is the Angel pointing at? A later painter added a reed cross (one of John's symbols) to the London version suggesting the Angel in the Louvre version is pointing at John. Does the Angel indicate the important child?

Before I try to convince you about the finger pointing in other paintings let me just mention a couple of things that strike me about these paintings. Am I mad or is that strange rock sticking up in the hole on the right, not the most phallic thing you have ever seen? And at the Virgin's feet in the London version there is another phallic symbol, an Arum Lily, the traditional flower of the bridal bouquet with an exaggerated erect, male stamen. Virgin or what? Sex, sex, sex that's all you think about!

To defend myself, I have to correct something from Dan Brown's 'Da Vinci Code'. He says, the painting was commissioned by the Nuns of the Church of San Francesco in Milan. A natural mistake because the commissioners sound like nuns, but in fact Leonardo received his brief on 25th April 1483 from the Confraternity of the Immaculate Conception. Not nuns at all but a small brotherhood of Franciscan monks, elected to promote the newly invented Vatican doctrine of the Virgin Mary's Immaculate Conception. Now who's talking about sex? And what Immaculate Conception is Leonardo talking about in this painting, which I see full of phallic symbols? Surely this must be all in my mind. Or is it?

Want some more mischievous finger pointing by Leonardo? What the hell do you make of this painting of John the Baptist smiling knowingly?

If you can make head or tale of all this, please look back and tell me what the statue outside St. Sulpice is all about.

And what do you make of Leonardo's painting of the Last Supper, (or is it the 'Penultimate' Supper?) where a disciple is thrusting the one finger up into Jesus' face. Is he saying you are not number one?

Alright, that's enough 'Da Vinci Code' type stuff, let's just examine people who were fans of John the Baptist and may have considered him more important than Jesus.

The Gnostic Christians believed the Biblical stories were not to be taken literally but were for education and initiation. They were strong in Egypt and could well have been the priests who buried the Nag Hammadi Scrolls when their beliefs were termed heretical by the rising power of the Roman Church. Their influence, however, stretched to the South of France where the Cathars seem to have held similar beliefs. They both had woman priests, and saw Mary Magdalene as a major religious teacher. They had a dualist view of the world like the Zoroastrians. They saw John the Baptist as the major character and Jesus to be secondary.

Whereas the Egyptian Coptic Church seemed to succumb to the beliefs of the Roman Church, the Cathars refused to follow this simplistic view of Christ's teachings and the Roman Church's attempt to suppress women. So what did they do about these true Christians? The Roman Church led a crusade against the area and wiped out the population en masse, burning their Prefects (the priests) at the stake for heresy. The Albigensian Crusade murdered over half a million men, women and children.

Just like the Gnostic Christian sects, who did not believe Jesus was the Messiah, so Terry's Hermit does not believe that Brian is the Messiah, and so as a heretic he is carried off to be burnt at the stake. Isn't that just typical?

A postscript I have to add to this chapter is that until recently there were around 65,000 Mandaeans worldwide. Almost all of them lived in Iraq, where they were protected by Sadam Hussein, who kept a lid on Muslim fundamentalism. Since Bush and Blair's invasion of Iraq in 2003, Mandaeans have been attacked, murdered, the boys kidnapped and forcibly circumcised, till now most have fled the country. By 2007, the population of Iraqi Mandaeans had fallen to approximately 5,000. Most Iraqi Mandaeans now live in fear in Syria and Jordan where they are still outcasts. They are ostracized, by both Christians and Muslims, and so nobody wants to help them. Please will someone come to their aid before this extraordinary ancient group, are completely wiped out?

16

THE MORNING AFTER

The sun rises over a rather bad model of Jerusalem. Terry had made a cock crowing sound, which I had on my cutting copy. We then dubbed the film and replaced it with a real cock-crow. With the bad model it didn't seem to work, so Terry insisted we put his fake cock-crow back.

Brian, acclaimed by all as the Messiah, has now had his evil way with the impressionable Judith. I suppose here we have to confront the question of whether Jesus, like Brian, had sex. The whole debate was begun with the publication of the controversial 'Holy Blood, Holy Grail', which suggested Jesus was married and had offspring. This was then picked up in the 'Da Vinci Code'.

One must say that if Jesus was a Jew, who is sometimes called a Rabbi, then it would be surprising if he was not married, unless he was a monastic Essene.

The Bible does not say that he was married, but equally it doesn't say he wasn't. But there are some clear pointers that something odd was going on. To clarify this we have to look at which Gospels were selected for our Bible and which ones were left out, and on what basis were they selected or deselected. Bishop Athanasius made the initial selection, 360 years after Christ, and it was he who invented the word 'canon' (approved law). Prior to this there had been just a series of Christian texts of varying popularity in different parts of the Empire. After 35 years, Athanasius' shortlist was presented to the Council of Hippo and after another 4 years of deliberation the Council of Carthage came to the final selection. The first oddity is that they disregarded one of their own criteria, that the Gospels selected should be written in the names of, or attributed to the apostles. Matthew and John were apostles, but Mark and Luke were not, they appear in Acts as being later colleagues of Paul, and had never met Jesus. Okay, the selection was made, but what was done to the Gospels of Peter, Thomas and Philip, not to mention the 'Gospel of Mary' and the 'Words of our Saviour', which we know existed because they are mentioned as Holy Scripture by Church fathers before the Council of Hippo? They had to be destroyed!

They what??!! Works attributed to the apostles were considered heretical and were to be burnt. What I can't believe is that the Vatican didn't keep copies and if they did, then they have never, to this day, admitted it. But these outlawed books were found amongst the Nag Hammadi Scrolls. So what in hell's name was so awful in these Gospels? Before we answer that, we might get a clue from the bits that were added and subtracted from the selected Gospels themselves. Yes, we know they were tampered with.

The Gospel of Mark might possibly have been written by the Mark mentioned in Acts of the Apostles but the Gospels of Matthew and Luke are written well after the actual apostles were dead, and are clearly just cleansed versions of Mark and in reality can be ignored; except to find out what the Roman Church wanted to change. John is the other original document. However although it is attributed to the Apostle John it is written too late to actually be by him.

Now have a quick look at Mark and you will find in modern translations an odd statement between Mark 16:8 and 16:9. Old translations, like the King James' version have nothing, but in the New Living translation we find something odd in brackets:

16:7 *'The women fled from the tomb, trembling and bewildered, and they said nothing to anyone because they were too frightened.'*
[Shorter Ending of Mark]

16:8: *'Then they briefly reported all this to Peter and his companions. Afterward Jesus himself sent them out from east to west with the sacred and unfailing message of salvation that gives eternal life. Amen.'*
[Longer Ending of Mark]

16:9: *'After Jesus rose from the dead early on Sunday morning, the first person who saw him was Mary Magdalene, the woman from whom he had cast out seven demons.'*

Confused? You should be. What is going on here? It becomes clearer in the English Standard version, which has this little note between verses 8 and 9: *'Some of the earliest manuscripts do not include 16:9-20'*

That is a little more honest but you have to look at the New International version for total clarity: *'The most reliable early manuscripts and other ancient witnesses do not have Mark 16:9-to-20'*

In other words, 16:9 to 20 is a forgery and Mark had the body missing but never had Jesus resurrecting. But can we learn anything about Mary Magdalene from this dishonest addition? Lets look at 16:9 the first verse of the forgery.

> *'After Jesus rose from the dead early on Sunday morning, the first person who saw him was Mary Magdalene, the woman from whom he had cast out seven demons.'*

This description of Magdalene does not come from Mark's Gospel but from Luke's: it is exactly the way he describes her in his Gospel. Mark has nothing bad to say about Magdalene but then suddenly someone has added this bit of skulduggery.

If bits are added that blacken the name of the Magdalene, what about the bits cut out? *'Bits cut out?'* you may well ask? But yes, if Mark is authentic, then obviously there are going to be things that are not compatible with later official Church teachings. Look at Mark 10:46 and tell me you don't spot a cut:

> *'Then they came to Jericho. As Jesus and his disciples, together with a large crowd, were leaving the city, a blind man, Bartimaeus....'*

What the hell happened in Jericho? One minute he arrives, next minute he's leaving. Well we can tell you what happened because in 1958 Morton Smith, a professor of ancient history, found a letter in the Monastery of Mar Saba with the missing sections in it. Luckily he photographed the letters in black and white and 4 scholars who visited in 1976 photographed them in colour. I say luckily because subsequent attempts by scholars to view the manuscripts have been unsuccessful. I wonder why?

The hidden letter was written by Clement of Alexandria, whom I quoted earlier about the secret teachings of Christ in Mark's Gospel. But before we get to the Jericho bit, let's look at the large section that Clement states was between verses 34 and 35 of Mark 10. You will recognize the story:

'And they come into Bethany. And a certain woman whose brother had died was there. And, coming, she prostrated herself before Jesus and says to him "Son of David, have mercy on me." But the disciples rebuked her. And Jesus, being angered, went off with her into the garden where the tomb was, and straightway a great cry was heard from the tomb. And going near Jesus rolled away the stone from the door of the tomb. And straightway, going in where the youth was, he stretched forth his hand and raised him, seizing his hand. But the youth, looking upon him, loved him and began to beseech him that he might be with him. And going out of the tomb they came into the house of the youth, for he was rich. And after six days Jesus told him what to do and in the evening the youth comes to him, wearing a linen cloth over his naked body. And he remained with him that night, for Jesus taught him the mystery of the kingdom of God. And thence, arising, he returned to the other side of the Jordan.'

Let us take this bit by bit. *'And they come into Bethany. And a certain woman whose brother had died was there.'*

I'm sure Mark would not have been so coy with the names, so it looks like they edited it first and then decided they just couldn't stomach any of it, so they cut it all out. (Researchers found some sections of the New Testament had been edited up to 6 times.) But we know Bethany is where Mary Magdalene lived and her brother was Lazarus and we recognize the story that is in John's Gospel:

'Now a man named Lazarus was sick. He was from Bethany, the village of Mary and her sister Martha. This Mary, whose brother Lazarus now lay sick, was the same one who poured perfume on the Lord and wiped his feet with her hair. So the sisters sent word to Jesus, "Lord, the one you love is sick." (John 11:1)

Both Matthew and Luke have omitted this important event from their Gospels which we know are versions of Mark's Gospel. But somebody has even cut it out of Mark. Why?

'And, coming, she prostrated herself before Jesus and says to him,

'Son of David, have mercy on me.' But the disciples rebuked her.
And Jesus being angered went off with her.'

Just ask yourselves, why would the disciples rebuke a grieving woman for that? And who is Jesus angry with, the disciples? There is only one explanation that anyone has given and that relates to a Jewish custom. When someone dies, it is customary to sit Shiva for the dead. If a wife is sitting Shiva, she is not allowed to leave the house without her husband's permission. So one of the sisters, Martha or Mary, seems to have come out from sitting Shiva for her brother without her husband's permission. With the names removed we have to look at John's version of the story to find Martha come out and get permission from Jesus for Mary to leave the house.

'And after she had said this, she went back and called her sister
Mary aside. "The Rabbi is here," she said, "and is asking for you."
When Mary heard this, she got up quickly and went to him.'

Now the disciples don't have reason to rebuke her because Martha has told Mary, Jesus has asked for her, thereby satisfying the needs of the Shiva ritual. So John and secret Mark don't quite agree but either way they both suggest Mary Magdalene is married to Jesus. We will look further into this later but this cut section does reveal some more un-welcomed speculations.

And Jesus, being angered, went off with her into the garden where
the tomb was, and straightway a great cry was heard from the tomb.

Well I can see why they cut that out. It is clear that Lazarus is not dead. So what is this all about? Perhaps the clue lies in John's version of the story. When Jesus is told Lazarus is dead, it all gets a bit surreal:

'So he told them, "Lazarus is dead, and for your sake I am glad I
was not there, so that you may believe. But let us go to him."
Then Thomas called Didymus said to the rest of the disciples,
"Let us also go, that we may die with him."'

Any ideas? I can only compare this to the third degree initiation in Masonry where the novitiate is laid to death on a shroud and then resurrected back to life as a Mason. That would certainly make sense as to why the others want to die as well. The next section does seem to reinforce this theory as well as raising a whole new outrageous idea:

> *'And straightway, going in where the youth was, Jesus stretched forth his hand and raised him, seizing his hand. But the youth, looking upon him, loved him and began to beseech him that he might be with him. And going out of the tomb they came into the house of the youth, for he was rich. And after six days Jesus told him what to do.'*

That seems to confirm the initiation idea. Now the outrageous bit:

> *'... and in the evening the youth comes to him, wearing a linen cloth over his naked body. And he remained with him that night, for Jesus taught him the mystery of the kingdom of God.'*

In my film 'Chemical Wedding' I hinted at the possibility of homosexual activities of Jesus by quoting another part of Mark's Gospel. After the last supper, Jesus goes to the Garden of Gethsemane. There, after some odd goings on, he is captured:

> *'A young man, wearing nothing but a linen garment, was following Jesus. When they seized him, he fled naked, leaving his garment behind.' (Mark 14:51)*

I like the ways Biblical films skip this little moment, even Mel Gibson is happy to show much flagellated bare skin but a young naked man? No way. The word used for the young man is the Greek 'neaniskos', the same word Mark uses for Lazarus at the tomb. So could this be Lazarus again, up to something strange with Jesus? Interestingly, Mark uses the word 'neaniskos' again at the original ending of his Gospel when Mary and Salome go to the tomb:

> *'But when they looked up, they saw that the stone, which was very large, had been rolled away. As they entered the tomb, they saw a young man (neaniskos) dressed in a white robe sitting on the right side, and they were alarmed.*

160

"Don't be alarmed," he said. "You are looking for Jesus the Nazarene, who was crucified. He has risen!"

Was this Lazarus again who seems to spend half his life either in the tomb or naked in a white linen cloth?! Before we move on, I should tell you what occurred in Jericho. Well I can't tell you much, as it was edited out in the first cut, but here is the remainder in Clement's own words.

'And after the words, "And he comes into Jericho," the secret Gospel adds only, "And the sister of the youth whom Jesus loved and his mother and Salome were there, and Jesus did not receive them." But many other things about which you wrote seem to be falsifications.'

Okay, he's a liar, there was clearly more to this and Theodore, whom the letter is addressed to, seems to have been told, by a group called the Carpocrations, that there is more. Clement's letter starts:

To Theodore.
You did well in silencing the unspeakable teachings of the Carpocrations. For these are "wandering stars" referred to in the prophecy, who wander from the narrow road of the commandments into a boundless abyss of the carnal and bodily sins.

We don't have any record of who the Carpocratians are, but from what is written here, they sound like a Christian sect who seem to be involved in some sort of sexual rites and are quoting the secret Gospel of Mark to justify themselves. Christian sexual rites may sound strange nowadays, but a heretical group, 'the Bulgari' had their name associated with sodomy by Catholic propagandists, and 'bugger' is still in use today. Obviously the Carpocratians were quoting something odd going on at Jericho, and Clement is denying it. Instead he gives us this nonsensical section that, *at Jericho there were these people who Jesus never met!* Could the Carpocrations have seen the original text of Mark's Secret Gospel that included something explicit going on in Jericho? You bet they did. Clement accidentally lets this slip:

'[Mark] brought in certain sayings of which he knew the

interpretation would, as a mystagogue, lead the hearers into the innermost sanctuary of truth hidden by seven veils. Thus, in sum, he prepared matters, neither grudgingly nor incautiously, in my opinion, and, dying, he left his composition to the church in Alexandria, where it even yet is most carefully guarded, being read only to those who are being initiated into the great mysteries.'

Clement now admits that the leader of the Carpocrations, one Carpocrates, has seen it.

'But since the foul demons are always devising destruction for the race of men, Carpocrates, instructed by them and using deceitful arts, so enslaved a certain presbyter of the church in Alexandria that he got from him a copy of the secret Gospel, which he both interpreted according to his blasphemous and carnal doctrine.'

Wow, something really carnal was in it. What I wouldn't give to see it. We can only hope that, one day, an archaeologist will find it. If you think I'm being a bit strong calling Clement a liar, then listen to this next section of his letter:

'They (the Carpocrations) do not know that they are casting themselves away into "the netherworld of the darkness" of falseness, and boasting that they are free, they have become slaves of servile desires. Such men are to be opposed in all ways and altogether. For, even if they should say something true, one who loves the truth should not, even so, agree with them. For not all true things are the truth, nor should that truth which merely seems true according to human opinions be preferred to the true truth, that according to the faith.'

What an out and out liar! 'If they say something that is true, deny it!' These lying b.... are the sort of people who collated the Bible we read today and it is with great difficulty and research that we try to find out who the real Jesus was. My computer is in real danger of being smashed here so I had better move on.

Actually the little bit that Clement gave out about Jericho does tell us something:

> *'And the sister of the youth whom Jesus loved and his mother and*
> *Salome were there,'*

This torturous identification yeals three people:

1.   Salome
2.   Mary the Mother of Christ
3.   Mary Magdalene or Martha, the sisters of Lazarus.

3 is probably Mary Magdalene because if Clement can't even reveal to Theodore what happened, then it was probably something to do with her, perhaps even something that revealed that she was married to Jesus. Or if the Carpocrations were quoting it, maybe something carnal happened between them.

Here you should become aware that Dan Brown is wrong when he suggests the 'disciple who Jesus loved' was Mary Magdalene when in, secret Mark, he refers to, *'the sister of the youth Jesus loved.'*, which suggests it is not a woman. This is confirmed by the four references to the Beloved Disciple in the Gospel of John: The one that Dan Brown quotes is from John's version of the Last Supper.

> *'Now there was leaning on Jesus' bosom one of his disciples,*
> *whom Jesus loved. Simon Peter therefore beckoned to him, that he*
> *should ask who it should be of whom he spake. He then lying on*
> *Jesus' breast saith unto him, Lord, who is it? (John 13:23)*

I love this because different translations have attempted to muddy it up. The English Standard version has him reclining at the table and another leaning on Jesus' back. And if you want a real laugh, have a look at how artists have attempted to portray this. I was in Toledo Cathedral in Spain and there, carved in a wooden screen is the Last Supper with one disciple leaning over on to Jesus' breast. It is very tortuous trying to get a man leaning on a breast at table; it looks better when paintings show the Last Supper not on chairs but reclining, like a Roman banquet.

Many paintings make this disciple sleeping, but how can he be sleeping if he is talking to Peter? I like the ones that get over the problem by making the disciple a small boy sitting on Jesus' lap. Here's a funny one by Jacopo Bassano that has him both a boy and sleeping.

Of course in movies they never dare try to show it. The cowards! Dan Brown makes a big point that this disciple in Leonardo's Last Supper looks like a woman. I would just point out that Leonardo was probably gay (he was never married and was had up for Sodomy charges at the age of 24).

Look at this painting by another gay painter Caravaggio.

In John Berger's 'Ways of Seeing' this painting was shown to adults who said it was Jesus, while children shown the same painting said it was a woman! When

I do film directing master classes, I show them this painting and tell the potential directors that they need to look at things with the eyes of a knowledgeable child. By the way I also show them Michelangelo's 'David'. If this has anything to do with the biblical character, I'll eat my hat. This is a gay guy, enjoying sculpting a gorgeous young man's body: and why not? I get the same feeling of adoration when I photograph beautiful young naked women.

As I mentioned before, the so-called penultimate supper has the correct people present and tells us clearly who was reclining with Jesus.

'Jesus arrived at Bethany, where Lazarus lived, whom Jesus had raised from the dead. Here a dinner was given in Jesus' honour. Martha served, while Lazarus was among those reclining at the table with him.' (John 12)

It is so obvious that the Magdalene was at the Last Supper in Bethany that she is shown in many paintings of the event. *'Eucharist of the Last Supper'* by Fra Angelico shows her as well as the 12 disciples, so it would have been no big deal for Leonardo to add her to the 12 instead of turning one of the disciples into a 'her' in some sort of conspiratorial way, leaving only 11 disciples.

Let's look at Mary Magdalene in another way. She is a constant in Jesus' life; she lives in Bethany which is where Jesus seems to spend all his time, eating Last Suppers, being anointed, raising people from the dead, having his feet washed with her hair, and getting a donkey to ride triumphantly into Jerusalem. She sponsored him, travelled with him, anointed him, confided in him, was companion to his mother and sisters. She was at the foot of the cross and she went to attend Jesus' body in the tomb. If you add what is in the other unselected Gospels, where she is described as the 'Apostle of the Apostles', she kisses Jesus on the mouth, he 'loves her' and she is even clearly described as 'his consort'! If he wasn't married to her, then they were obviously having an affair. As I say, you pays your money and you takes your choice.

I think I agree with those who suggest the Wedding at Cana was his wedding because how else can one explain how a so-called 'carpenters' wife is giving orders to the household servants? Come on, give us a break!

Like Brian and Judith, I go for Jesus having had sex and the big question then is, did they have children?

One thing Josephus says about the Essenes is, that they do not marry out of pleasure but for the sake of posterity. Jesus being from the bloodline of David would have been expected to procreate for 'posterity'.

So if they had a child, where is it? After Jesus' death, Mary, her brother Lazarus, Maximinus, and some companions appear to have been expelled by persecutions from the Holy Land, and went to Alexandria. From there, with Joseph of Aramathea, they crossed the Mediterranean in a frail boat to the Jewish Kingdom of Septomania in the South of France. Right up to the middle ages Royalty from the area, like the Duke of Toulouse, were recognized by the Caliph of Baghdad and Pepin as 'the true seeds of the Royal House of David.' They kept strict observance of Jewish Sabbaths and Holy Days, spoke Hebrew and Arabic and used the Lion of Judah as a heraldic device on their shield. Whether these descendents of the 'Royal line of David' came from Jesus and Mary, or other Jewish Royal family members that went there, is another thing. We do know that Herod also retired to France.

Our boat with Mary and Joseph of Aramathea seems to have been blown off course to the East and landed at the place now called Saintes-Maries-de-la-Mer, which is the capital of the Camargue. According to longstanding legend, on the boat were three Marys: Magdalene, Mary Salome, and Mary Jacobe as well as Aramathea, and intriguingly a Sarah. The town is a pilgrimage destination for Gypsies who gather yearly for a religious festival in honour of Saint Sarah. The French believed she was Mary Magdalene's daughter, and she was also known as Sara-la-Kali (Sarah the black). Others believe that dark-skinned Saint Sarah was the Egyptian servant of the three Marys. All one can say is that Sarah was probably not her name but her title as it translates in Hebrew as Princess! Black Madonnas are found all around the area, but these statuettes were disliked by the Roman Church who claimed they were turned black by candle smoke. Churches named Notre Dame sprang up throughout France and the one at Chartres is clearly celebrating Magdalene and her spiritual name Sophia (wisdom). Even the Knights Templar whose founders are thought to relate to the Bloodline, venerated her and kept her relics and paid homage to a skull, called Baphomet, a simple code for 'Sophia'. The Roman Church refused to make her a Saint till recently. I filmed in Lourdes where there was a very fakey sighting of a Virgin but the site is venerated by the Roman Church who encourage mass pilgrimages. But what about Saintes-Maries-de-la-Mer? Nothing. When I was there, all I saw was a plaque celebrating the visit of Pope John 23 to the town. No massive celebration of this Holy site, just the one good Pope John 23 who broke all the rules (and is oddly named John 23 when there had already been a

Pope John 23) and who Malachi Martin (Appendix 4) suggests was a Mason.

While I remember, when we were in Tunisia filming, 'Brian', John 23 had died and Pope John Paul was elected. I remember sitting round the hotel pool and hearing that after just 33 days he had died. At the time, I thought this was funny, that being Pope didn't get him very far with God. I am sorry now that I joked about it because this was the other 'good' Pope (called the smiling Pope), who lived a humble and truly Christian Life, a wonderful human being. He was about to make some revolutionary changes to the Papacy. He was the first Pope to choose an investiture to commence his papacy rather than a coronation, and the world would have been a better place had he survived. But he was poisoned by a cup of coffee, by those who hung the Italian banker under Blackfriars bridge. The Church tried to cover it up, firstly saying it wasn't a nun who found him, and then making Sister Vincenza take a vow of silence before being sent to a nunnery. If you have any doubts, read David Yallop's book, 'In God's Name'. Although written some time ago, it gives a clear picture of how the Catholic paedophile cover-ups would come about.

Oh, I forgot to mention, there is yet another painting of the 'Virgin of the Rocks'! I think it might throw light on the others and this chapter. The brief for the Louvre painting from the Confraternity was very specific, with a line up of *God in a cloak of gold brocade*; above 4 angels *in garments fashioned in the Greek style*; Mary and Jesus and two prophets. You can imagine their surprise when Leonardo turned up with two naked babies and a couple of ladies in a cave! You can understand why they refused to pay him and the painting ended up in a lawsuit. Who can make any sense of this? Laurence Gardner suggests that Leonardo was asked to complete the painting so that it could be unveiled for the Feast of the Immaculate Conception on the 8th December, in just 8 months. Given the deadline it is a wonder that he undertook the commission, but he decided to ignore the brief and use a composition he had already prepared for another brief. Taking photos of the paintings and scaling them to match, the topographical surveyor David Wood found that the background features matched so perfectly, in fact too perfectly for a copyist or measurement, he believes they were somehow traced. (Because they are different sizes I can only suggest some form of projection!) The third legitimate 'Virgin of the Rocks' is at the Musée des Beaux-Arts de Caen, and Laurence Gardner believes this is the first painting and was either finished by Leonardo, or by the School of Leonardo, after his death. It is not a copy of either the London or the Paris version in that it is subtly different

from both.

In basic construction, it resembles the original Louvre painting but the pointing Angel is looking out at us knowingly. In the Louvre she looks at the nearest child, and in the London one she appears to be looking at the other child. Laurence Gardner tells us that the central character in all paintings was never described by Leonardo as the Madonna; he called her La Nostra Signora – Our Lady. This is the term used for Mary Magdalene by the Templars and the Troubadours. Her hair is now red and her costume red and gold. Leonardo also never specified who the children were. The angel named by others as Uriel is strange since Uriel is always depicted as a man but this is a young girl. Laurence asks us to consider this Old Testament Song of Solomon translated from the original Greek:

> 'The vines put forth the tender grape... Arise, come my consort, my fair one... Thou art my dove in the shelter of the Rocks.' (Song of Solomon 2:13)

From all this, he concludes that this is Mary Magdalene with her eldest daughter and two sons living in the cave where she is thought to have inhabited in the South of France. By a tortuous translation he suggests that the lily flower

**Here is the cave where Mary was alleged to have spent her final years.
Notre Dame of the Rocks?**

is known as Tamar, which was thought to be the name of Magdalene's daughter. David Wood however thinks the lily symbolizes the fleur-de-lis linking Magdalene to the Royal families of France. I can't decide myself what I believe, I can only tell you what I see: a woman whose clothes start in the first painting very Mary Magdaleneish and are slowly changed, as is her hair which starts as red, two babies, one blessing the other while the other has his hands together in a religious prayer, and a teenage girl who sometimes has wings and starts by pointing at the higher positioned child. I have to ignore the halos and the reed cross as these were later additions. The setting is not the Egyptian desert – so it is not a painting of the Flight to Egypt as sometimes suggested, but a cave in a fertile rocky landscape.

Whether you believe it or not, I am almost certain that Leonardo was involved with esoteric ideas and would have believed that after Mary's time of preaching in Marseilles, she lived in prayer and contemplation in a cave in the Sainte-Baume mountains nearby.

17

THE PYTHONESS

No this is not Carol Cleveland; although there is no doubt that it could well be a description of her as the female Python. Nor is it a female follower of the Pythons. The Pythoness was the Oracle Priestess at Delphi whose advice was sought by powerful statesmen and famous philosophers. She was one of many famous priestesses of the Pagan Mysteries. Other important women in ancient times include great mystical poets like Sappho and her sisters on Lebos and Diotima, the priestess who taught Socrates and philosophers such as Arignote and Themisto. And of course for me, and many groups, there is Mary Magdalene, who we believe understood the Gnostic nature of the teachings. I would like to suggest that we call a woman who, against all the odds, does great things a Pythoness. But what happened to women, that they were reduced to the status of children?

From what we can understand, women were even removed from the Holy Trinity, which was God the Father, God the Son and God the Holy Mother; the latter being switched to God the Holy Ghost. I like the Google translation of this to *'God the Holy Alcohol.'* Perhaps we should translate the whole Bible through Google to remove the prejudiced translations we get. I really like the Russian translation Google makes of *'Out of sight out of mind'* which when translated back to English becomes, *'invisible idiot'*.

Side by side with the decline of the status of women went the destruction of ancient wisdom and knowledge. Strangely, wisdom has a female name, 'Sophia', which is where the word philosophy comes from (philo – love of, sophia – wisdom). In long-standing tradition, Mary Magdalene was known as Sophia and we know the Knights Templar in France venerated a skull called Baphomet, which translates using the Atbash cipher to Sophia. Significantly the early Church spent much time attacking philosophers as well as trying to sideline Mary Magdalene. In the Egyptian city of Alexandria occurred three events that typified everything that was to befall the known world. Mankind lost the ancient world's single greatest archive of knowledge, the Library of Alexandria, which was destroyed by Christians. The famous philosopher and mathematician Hypatia of Alexandria was taken from her chariot as she was returning home from the Museum. Christian zealots dragged her into the cathedral of Alexandria, stripped her and proceeded to dismember her with sharp shells and burn the pieces of her corpse. Hypatia's violent death has come to mark the end of the age of great Greek mathematics. And finally the Temple of Serapis was converted into a Christian Church and many documents were destroyed. The Temple of Serapis was estimated to hold about ten percent of the overall Library of Alexandria's holdings.

Let me remind you of the beliefs of Serapis, which I referred to in the beginning:

1. A God made flesh.
2. His father is God, his mother a mortal virgin.
3. He is born in a humble cave on 25th December
4. He offers his followers a chance to be born again through the rites of baptism
5. He miraculously turns water into wine at a wedding.
6. He rides triumphantly on a donkey while people wave palms in his honour.
7. He dies at Easter-time as a sacrifice for the sins of the world.
8. After his death he descends to hell, then on the third day he rises and ascends in triumph.
9. His followers await his return as the judge during the last days.
10. His death and resurrection are celebrated by a ritual meal of bread and wine – symbolizing the body and blood.

And the philosophy of the Mystery religions?

1. Be pure of thought and deed.
2. Have a personal loving relationship with God.
3. Love your neighbour.
4. Love your enemies.
5. Embrace poverty and humility.
6. Believe in one God.

7.   Attack idolatry.
8.   The Son of God is the embodiment of the logos.
9.   Conceived of God as a Holy Trinity.

Undoubtedly you must think this is ridiculous because, if it were true, people at the time would have known that Christianity was just a copy of the Pagan mysteries. You are right. The philosopher and satirist Celsus criticized Christians for trying to pass off the Jesus story as a new revelation.

> 'How are they unique? Or ours are to be taken as myths and theirs believed.'

To answer this, Justin Martyr claimed that the story of Dionysis was 'invented by demons' to throw doubt on Jesus. Father Firmicus Maternus, complained that the resurrection of Dyonysis was an attempt to ridicule the true faith, claiming 'the devil too has Christians'. And the Church finally came up with the most ridiculous explanation ever invented. They called it, 'diabolical mimicry'. Can you believe the idea that the Devil had plagiarized Christianity by anticipation? The Church father Tertullian wrote:

> 'The Devil, whose business is to pervert the truth, mimics the exact circumstances of the divine Sacraments. He baptizes his believers and promises forgiveness of sins…. He celebrates the oblation of bread, and brings in the symbol of the resurrection. Let us therefore acknowledge the craftiness of the devil.'

And that same Tertullian writes another document attacking women:

> 'These heretical women, how audacious they are! They have no modesty. They are bold enough to teach; to engage in argument.'

I still cannot fathom from my position in the 21st century, how the Roman Church unlike Jesus, came to consider women as second-class inferiors? Did it come from the Jewish culture, which was dreadfully patriarchal?

> 'The words of the Torah will be destroyed in the fire sooner than be taught by women.' (Palestinian Talmud)

172

Or was it just the beliefs of the Roman Empire where, for example, the officially sanctioned ceremonies held women's legal status as, dependent minors.

Women were treated as equals by Jesus, Paul, the Gnostic Church, the Cathars and of course by the People's Front of Judea. But the Roman Church, which based its legitimacy on Peter didn't buy into this human view. Could Peter have been the culprit since he is often quoted with misogynous sayings, as in the 'Pistis Sophia',

"Let Mary leave us, for women are not worthy of life."

I once read an explanation for this attitude based on anthropology. As I am not an anthropologist, I cannot tell you if it has any validity but it has a logic. The book was by Frederick Engels and was enormously titled, *'The Origin of the Family, Private Property and the State'*. The argument went like this:

Original primitive communities were matriarchal as people traced their ancestry through their mothers, sometimes not being sure who in the tribe was their father. (In one legend women were thought to get pregnant by bending to the North wind). The central God was also a woman, probably because they were capable of the magic of creation, birth. We know the extremely ancient Temples of Malta were built to the Goddess we call the 'Fat Lady' from the sculptures. And the mother goddess was widespread in many civilizations.

Sheila-Na-Gig the Celtic Goddess of Creation

In ancient societies property was held in common and the men were hunters. If they happen to war with another group, there was only one thing worth doing with their prisoners, eat them! That was until agriculture developed and was able to produce a surplus of food. This meant that if you captured an enemy, instead of eating him you could put him to work and they could make enough food for themselves and a surplus for you. At that point slavery was created and this complex society built on surplus was able to sustain cities. As it was the males who captured the slaves, it meant they became the dominant force, and how many slaves they owned made them richer in the surplus the slaves produced. This wealth the male wanted to pass on to his children, so he needed to make a woman his personal property for procreation. He needed to own her. And this, Engels argued, was the origin of marriage, private property and the state and resulted in the second-class status of women.

Perhaps Engels was right as the idea of celibate priests has nothing to do with scripture but everything to do with property rights. Originally, in the Catholic Church priests were allowed to marry till 1095 when Pope Urban II ruled that those seeking ordination should not be married. A later edict by Pope Innocent II in 1139 required married priests to abandon their wives and families. The reason stated for this unchristian act, was to insure that Church property would not be inherited by children of priests but would remain in the hands of the Holy See. Property again raises its ugly head, and gave rise to the conditions for the propensity of paedophiles in the Catholic priesthood.

Okay that's the reason for celibacy but if Jesus treated women as equals why did the official Church want to suppress them?

When Luke writes his cleansed version of Mark's Gospel, what is the main change he makes from the original? A clear attempt to blacken the name of a particular woman, Mary Magdalene, and not only when he mentions her by name but when he takes stories that we know are about her and corrupt them into slanderous rubbish.

'Now one of the Pharisees invited Jesus to have dinner with him, so he went to the Pharisee's house and reclined at the table. When a woman who had lived a sinful life in that town learned that Jesus was eating at the Pharisee's house, she brought an alabaster jar of perfume, and as she stood behind him at his feet weeping, she began to wet his feet with her tears. Then she wiped them with her hair, kissed them and poured perfume on them.' (Luke 7:36)

174

All I can say about whoever this person pretending to be Luke happens to be, is 'what a bastard!' and the style suggests he is probably the same bastard who forged the end of Mark's Gospel. He knows he is not going to get away with calling Magdalene those names, so he does it in this slimy way. I wish he would take a drop of his own medicine because in his added section in Mark he writes:

> *'In my name they will drive out demons; they will speak in new tongues; they will pick up snakes with their hands; and when they drink deadly poison, it will not hurt them at all.'*

Please pick up a snake and drink some poison for my sake. Let's move on before I really do smash my computer. What else has been added to the Bible?

What about the letters attributed to Paul but are now thought by the majority of modern scholars to be forgeries:

First Timothy
Second Timothy
Titus
Ephesians

These forgeries include vitriolic rubbish against believers who might not follow the party line:

> *'Some have wandered away from these and turned to meaningless talk. They want to be teachers of the law, but they do not know what they are talking about or what they so confidently affirm. We know that the law is good if one uses it properly. We also know that law is made not for the righteous but for lawbreakers and rebels, the ungodly and sinful, the unholy and irreligious; for those who kill their fathers or mothers, for murderers, for adulterers and perverts, for slave traders and liars and perjurers—and for whatever else is contrary to the sound doctrine that conforms to the glorious gospel of the blessed God, which he entrusted to me.'*

Yuk! Is this anything to do with Christ or what? But more. Titus 1:16
> *'They claim to know God, but by their actions they deny him. They are detestable, disobedient and unfit for doing anything good.'*

175

Because they 'think for themselves, they're all individuals'. And now we come to women in the forged letters. 1 Timothy 2:9

> '*I also want women to dress modestly, with decency and propriety, not with braided hair or gold or pearls or expensive clothes, but with good deeds, appropriate for women who profess to worship God. A woman should learn in quietness and full submission. I do not permit a woman to teach or to have authority over a man; she must be silent. For Adam was formed first, then Eve. And Adam was not the one deceived; it was the woman who was deceived and became a sinner. But women will be saved through childbearing— if they continue in faith, love and holiness with propriety.*'

Pretty sick stuff, but not written by Paul because in the authentic letters of Paul we find women are extremely important to his mission.

> '*I commend to you our sister Phoebe, a servant of the church in Cenchrea. I ask you to receive her in the Lord in a way worthy of the saints and to give her any help she may need from you, for she has been a great help to many people, including me. Greet Priscilla and Aquila, my fellow workers in Christ Jesus. They risked their lives for me.*' (Romans 16:1)

You don't have to be an expert to work out that, these two letters have not been written by the same man, unless he's a schizophrenic. But you do need to be an expert to know what has been mistranslated as '*servant of the church*' is in fact '*deacon of the church*'. Someone with authority to preach!

Okay, so I hope you are getting the picture that the additions to the text of the Bible, as we know it, seem to be to:

1. Castigate deviants,
2. To subjugate women.
3. To blacken the name of Mary Magdalene.

Side by side with this attack on women seems to go an assault on knowledge leading directly to the dark ages. Unfortunately, the present day Catholic Church has not moved out of these dark ages. As I write, the Vatican has just issued a statement:

'The ordination of women as Roman Catholic priests is a 'crime against the faith,' the Vatican said as it issued a raft of new disciplinary rules.

Cases of 'attempted ordination of women' will henceforth be handled by the Vatican's doctrinal watchdog, the Congregation for the Doctrine of the Faith.

The new rules put attempts at ordination of women among the 'most serious crimes,' along with paedophilia. Those who attempt to ordain women — and the women concerned — are subject to automatic excommunication.'

Great. Not only on a par with paedophilia but worse because paedophiles are not automatically excommunicated but hidden and excused where possible.

To conclude this chapter, let me tell the story of a painting. It is in the National Gallery and it seems both too alien to grasp, and at the same time entirely straightforward, encouraging scholars of every variety to register their own different interpretations in print. Because it is so photographic it might appear that, objects are there because they happen to be in the room. But no, there is nothing in a painting that was not intentionally put there by the painter. *(see fig 13 for important colour details)*

I can't give you all the answers but I can tell you the extraordinary nature of the mystery and you can puzzle with the answers for yourself. First, think about when this could have been painted. Well a date and the artist's name are painted on the wall above the mirror. The date is before Leonardo Da Vinci was born! It says 1434 and in Latin *'Johannes de eyck fuit hic'*, which translates like something scrawled on a toilet door, *'Jan van Eyck was here'*. Like many bits of information, I cannot tell you if this is relevant, but van Eyck means *'of the oak tree'*. Throughout Europe, the oak was once viewed as a sacred tree, linked with the sky God who sent thunder and lightning, whether his name was Zeus, Jupiter, Taranis or Thor. Zeus was even crowned with a wreath of oak leaves. And the oak was important to the Druids of Britain and is the sacred tree of Wicca. We find it features as a sacred tree from Israel to North America, and is important to Basque culture where the bombing of Guernica was on the site of their sacred oak. If you look back at the Bosch painting featured earlier you will see that the figure 'Air' has a twig of oak in his hat and the cross beam of the cross in his hand which will join the upright held by 'Water' somewhere outside the painting.

In 1425 van Eyck entered the service of the powerful and influential Duke Philip the Good of Burgundy, making him quite well off. The history of the painting and how it got to the National Gallery in London is fascinating. It originally was in the possession of Don Diego de Guevara, a Spanish career courtier of the Habsburgs. He lived most of his life in the Netherlands. By 1516 he had given the portrait to Margaret of Austria, Habsburg Regent of the Netherlands. An inventory of Margaret's paintings lists it as, *'a large picture, which is called 'Hernoul le Fin' with his wife in a chamber, which was given to Madame by Don Diego, whose arms are on the cover of the said picture; done by the painter Johannes.'* A note in the margin says, *'It is necessary to put on a lock to close it: which Madame has ordered to be done.'*

In 1524 another inventory gives a similar description, but the name is now given as 'Arnoult Fin'. In 1530 the painting was inherited by Margaret's niece Mary of Hungary, who in 1556 went to live in Spain. It is clearly described in an inventory taken after her death in 1558, when it was inherited by Philip II of Spain. In 1599 a German visitor saw it in the Alcazar Palace in Madrid. Now it had verses from Ovid painted on the frame: *'See that you promise: what harm is there in promises? In promises anyone can be rich.'* In an inventory after the death of Carlos II in 1700, it was still in the palace, but by 1794 it had moved to the Palacio Nuevo in Madrid.

Then suddenly in 1816, the painting appears in London, in the possession of Colonel James Hay, a Scottish soldier. He claimed that after he was seriously wounded at the Battle of Waterloo the previous year, the painting hung in the room where he convalesced in Brussels. He fell in love with it, and persuaded the owner to sell. This is probably a lie. The fact is that in 1813, Hay was at the Battle of Vitoria in Northern Spain, where Wellington fought the retreating French army led by Napoleon's brother, Joseph Bonaparte. We know a large coach loaded with artworks looted from the Spanish royal collections was captured and plundered by British troops, before what was left was recovered by their commanders and returned to the Spanish. On his return to London, Hay offered the painting to the Prince Regent, later George IV of England, via the fashionable painter, Sir Thomas Lawrence. The Prince had it on approval for two years at Carlton House before eventually returning it in 1818. Hay gave it to a friend to look after, until he arranged for it to be included in a public exhibition in 1841. A year later it was bought for £600, by the newly formed National Gallery. The shutters had gone, along with the original frame and it was catalogued as 'A Gentleman and his Lady'.

What a story, and when one researches the different owners it reads like a history of Europe. But what the hell is it about? In 1862 the gallery renamed the painting, 'The Arnolfini Marriage' after research by W.H. James Weald, an expert on Dutch art. This is the present day Catalogue description:

> 'This work is a portrait of Giovanni di Nicolao Arnolfini and his wife, but is not intended as a record of their wedding. His wife is not pregnant, as is often thought, but holding up her full-skirted dress in the contemporary fashion. Arnolfini was a member of a merchant family from Lucca living in Bruges. The couple are shown in a well-appointed interior.'

Hold on, the Burgundian State archive dates the marriage of the Arnolfinis as 1447, thirteen years after the date on the picture and by that time Jan van Eyck was dead! And how the hell do they know the wife is not pregnant? Are they doctors or have they had a doctor do a pregnancy test on the painting? She could be just three months pregnant or calculate for yourself if holding that quantity of skirt produces that much bulge. The argument for it being the fashion comes from a painting by Jan called the Dresden Triptych. The central panel is the Madonna and Child, and the small right panel is St. Catherine who has a similar bulge to Mrs. Arnolfin.

But wait, the young lady is not holding up her skirt to produce the bulge. Maybe this Saint is actually pregnant! And anyway what is Saint Catherine doing in a Madonna and Child? This is her tale, she dreamt she was the bride of Christ and woke up with His ring on her finger. The bride of Christ; is Jan telling us something about the real person who was the bride of Christ, perhaps even that she was pregnant. More about this later. In our bedroom scene, the lady may or may not be pregnant but what is the National Gallery trying to do with such a definitive statement, protect her honour?

Here is what I think we actually see. Firstly the painting is a study in detail. Jan was described, by his patron, as a scientist and I get the feeling that he is trying to investigate right down to the molecules of the objects. Carpets, clothing, jewellery, if you can make it, I can paint it: the very opposite of the impressionists. For those of you who want to be photographers, let me talk you through the lighting. The key light is meant to be from the window on the left. If this was the only source of light, then the man's face would be darker on the opposite side and the joined hands would also be very dark. For me to get this particular look, I would have to have another source of light from the camera position, what we call a fill light. The lady is lit by a light or a window around where the man's upraised hand is. You can tell exactly where by the shadow of her nose. This is always how we light the leading ladies, a soft light which does not allow the nose shadow to stream across the face. Something else that I notice is that her white headdress is bouncing light under her chin. A detail, which makes me believe he was painting what was there. I mention soft light, which we produce by putting light through a large piece of tracing paper. For me to light the chandelier the way it looks would take a soft light with a piece of trace as big as a man. The hardest thing to light is a silver teapot because it makes hard pinpoints of light and reflects everything in the room, including your lights.

You have to build a white tent, which you light through. The chandelier is almost impossible to get like that.

Now off the technical stuff, what about the details? Firstly he is in outdoor clothes and is poised unnaturally. It looks like he has just come in and kicked off his clogs. What do you think? I noticed in Russia, it is common practice to take off your shoes when you enter the house. But why paint them into the foreground? Do the clogs indicate this event is taking place on holy ground, especially as she also seems to have removed her indoor slippers, which are also in the picture. If there were more objects on the floor we could suggest the artist thinks these two are untidy, but there is nothing else. What about the hat, could it represent a crown or just that he is bald and thinks he looks best in his hat? He holds one hand as if he is taking a religious vow and holds her offered hand in an odd way. A marriage vow? Not according to the British Museum. But how do they know? Is the little dog their pet, or does it symbolize fidelity? 'Fido' originated from the Latin 'to trust'. Behind the pair, the curtains of the marriage bed have been opened. The bedpost's finial is a tiny statue of Saint Margaret, the patron saint of childbirth. But of course she is not pregnant. From the finial hangs a whiskbroom, a symbol of domestic care, perhaps. The three oranges on the chest below the window may refer to fertility, and the apple on the sill could be there to remind us of Eve. Outside the window is a tree with bright red fruit, which makes the season autumn. Although daytime, a single candle is burning in the left rear holder of the chandelier, adorned with upturned fleur-de-lis, crosses and crowns. A string of amber pearls with green tassels hangs on the wall. Beside them in the mirror we see reflected their backs and the door of the room, where there are two people standing or entering. The small medallions set into the mirror's frame show tiny scenes from the Passion of Christ and possibly represent God's ever-present promise of salvation. This is all very vague, and everybody seems to feel there is something more to the painting; something hidden.

Suppose I say that Bruegel painted the 'Biblical Census at Bethlehem' in a severe snowy landscape with Flemish peasants, totally un-Holylandish. Or consider the painting next to the van Eyck, in the National Gallery. Called the 'Holy Family', by Joos van Cleve it has Joseph in straw hat and anachronistic glasses.

The section of a painting by Rogier van der Weyden shows a typical Dutch scene with book and furniture of the period. But the ointment jar tells us this is Mary Magdalene and so does the fact that she is wearing Magdalene's typical green.

Holy Family   Van der Weyden

If you look back at the *'The Arnolfini Marriage'*, Laurence Gardner in his book the 'Magdalene Legacy' suggests that this is exactly what the woman is wearing. To this he adds that the couple are surrounded by symbols of fertility and royalty, especially French royalty with the fleurs-de-lis in the chandelier and upturned crowns. The single candle and removed shoes suggest the sacred, and he believes that the miniature paintings of Jesus' passion round the mirror, make this couple Jesus and Magdalene.

But what about the hat?

When Mary Magdalene sees Jesus outside the tomb she does not recognize him:

'She turned herself back, and saw Jesus standing, and knew not that it was Jesus.

Jesus saith unto her, "Woman, why weepest thou? whom seekest thou?"

She, supposing him to be the gardener, saith unto him, "Sir, if thou have borne him hence, tell me where thou hast laid him, and I will take him away."

Jesus saith unto her, "Mary."

She turned herself, and saith unto him, "Rabboni"; which is to say, Master.

Jesus saith unto her, "Do not touch me; for I am not yet ascended to my Father."

Why would she think he is a gardener? Perhaps he was dressed like a gardener. Perhaps in the Netherlands at the time, gardeners wore wide brimmed hats. Maybe this is not as silly as it sounds; Laurence offers several Dutch paintings, which strangely show Jesus, as the gardener, meeting Magdalene outside the tomb, with a wide brimmed hat.

Caracciola   Rembrandt

This all goes to make the '*Arnolfini Marriage*' painting a bedroom heresy, suggesting not only a marriage between Jesus and the Magdalene but with sacrilegious emphasis on her fertility.

I have points for and against such a theory. My main point for is based on the inset pictures around the mirror. There are ten miniatures of Christ's Passion starting at the top with the crucifixion, then round the sides are other populated scenes from his life. At the very bottom is the resurrection scene at the tomb where Magdalene meets Jesus and thinks he is the gardener. The problem is that the characters are not there! Where is Jesus and where is the Magdalene? Perhaps they have stepped out of the miniature and are standing before us. Boy, do I like this theory of mine, but unfortunately I have a couple of problems with it. Firstly, in the biblical scene Jesus says '*Noli me tangere*', do not touch me. This is the title of many paintings so would be known to Jan van Eyck. Yet in his painting it is the man who is actually touching the woman.

Secondly the alabaster jar of the Magdalene is absent, and thirdly her hair is not really red. Does Jan know and use the convention of showing Mary Magdalene with red hair? At the base of Jan's painting of the Crucifixion, *(see colour plate fig 14)* you will see the Magdalene identified by her very red hair. It is a shame but perhaps the inclusion of the alabaster jar or the red hair would have made it too obvious and maybe the touching hands, is not such a big deal.

Okay, I am desperately trying to convince myself but there is more from Laurence Gardener that is of interest in the '*Arnolfini Marriage*'.

When Jan painted the Ghent altarpiece, his wife Margaretta helped him. Art books say Jan had an older brother called Hubert who actually assisted Jan with this commission. Laurence insists Hubert is a myth! His name never appears for a hundred years then suddenly, there is a Hubert. And as his name became established, Margaretta's was sidelined. The switch began when the Altarpiece won praise and awards, which led to greater public awareness. The Cathedral authorities had a problem in admitting that a woman might have been involved in the painting. By 1568 a brother had been invented and who could complain, since the originators were all long dead. A painting by Margaretta van Eyck entitled '*Madonna with Mary Magdalene with a Donor*' was catalogued at the Bruges Exhibition in 1867 and another at the London National Gallery at its opening. Later, without explanation the National Gallery removed her name from the catalogue and the painting was reassigned to an unknown artist. I cannot tell you how accurate this story is because Hubert lives on and Margaretta has successfully been expunged from art history.

What I do like about this theory is that it presents us with yet another possibility about the 'The *Arnolfini Marriage*' painting. Let's suppose the painting is of the Arnolfini couple, created when they got married in 1447, after Jan was dead. Then the inscription on the wall '*Jan van Eyck was here 1434*' was put there to commemorate Jan, by the real artist who created the work, who was actually – his wife. Nice one, Margaretta! You are a Pythoness.

18

HE'S NOT THE MESSIAH HE'S A VERY NAUGHTY BOY

After a full frontal to the multitude, there follows an absolutely great interaction between Mandy, Brian and the crowd. I love the way it develops from simple chants to crowd reactions with character.

MANDY: *Now, you listen here! He's not the Messiah. He's a very naughty boy! Now, go away!*

CROWD: *Who are you?!*

MANDY: *I'm his mother. That's who.*

CROWD: *Behold His mother! Behold His mother! Hail to thee, mother of Brian! Blessed art thou, Hosanna! All praise to thee, now and always!*

MANDY: *Well— Now, don't think you can get around me like that. He's not coming out, and that's my final word. Now, shove off!*

CROWD: *No!*

MANDY: *Did you hear what I said?*

CROWD: *Yes!*

MANDY: *Oh, I see. It— it's like that, is it?*

CROWD: *Yes!*

MANDY: *Ohh. Oh, all right, then. You can see him for one minute, but not one second more. Do you understand?*

CROWD: *Yes.*

MANDY: *Promise?*

CROWD: *Well, all right.*

And then after Brian addresses them.

CROWD: *Oohhh, that wasn't a minute!*

The film's satire on unthinking religious devotion is epitomized by Brian's attempt to persuade the crowd to think for themselves:

BRIAN: *Look, you've got it all wrong! You don't need to follow me, you don't need to follow anybody! You've got to think for yourselves! You're all individuals!*
THE CROWD: *Yes! We're all individuals!*
BRIAN: *You're all different!*
THE CROWD: *Yes, we are all different!*
TERRY BAYLER: *I'm not.*
CROWD: *Shhh!*

Brian tries to deny he is the Messiah, Mandy knows he is not the Messiah, but there were many in ancient Israel who claimed they were. Interestingly, the historian Josephus writes of a prophet whom he calls the Egyptian.

> *'There was an Egyptian false prophet that did the Jews more mischief than the former; for he was a cheat, and pretended to be a prophet also, and got together thirty thousand men that were deluded by him; these he led round about from the wilderness to the mount which was called the Mount of Olives. He was ready to break into Jerusalem by force from that place; and if he could but once conquer the Roman garrison and the people. Now when Felix heard he ordered his soldiers to take their weapons, and came against them with a great number of horsemen and footmen from Jerusalem, and attacked the Egyptian and the people that were with him. He slew four hundred of them, and took two hundred alive. The Egyptian himself escaped out of the fight, but did not appear any more'.* [Flavius Josephus, *Jewish War* 2.261-262]

Why is this guy never mentioned as a possible Christ? In his other book, 'Antiquities' Josephus tells the same story.

> *'About this time, someone came out of Egypt to Jerusalem, claiming to be a prophet. He advised the crowd to go along with him to the Mount of Olives, as it was called, which lay over against the city, and at the distance of a kilometre. He added that he would show them from hence how the walls of Jerusalem would fall*

down at his command, and he promised them that he would procure them an entrance into the city through those collapsed walls. Now when Felix was informed of these things, he ordered his soldiers to take their weapons, and came against them with a great number of horsemen and footmen from Jerusalem, and attacked the Egyptian and the people that were with him. He slew four hundred of them, and took two hundred alive. The Egyptian himself escaped out of the fight, but did not appear any more.'
[Flavius Josephus, *Jewish Antiquities* 20.169-171]

This sounds so much like the events in the Bible. Why does nobody see it? I suppose, firstly, the fact that he is called the Egyptian and second that it occurred during the time of the Governor Felix.

But think, obviously the Jews would not follow an Egyptian, so what could Josephus mean by the Egyptian? It has to be a Jew who has lived in Egypt and has an obvious Egyptian accent and maybe style. And we are told in the Bible that the family went to Egypt just after his birth.

What about Felix being the Procurator? Well you may think this is impossible, since it is quite clear in the Bible that Pilate is the Procurator at the time. Perhaps the fact that Pilate was well known to the Jews for his activities is why it was suggested he was the procurator at the time, by those writing many years after the event. There is also the possibility suggested by Daniel Unterbrink's theory, that Pilate crucified Judas the Galilean, and the story was usurped to be the death of Jesus.

You think I'm plucking at hairs do you? Well just wait. Jesus was said to begin his mission after the death of John the Baptist. But Josephus writes that Pilate was dismissed before he relates the story of the Baptist's death at the hands of Herod. If his chronology is right then Pilate was not the Procurator during the time of Jesus' mission.

And that's not the only evidence; when Paul is arrested, it states in Acts of the Apostles:

'As Paul was to be led into the castle, he said unto the chief captain, "May I speak unto thee?"

Who said, "Canst thou speak Greek? Art not thou that Egyptian, which before these days made an uproar, and led out into the wilderness four thousand men that were murderers?"

But Paul said, "I am a man, which am a Jew of Tarsus."' (Acts 21 – 38)

So Paul is accused of being 'The Egyptian' suggesting that the Egyptian was functioning at the time of Christ. Not only this but when Paul is brought to trial before Felix, the prosecuting lawyer proclaims:

'Tertullus presented his case before Felix: "We have enjoyed a long period of peace under you, and your foresight has brought about reforms in this nation. Everywhere and in every way, most excellent Felix, we acknowledge this with profound gratitude.... We have found this man to be a troublemaker, stirring up riots among the Jews all over the world. He is a ringleader of the Nazarene sect and even tried to desecrate the temple; so we seized him."'

Felix has been Procurator for some years, as Paul in his defence confirms:

"I know that for a number of years you have been a judge over this nation; so I gladly make my defence."

All very intriguing, but remember that the opening quote from Josephus began with: *'There was an Egyptian false prophet that did the Jews more mischief than the former.'* I should quote the *'former'* to let you know how common this all was.

'More evil were the cheats and deceivers claiming inspiration, they schemed to bring about revolutionary changes by inducing the mob to act as if possessed, and by leading them into the desert on the pretence that their God would show them a sign of approaching freedom.'

So people claming to be mystic deliverers are appearing everywhere, it is only Brian who does not claim any divinity. However on leaving the window, Brian finds his house full of followers being organized by John, who is clearly exploiting people's gullibility.

JOHN: *Don't push that baby in the Saviour's face. He'll touch it later.*

TERRY BAYLER: I say. I say, could He just see my wife? She has a headache.
JOHN: She'll have to wait, I'm afraid.
TERRY BAYLER: It's very bad, and we've got a luncheon appointment.
JOHN: Look, the lepers are queuing.
TERRY BAYLER: Her brother-in-law is the ex-mayor of Gath, you know.

Then comes the moment where 'our saviour', George Harrison makes a swift appearance.

JOHN: Brian, can I introduce the gentleman who's letting us have the Mounts on Sunday?
GEORGE HARRISON: Hello.

George didn't actually say 'Hello', the problem was that with all the bustling you hardly noticed him. So Mike Palin dubbed the 'Hello' on, in his best Liverpudlian accent.

It was quite an honour meeting George, like meeting Royalty at the time. Later I directed a video clip for him and got to know him quite well; he had a wonderfully gentle, offbeat humour that always made me laugh. It was real sad when he died. The last time I met him was at Terry Gilliam's 60th Birthday Party. As a present, George gave Terry a ukulele that had belonged to George Formby and proceeded to sing "When I'm Cleaning Windows" on it. He followed that with 'Happy Birthday' to which we all joined in. So I can now claim I sang with George Harrison. Talking about singing birthday wishes, a few years back I got a message on my answer-phone, which was some lady singing 'Happy Birthday' to me. As it was playing I kept wondering, 'who the hell is this, I don't know anybody who sings in tune!' It finished with love from Kate. Kate Bush, that was: I'd recently directed a video clip for her. It convinced me that not many people actually sing in tune.

Back to Brian who, after leaving George and the other acolytes goes outside where you just catch some of the dialogue.

JOHN: And keep the noise down, please! Those possessed by devils, try and keep them under control a bit, can't you? All right. Now, those with gifts come forward, please. Incurables, you'll just have to wait for a few minutes.
MAN: Will he endorse fish?

JOHN: Ahh, you'll have to speak to sibling Francis about endorsements. Um, women taken in sin, line up against that wall.

I liked the incurables but Terry thought they were too silly, so out they went.

A typical incurable

When Brian leaves he comes down some steps, sits down in a courtyard and is followed by Judith. In fact she didn't follow, there was a scene cut out here called the 'Otto' scene. It was written by Eric who said, *"It's essentially a pretty savage attack on rabid Zionism, suggesting it's rather akin to Nazism, which is a bit strong to take, but certainly a point of view."* Terry Gilliam, thought it should have stayed, joking "we've alienated the Christians, let's get the Jews now." Don't take this literally. Python humour is not based on 'getting' people, Terry knows full well that intelligent Christians or Jews would accept a Pythonesque view of certain nonsensical attitudes. Remember even left-wing groups are 'got at' in the film for their tendency to split into tiny, antagonistic factions over minor theoretical points. 'Splitters!' When the Roman Church, who never condemned capital punishment, led a crusade for the sanctity of the unborn baby, the Pythons took the idea to the ridiculous, singing the satirical song 'Every Sperm is Sacred'. With Otto I think the Pythons felt the criticism was valid but they felt uncomfortable criticizing Israel at that time and so the scene was cut. I wanted it in, but then it was easy for me, I wasn't going to take the flack. I also thought it was important for the structure of the film. Looking back on it historically, who knows, if we had made those criticisms of rabid Zionism at that time, it might have helped the liberal forces in Israel and created an atmosphere where religious fundamentalism would have been ridiculed leading to a better relationship between Jews and Palestinians.

Anyway this is how it went. Brian sits down and a voice behind him says, "Hail leader." He turns and finds Eric, as Otto, in bamboo armour standing there with his arm raised in a Nazi salute. He also has a little Hitler moustache.

OTTO: *Hail, Leader!*
BRIAN: *What?*
OTTO: *Oh, I— I'm so sorry. Have you seen ze new Leader?*
BRIAN: *The what?*
OTTO: *The new Leader. I— I wish to find him and hail him. (RAISES ARM) Hail, Leader. See?*
BRIAN: *Who are you?*
OTTO: *Uh, my name is... Otto.*
BRIAN: *Oh. Otto.*
OTTO: *Yes. Otto. It's time, you know. .*
BRIAN: *What?*
OTTO: *Time that we Jews racially purified ourselves.*
BRIAN: *Oh.*
OTTO: *He's right you know. The new leader. We need more living room. We must move into the traditionally Jewish areas of Samaria.*
BRIAN: *What about the Samaritans?*
OTTO: *Oh, We'll put them in little camps.*
BRIAN: *Shh! Otto!*
OTTO: *What? The Leader? (SALUTES AGAIN)*

Eric as Otto

191

Hail Leader!
BRIAN: *No, no; it's dangerous.*
OTTO: *Oh. Danger? There's no danger. Men!*

A squad of men march in to the courtyard and come to attention opposite Otto.

OTTO: *Impressive, eh?*
BRIAN: *Yes.*
OTTO: *Oh, yes! We are a thoroughly trained suicide squad.*
BRIAN: *Oh.*
OTTO: *Oh, yes! We can commit suicide within twenty seconds.*
BRIAN: *Twenty seconds?*
OTTO: *You don't believe me?*
BRIAN: *Yes.*
OTTO: *I think you question me.*
BRIAN: *No, no, no.*
OTTO: *I can see you do not believe me.*
BRIAN: *No, no. I do.*
OTTO: *Enough! I'll prove it to you. Squad!*
SQUAD: *Hail, Leader!*
OTTO: *Commit... suicide!*

They open flaps in their armour and, on the count of three, thrust knives into their breast and drop down groaning.

OTTO: *I think now you'll believe me?*
BRIAN: *Yes. Very impressive.*
OTTO: *I think now I prove it to you?*
BRIAN: *Yes.*
OTTO: *All dead.*
BRIAN: *Yes.*

Otto struts proudly amongst them.

OTTO: *Not one living. He's dead... and he's dead. See? I tread on him. He's dead... and he's dead... and he's dead. They're all dead. All dead good Jewish boys. No foreigners! But their names will live forever! Helmut,*

Johnny,... er.. er the little guy,... the— er— the other fat one. Their names will live eventually forever.

A farting sound. Otto swings round.

OTTO: *Wait a minute. There's somebody here who's not dead. There's somebody here who is only pretending to be dead. Stand up, you.*

CHARLES McKEOWN: *Oow!*

OTTO: *Who said 'ow'?! You're not dead either. Neither are you! Stand up! Stand up. You're not dead. Ah— Eh— Oh, my heck! Stand up! Stand up, all of you! Oh, my heck, is there not even one dead?!*

CHARLES McKEOWN: *No, sir. Not one.*

OTTO: *Why not?!*

TERRY BAYLER: *We thought it was a practice, sir.*

OTTO: *But all the bleeding and the groaning?*

CHARLES McKEOWN: *Little secreted sheep's' bladders, sir.*

OTTO: *Oh— Oh, my cock! Sheep's' bladders?!*

CHARLES McKEOWN: *Yes.*

OTTO: *You are a shower! A non-Semitic, mutinous, racially impure, cloth-eared bunch of Roman-lovers!*

CHARLES M: *Sorry, sir.*

OTTO: *Tomorrow, as a punishment, you will all eat... pork sausages!*

SQUAD: *Oh no.*

Otto turns back to Brian.

OTTO: *Now. Tell ze Leader that we are ready to die for him ze moment he gives the sign.*

BRIAN: *What sign?*
OTTO: *The sign that is the sign. That shall be the sign. Men! Forward!*

Impressive military music as they march off singing.

SQUAD: *There's a man we call our Leader. He's fine and strong and brave, And we'll follow him unquestioning Towards an early grave. He-e gives us hope of sacrifice And a chance to die in vain, And if we're one of the lucky ones, We'll live to die again.*
BRIAN: *Silly bugger.*

That was it. It was a long, painful discussion but in the end the Pythons have a rule that if someone doesn't like their own stuff they can take it out. So Eric finally took it out. Fortunately Otto could not be totally removed because his suicide squad, were in every shot at the foot of the cross. It was decided to shoot (in a rather grey London) a shot of Terry, as a man tying up the crucified, turning and seeing Otto and his squad and telling the audience, who they are, before running away.

19

WELEASE BWIAN

Now with Brian arrested and brought before Pilate, we find that visiting Jerusalem is Pilate's fwend, none other than Biggus Dickus himself. What is extraordinary is that we get no feeling that this is Brian. Graham does a Mike Palin, and is a completely different person. When Graham died, I put together an assembly of all his best parts. From Oscar Wilde to the northern miner, to his pepperpot woman and the Protestant bigot in Sperm Song, they are extraordinary and no one, not I nor any of the Pythons, knows how he did it. Graham just seemed to be in his own world, a complete mystery to us all.

After sending Brian to be crucified, the trumpets sound and Pilate goes out to address the crowd. Our crowd were Tunisians and spoke no English, so the fun was to get them laughing at the right time and reacting together. The best bit was getting them to lie on the ground and kick their legs in the air in uncontrolled laughter. This is how Terry Jones remembers our attempts at this:

> 'We got a Tunisian comedian to tell jokes to the crowd but he didn't go down well. So after ten minutes I said to my Tunisian AD: "This isn't working. Just tell the crowd to do what I do." So I fell on my back and waggled my legs in the air and laughed hysterically. Then the AD told the crowd to do the same. They all went down in a cloud of dust and it was hysterical. The only trouble was that we weren't turning over!!! So we had to do it again and I swear it wasn't as funny the second time.'

I remember that all they got for lunch was a French loaf and a tin of sardines. But I hope they got paid well enough because they were great.

We cut a scene related to Otto here. Judith runs up to a rooftop and releases some doves, the 'sign that is the sign'. They are seen by a bush that becomes a man, who waves to John Cleese on a hill. John then does a 'silly walk' on the hilltop. This signal is received in Otto's camp where Otto rallies his troops to rescue Brian. Shame about losing John's silly walk.

Meanwhile, Judith returns to the forum to encourage the crowd to 'welease Bwian' and Pilate finally gives orders to 'welease' him. We can't actually find any evidence that Roman Governors offered the Jews a chance to release one of their convicted criminals. It can only be an attempt by the new Church of Rome to excuse the Romans for Jesus' death and blame the Jews who chose to release Barabbas, a rebel and a murderer. It is odd that Pilate would release a murderer like that, but even odder is the choice of name.

Barabbas' first name is not mentioned in the King James' version of the Bible or quite a few others, but in the New Revised Standard Version, they dare to put it.

> 'Now at the festival the governor was accustomed to release a prisoner for the crowd, anyone whom they wanted. At that time they had a notorious prisoner, called Jesus Barabbas. So after they had gathered, Pilate said to them, "Whom do you want me to release for you, Jesus Barabbas or Jesus who is called the Messiah?"'

First, ask yourself why so many translations cut this out? But while it is an interesting coincidence that Barabbas' first name was Jesus, what about that second name, Barabbas? Bar means 'son of' and abba means 'father', generating 'Son of the Father'. The other possible meaning of the name is 'Son of the Rabbi'. Either way the name suggests Jesus himself. It almost feels like a dualist concept here. The good Jesus and the criminal Jesus, one crucified the other released. This even gave ammunition to those who believed the twin heresy. More about this dualism later. (Confusingly Acts 1:23 has a chosen follower of Christ called, Joseph Barsabbas, and Acts 15:22 has a Judas Barsabbas, which some translations try to confuse by misspelling it as Barsabas. Well I'm confused.)

Meanwhile Mike as the kind Centurion is organizing his prisoners, '*Out of the door, line on the left, one cross each.*' Mike did this in two totally different ways. Firstly in the kindly way you see in the film and the other was more like someone who is efficiently getting on with his routine job. Absolutely no interest in the prisoners problems or what is about to happen to them. *'Yes fine ok, out of the door, line on the left, one cross each.'*

Both ways worked great and it was a difficult choice. I wish people could see both because it was quite amazing, how different they were. Surrounding him with the awful jailers, Eric and Terry Gilliam, was genius. I never understood what Terry Gilliam was saying and had to go back to the script to find it: *'There are lumps of it round the back.'*

That's one of the things that surprises people about the way I work. I read the script when I am offered the film and then try desperately to forget it. I also try not to watch rushes. On Brian, I had to watch them because we were running the projector out in Tunisia. Most editors sit with the director in rushes and the director tells them what take they like. When I am directing, I don't even watch rushes. I go into the cutting room, whiz a few takes through the editing machine, to see that everything is okay and then wait to see what the editor does with them. As a director, you should know what you've got artistically; you've seen the lighting, framing and performances on the set. It is up to the technicians to worry if there is something wrong technically. When we were shooting 'Brazil', Terry Gilliam was similar, he would come in to the cutting rooms in the morning and we would speed through a few rushes on the machine, before they were even sunk to the sound.

Okay why do I do this? I am desperately trying to see the material with as fresh an eye as possible. There is nothing worse than sitting through eight takes of a piece of dialogue. One of the worse things with some directors is for them to get bored with their own material. I am often asked to repair a film that has gone wrong in the editing. First thing I ask is what has been cut out. Usually it is a perfectly good scene; sometimes even a scene with crucial information that the director has got bored with, and in desperation cut out. Editing is a long process and requires every trick you can think of to keep the shots as fresh as possible.

Here I would like to tell every young person starting out in the world that you have character traits, which will help you if you can find the right job for them. Even traits, which people might have told you were bad! For instance I am very slipshod at the beginning, and slowly become a perfectionist. Let me explain. I cannot cut carpets or put up wallpaper. The problem is that I try to cut them roughly and then slowly trim them into place. It doesn't work. Terry Gilliam is great at laying a carpet because he does it right the first time, he's a perfectionist at the beginning. I can paint a wall but I don't prepare the wall well because I get bored, so that after the first coat I have to sand the wall again and then give it another coat. If it still has blemishes, it gets on my nerves and I have to do it again till it is right. By that time the carpet is down and I accidentally sprinkle paint on the carpet. As they say 'if a job's worth doing, it's worth doing well.' Okay that's one of my traits which people say is bad – BUT – it turns out to be perfect for editing. You should not, and cannot, make a perfect cut the first time you assemble the material. You need to throw it roughly together and then look at it in context and then later start to trim it up. Terry Gilliam can spend all night on trying to get a perfect cut. There is no perfect cut when you first assemble the material because there is no way yet of understanding the pace of the film. I should warn you here, the word 'pace' is used by film executives all the time in the wrong context. They watch a film in their plush studio cinema, they are bored in sections and they say it needs more pace; when actually what they mean is, *cut it faster*. Pacing a film is deciding which scenes to move quickly and which ones to slow down on. For instance at this point in 'Life of Brian', we have Brian heading for crucifixion, Judith trying to save him, the crowd demanding his release, the Centurion going to release him, etc; and on top of this, the audience know all the characters and the set up, and they are getting tired and fidgety. So like the ending of any action film, you would intercut these scenes faster and faster. Well you would think so, but 'Brian' is the only film I have edited, where I found it was naturally running faster and faster towards the end. It was like a runaway car down a hill. The reason was that when it becomes obvious that Brian is going to be crucified, the audience want to know how we are going to deal with it. They can't believe we might actually put him up on the cross. So I have an old axiom that 'if the audience don't want to know what is going to happen next – then cut fast: when they want to know what is going to happen next – slow down'. It's the same as what I said about Hitchcock at the beginning, once the bomb is in the bag and the bag is on the bus, slow time down. So I could feel from the very first showing of 'Brian' that it was careering out of control. I had to start adding frames to try to slow it down. The sort of scenes that helped me were our wonderfully grotesque jailers, who, when the Centurion comes looking for Brian, hold him up with a load of nonsense.

So there is no perfect cut first off, you can have a theoretical idea but until you show it to an audience you don't really know what the pace of each scene should be. And my worse trait, of being slipshod in the beginning, turns out to be one of my best characteristics for editing. Other jobs, like car maintenance where you have to tighten bolts to exactly 57 lbs per whatever – forget it! I also don't go up ladders much anymore because so often in the past, I have put up ladders and couldn't be bothered to secure them properly, and they have subsequently collapsed. Ouch! So to all young people, I say 'you are all individuals' with talents, and those talents may be criticized because they are not the norm. They are still talents, which you just need to find the right vocation for. I was listening to Daley Thompson talking, and what made him a terrible pupil at school, when channelled the right way, made him the greatest decathlete ever.

By the way, the reason I mention Terry Gilliam working all night on a cut is because I am a morning person and he's a night person. And because we are so typical of the types, I learnt the difference. Morning people like me wake up optimists, we have lots to do and things to achieve. By midday I'm beginning to flag and lose my optimism. Terry as a night person wakes up a pessimist. Oh God another day, how am I going to get through it? Finally he drags himself up and as the day progresses, he begins to feel better, till by the evening he is bubbling.

So back to Brian on his way to be crucified, and John appearing before the jailers. Again you will notice the incomprehensible and stuttering jailers get out of character for just one split second before we cut away:

ERIC: *Anyway, get on with your story.*
TERRY GILLIAM: *Well I knew she never really liked him, so I kiss..*

This works on the same principal, as "You haven't given us time to hide," cutting quickly before we step too long out of the film.

For those of you who know 'Holy Grail' you might remember one of these at the end of Tim the Wizard, where John is describing the Monster "with big sharp pointy teeth." King Arthur turns towards camera and says: "What an eccentric performance." Same principal applies, if you get out of character for a gag, cut quickly to the next scene. I should warn you again that in art there are no laws, so don't take what I say as Gospel. You may find a style of film, which allows you to drop out of character for large stretches. I'm thinking here of Bob Hope and Bing Crosby's 'Road' movies. So whenever anyone tells you this or that law in art, they are mistaken. What there is, is an effect. For instance the first rule everybody is told when they go to film school, to learn how to direct, is 'don't cross the line'. For those of you who have never heard the expression, let me explain quickly. If you are filming a football match you have your cameras generally on one side of the pitch; so that the reds are always kicking left to right. If you put a camera on the other side of the pitch, the reds are now kicking right to left. If you cut these camera shots together during the course of the game, the audience will get totally confused as to what is going on. If you do have a camera on the other side then you can use it only once play has stopped, like to review a goal. So the rule is don't cross the line because it confuses the audience's sense of direction. Except that it is not a rule. I actually cross the line when I want the audience to lose their sense of direction. In my film 'Love Potion' a girl runs into a basement with her friend. Something suddenly happens to her friend. I don't want the audience to understand exactly what is going on, so I 'cross the line', to throw the audience's sense of direction. I have seen this used in other films. There is a great film called 'Starting Over' (it got terrible reviews as usual). It starred Burt Reynolds, who I think is a great comedian and actor. 'Starting Over' is a romantic comedy, but one where every attempt is made to make the romance awkward and excruciating. So our couple are about to kiss and instead of being in close up, Alan J. Pakula films it from the other side of the room. Another romantic moment, Pakula crosses the line to stop us getting involved.

Just to add, if Alan J., Burt Reynolds, Jill Clayburgh or Candice Bergin read this I want to tell them 'Starting Over' is a great piece of work that they can justifiably be proud of and to hell with the critics!

20

CRUCIFIXION PARTY

Heading for Calvary, the 'lucky bastards' who are about to be crucified pass through the streets of Jerusalem. I like the little cameo by Mike selling crucifixion knick-knacks.

> MIKE: *Souvenir of Calvary. Very nice little item, this. Wrap it 'round a lamp and the crosses twinkle on and off. Very nice. Doubles as a tablecloth or a curtain. Totally washable. Well, how about this, then? A couple of crosses, one slightly damaged.*

I once did a documentary in Lourdes and was amazed by the hundreds of stalls selling statuettes of Bernadette's Virgin and water bottles in her shape to capture the spring water.

One poor soul in the crucifixion party finds his cross too heavy and collapses and a very kind passer-by, Terry Jones, picks up his cross to help. *(See fig 20)* There is a very odd parallel to this in the Bible:

> 'And they compel one Simon, a Cyrenian, who passed by, coming out of the country, the father of Alexander and Rufus, to bear his cross.' (Mark 15:21)

As usual the Gospels contradict themselves as John says that Jesus carried the cross himself, and there is no mention of a Simon. But what is odd about the quote in Mark's Gospel is that he seems to know an awful lot about this casual passer-by! He knows his name, Simon: his origin Cyrene a town in Libya, which had a big Jewish community, and even his children, Alexander and Rufus. How strange is this? Did this casual passer-by give an interview to the press after the event? It clearly says he did not act out of kindness but was forced by the Romans to help, although in films he is nearly always shown as being a caring person who takes on Jesus' burden. Also because Simon's home town is in Libya north Africa, a connection arose making Simon of Cyrene the first African saintly Christian. So in films he has often been played by black actors, including, Sidney Poitier, in 'King of Kings'. At least in 'The Passion', Mel Gibson portrays Simon as a Jew being forced by the Romans to carry the cross, but even then, as the journey to Mount Calvary continues, he shows compassion to Jesus and helps him make it to the top.

Okay, Simon is remembered sympathetically, and we have lots of information about him; but there must be more to this story than meets the eye. Suppose he wasn't an innocent passer-by, and suppose he was someone crucially involved in the events. I think this is where 'Life of Brian' might have evidence. Our 'Simon' makes it all the way to the top and then:

BERNARD: Right. Next!
TERRY JONES: Ah, look. It's not my cross.
BERNARD: What?!
TERRY: Um, it's not my cross. I was, ah, holding it for someone. Um—
BERNARD: Just lie down. I haven't got all day.
TERRY: No, of course. Um, look. I hate to make a fuss—
BERNARD: Look. We've had a busy day. There's a hundred and forty of you
*   lot to get up.*
TERRY: Uh, will you let me down if he comes back?
BERNARD: Yeah. Yeah, we'll let you down. Next!

So our Simon gets crucified. Amongst the Gnostic Christians, Simon of Cyrene, by mistaken identity, suffers the events leading up to the crucifixion, and dies on the cross instead of Jesus. This is the story presented in the 'Second Treatise of the Great Seth', although it is unclear whether Simon or another man actually died on the cross. This is part of a belief held by some Gnostics that Jesus was not of flesh, but only took on the appearance of flesh. The idea that there was a substitute for Jesus on the cross is also a belief held by many Muslims, as the Qu'ran seems to suggest a substitution. So, however confusing this all is, it seems Simon is an insider who had a more important role in the crucifixion and that is why they know so many details about him.

In 1941 in the Kidron Valley outside Jerusalem, a burial cave was discovered belonging to Cyrenian Jews and dating before AD 70. Within it they found an ossuary inscribed in Greek, "Alexander Son of Simon." Obviously one cannot, however, be certain that this refers to the same person as the son of Simon the Cyrene mentioned in the Bible, but it is a nice possibility.

As Mike goes up on his cross we get the following.

MIKE: *I'll get you for this, you bastard.*
BERNARD: *Oh, yeah?*
MIKE: *Oh, yeah. Don't worry. I never forget a face.*
BERNARD: *No?*
MIKE: *I warned you. I'm going to punch you so hard, you Roman git!*
BERNARD: *Shut up, you Jewish turd!*
MIKE: *Who are you calling Jewish?! I'm not Jewish! I'm a Samaritan!*
TERRY BAYLER: *A Samaritan? This is supposed to be a Jewish section.*
BERNARD: *It doesn't matter! You're all going to die in a day or two.*
TERRY BAYLER: *It may not matter to you, Roman, but it certainly matters to*
    us. Doesn't it, darling?
CAROL: *Oh, rather.*
TERRY BAYLER: *Under the terms of the Roman occupancy, we're entitled to*
    be crucified in a purely Jewish area.
TERRY GILLIAM: *Pharisees separate from Sadducees.*
TERRY JONES: *And Swedish separate from Welsh.*
BERNARD: *All right! All right! All right! We'll soon settle this! Hands up, all*
    those who don't want to be crucified here.
VICTIMS: *Ooh. Oh. Uh. Uh...*
BERNARD: *Right. Next!*

Not only does this reflect the sectarianism and infighting that was prevalent at the time but there is an extremely interesting point here.

When Mike, as the Samaritan, is accused of being a Jew he responds indignantly, *"I'm not Jewish I'm a Samaritan."* The Samaritans did in fact refuse to be called Jews, and for a very good reason, but we need to look at their history to find out why.

The Samaritans derive their name not from a geographic area but from the ancient Hebrew term for 'keepers of the Law'. They insist that they are direct descendants of the Northern Israelite tribes who survived the destruction of Israel by the Assyrians in 722 BC. The inscription of Sargon II records the deportation of a relatively small proportion of the Israelites probably from around Jerusalem and therefore from the tribe of Judah. So it is quite possible that a sizeable population remained that could identify themselves as 'Israelites', the term that the Samaritans prefer for themselves as opposed to 'Jews'.

The Samaritans claim to worship the true religion of the ancient Israelites prior to the Babylonian Exile, which was preserved by those who remained in the Land of Israel, as opposed to the amended Judaism, brought back by the exiled returnees.

Although historically the Samaritans were a large community, more than a million in Roman times, they gradually reduced to several tens of thousands up to a few centuries ago. Their unprecedented shrinkage was the result of various historical events, most notably the bloody repression in AD 529 by the Christian rulers. As of November 2007, there were just 712 Samaritans living almost exclusively in two localities in Israel, Kiryat Luza on Mount Gerizim and the city of Holon. That they occupy Mount Gerizim is key to understanding their division from the Jews. Here are the relevant bits from John's Gospel, verse 4.

> 'So Jesus came to a town in Samaria called Sychar, near the plot of ground Jacob had given to his son Joseph. Jacob's well was there, and Jesus, tired as he was from the journey, sat down by the well. A Samaritan woman came to draw water and Jesus said to her, "Will you give me a drink?"'

There is an interchange that concludes with:

> "Sir," the woman said, "I can see that you are a prophet. Our fathers worshipped on this mountain, but you Jews claim that the place where we must worship is in Jerusalem."
> Jesus declared, "Believe me, woman, a time is coming when you will worship the Father neither on this mountain nor in Jerusalem."

The mountain referred to here is Mount Gerizim and it was selected by Joshua after the conquest of Canaan as a Holy site, when he 'set up a stone as a witness, placing it next to the sanctuary of Yahweh, under the oak tree.' And this then is the cause of the split. After Joshua's death, 'The Children of Israel split into two factions: a loyal faction on Mount Gerizim; and the faction that followed a priest called Eli. A terrible civil war then broke out between Eli and the sons of Pincus.'

So what do the Samaritans say when they are called Jews? *'We are not Jews because we are not from the tribe of Judah.'* What I cannot understand is why all the other people who are called Jews don't say the same. For instance the Levites are not from the tribe of Judah, they are from Aaron's family who are the legitimate priests of the Israelites. Why do so many Israelites allow themselves to be called Jews when it is the tribe of Judah that usurped the whole kingdom. I have already explained how David fought with the Philistines to conquer Israel. Now ask yourself, how did he and then his son Solomon become so fabulously rich? The Bible tells us, for when Solomon dies his son Rehoboam takes over and:

> *'Israel went to Rehoboam and said: "Your father put a heavy yoke on us, but now lighten the harsh labour and the heavy yoke he put on us."' (Kings 12:3)*

And what does Rehoboam answer?

> *"My father made your yoke heavy; I will make it even heavier. My father scourged you with whips; I will scourge you with scorpions." (Kings 12:14)*

Well you can imagine their response.

> *'So Israel has been in rebellion against the house of David to this day. When all the Israelites heard that Jeroboam had returned, they made him king over all Israel. Only the tribe of Judah remained loyal to the house of David.' (Kings 12:18)*

So the tribe of Judah (the Jews) became rich by ruthlessly exploiting the rest of the tribes of Israel which led to the division of the land into two kingdoms. Judah is one of Isaac's sons and it is he who sells Joseph of the many coloured coat, into slavery. So maybe this tribe of Judah just has bad genes.

You don't believe Judah could have bad genes? How about this then; after the account of Judah selling Joseph into slavery, there is the most odd section in the Bible about Judah. It starts in Genisis 38, which perhaps you remember says Judah married a Canaanite woman, called Shua. Hold on! This by definition makes no person from the tribe of Judah even Jewish, because the rule is that you are Jewish through your mother not your father. But leaving this rather important issue aside, Judah and Shua marry and have a boy called Er.

> 'But Er, Judah's firstborn, was wicked in the Lord's sight; so the Lord put him to death.'

Wow, even God seems to think they are a bad lot, but it gets worse. Judah asks his second son Onan, to take on the dead Er's wife Tamar, as is the custom. But:

> 'Whenever Onan lay with his brother's wife, he spilled his semen on the ground to keep from producing offspring for his brother. What he did was wicked in the Lord's sight; so he put him to death also.'

Are you finding all this as odd as I do? But more:

> 'Tamar took off her widow's clothes, covered herself with a veil to disguise herself, and then sat down at the entrance to Enaim, which is on the road to Timnah. When Judah saw her, he thought she was a prostitute, for she had covered her face. Not realizing that she was his daughter-in-law, he went over to her by the roadside and said, "Come now, let me sleep with you."'

The word prostitute is translated variously in different versions, 'harlot', 'shrine prostitute' but the most accurate is Temple Prostitute. A sort of Vestile Virgin that existed in the Canaanite religion. So Judah is making use of women made available for followers of Astarte. Make of that what you will, but Tamar becomes pregnant.

> 'About three months later Judah was told, "Your daughter-in-law Tamar is guilty of prostitution, and as a result she is now pregnant."
> Judah said, "Bring her out and have her burned to death!"'

The hypocrite! But then he finds out he is the evil doer and guess what, Tamar gives birth to twins.

'As she was giving birth, one of them put out his hand; so the midwife took a scarlet thread and tied it on his wrist and said, "This one came out first." But when he drew back his hand, his brother came out.' (Genesis 38:27)

This bloody tribe of Judah even fight in the womb so why do people from the Kingdom of Israel allow themselves to be called after this bad lot? And why is Jerusalem, which is the capital of Judah, considered by them to be the Holy City when David steals the 'Arc of the Covenant' and takes it there: dancing in front of it like a conquerer? Why do they not call themselves Israelites or Hebrews (from the ancient Egyptian term Habiru) or Galileans if they are from the tribes of Zebulon, Naphtali, Issachar and Asher who inhabited this area? This, rather unpleasant tribe of Judah have kept their superiority over the rest of the Israelites right up to this present day.

A few years back, George Tamarin a lecturer at Tel Aviv University, decided, like the Samaritans, that he did not want to be called Jewish on his identity card, but Israeli. He took his case to the Supreme Court of Israel. Unanimously, the Judges ruled that he could not change his identity card because there is a Jewish nation but no such thing as an Israeli nation. How the rest of the ancient tribes must weep in their graves at this complete domination of the people of Israel by one tribe who are mainly of Canaanite blood!

How did it happen? Now please don't issue a fatwa on me if I throw my theories out for discussion.

Let me start by telling you of three experiences that may be relevant. First, a few years back I was asked to give advice to Zoe Neirizi, an Iranian film director. Her film was about her experiences during the Iranian revolution. She was one of the many left-wingers who revolted against the Shah but when he was toppled, the Ayatollah and religious fundamentalists then turned on their left-wing allies in the revolution. Tragically, Zoe's husband was killed and she was jailed. She was pregnant in jail and she describes how women were not allowed to scream during childbirth because, under the strict rules of the Ayatollah, a woman's pains should not be heard by the male jailers. If they made any noise they were beaten! Anyway I looked at her film and suggested she should add some winding Arabic music over a particular section. Like Mike's Samaritan she was quick to correct me. "We are not Arabs!" It exposed the lack of knowledge, which made me think of all those Middle Eastern Islamic countries as Arab. So, later, I will have to try to define Arabs.

Secondly, many times in my life I have been asked: "You are Jewish aren't you?" I must look a bit Jewish but it still surprises me that with such a typical Irish name (Doyle), people can still think this. Maybe I've become more Jewish from having had two long-term relationships with Jewish girls. (One of these originally thought I was Jewish too.) My answer to, 'are you Jewish?' is, 'Perhaps!' Why do I say this? Well my mother was Spanish. At the beginning of the eighth century, under the Muslims, many local Spaniards embraced Islam. Christians and Jews were free in all aspects of their lives as the Muslims respected their religion and institutions. The result was the birth of the first truly cosmopolitan culture in the West. But this success in wealth, knowledge and co-existence came to an end in a violent and very sad way when Christian Crusaders destroyed the Muslim civilization which had taken centuries to build. The Jews were expelled and the Muslims were forced to convert to Christianity. Millions died as tolerance was replaced by something that *'No one expects!' the Spanish Inquisition*. A suspected Muslim could be killed for the smallest act resembling Islamic tradition – such as taking a bath on Friday.

I was in Andalusia for Holy Week where guys dressed like the Klu Klux Klan carry Christian statues through the town while incense and drums pound the air. One can only imagine what happened in early days if you didn't bend your knee to the statue.

Although many Jews left Spain, presumably some Jews converted and stayed. My mother told me a story, which unfortunately I didn't take much notice of at the time, and now she is dead, I can't ask her if it was a personal experience or something she read about. Anyway as I remember it, she said a friend in Spain told her that, at the age of 13 (about 1916 if she was my mum's

Spain Holy Week

age) she was taken into a secret room in the house, where she found Jewish regalia, and was told about her Jewish ancestry, but had to keep quiet about it. So perhaps I'm Jewish. (see Appendix 6 for my DNA analysis)

Thirdly, I was in Paris with a friend, Tony, on his first visit to the city. We were taking a walk when he stopped, looked around and said: "They are all Yids!" Sorry about the term, Tony is not a rascist, he just tends to use provocative terms, as is typical of Londoners. We were not in the Marais, the Jewish area of Paris but near l'Etoile. "Perhaps you're right," I answered. Unlike Spain the Jews of France, of which there were many, were not expelled from France but forced to convert to Christianity.

Now, before I comment on all this, let me give you four facts. to add to these anecdotes:

1. In the Bible, Paul's letters are sent to well established Jewish communities scattered round the surrounding countries. There are letters to the Romans, to the Galatatians in Anatolia, to Corinthians in Greece, to Philippians in Macedonia, to Colossians, a Phrygian city in Turkey. His first letter was in AD 52 to the Thessalonians probably written from Athens. When Paul travelled to these countries he preached in Synagogues.

2. Mary Magdalene and other Jews who were proto Christians left Israel before the war with the Romans in AD 66.

3. When the Jews were chucked out of Spain, most went to live in areas of the Ottoman empire, like North Africa and Turkey, not Israel.

4. There was a Golden age of Jewish culture in Israel during the time of Rabbi Judah ha-Nasi 200 years after the AD 66 rebellion.

Okay, let's piece this all together. The basic biblical story of the Israelites (my additions in brackets) is that Abraham and his family left Mesapotamia as nomads and travelled to Canaan. Abrham begot Isaac who begot Jacob who had 12 sons. Because of one brother, Joseph, the family moved to Egypt where they grew and prospered. Many years later the Egyptians oppressed them; but (after the Thera Volcano around 1,500 BC) the tribes of the 12 brothers led by Moses, escaped and for 40 years led a nomadic existence in the desert. (After an earthquake) they entered Jericho and Joshua led them to burn, kill and plunder the local population till they controlled Canaan and eleven of the tribes were given a portion of this new land of Israel. The tribe of Levi were priests and took tithes from the eleven. Judges ruled the land till Saul was made King. David of the tribe of Judah usurped the throne, kidnapped the arc of the covenant and brought it to Jerusalem where his son Solomon built a Temple to house it. When Solomon died the rest of the tribes split from the oppressive tribe of Judah making two kingdoms. Around 600 BC Nebuchadnezzar invaded Judah and destroyed the Jerusalem Temple.

I believe the story so far, based on the Egyptologist David Rohl's book 'A Test of Time'. (worth reading just for the evidence he brings to the story of Joseph and his coat of colours). But now I begin to have problems. After the destruction of the Temple, the Jews were taken as slaves to Babylon. When the Persians defeated the Babylonians, Cirus the Great allowed the Jews to return to Israel and rebuild the Temple.

My first problem is, who was taken to Babylon by Nebuchadnezzar? In the Bible it suggests it was the leaders from the tribe of Judah who were taken, not the other Israelites who seemed to have been in perpetual conflict with the tribe of Judah. Perhaps this story of the captives going to Babylon and returning to rebuild the Temple is the beginning of the term 'Jew' being used abroad, wrongly representing all the 12 tribes. The Samaritans clearly said they were Israelites who were not sent to Babylon and refused to be called Jews. Their land is just north of Judea so perhaps they were more sensitive than say, the Galileans, who lived much further from the territory of Judea.

Continuing the story, we now have the arrival of Alexander the Great. It is believed that many Jews helped him in his conquest of Egypt. I would suggest Jews as opposed to Israelites because Judah is next to Egypt. They were rewarded with their own quarter in the Emperor's new town of Alexandria. That was a Jewish quarter not an Israelite quarter because, presumably, it was predominant inhabited by members of the tribe of Judah.

Now it is suggested that the land comes under the control of Rome but a revolt in AD 66 led to liberation. This was short lived as Titus conquered the land and destroyed the Temple. The Jews were expelled from Israel and have since desired to return to their homeland to re-establish the state of Israel which they finally succeded in doing in 1947.

I have a problem with this; I do not believe the Israelites were expelled by the Romans after the rebellions. Josephus writes that the Galileans did not come to the aid of Jerusalem so they clearly stayed put. The letters of Paul are to well established communities with Synagogues before the rebellion. Also, as mentioned in fact 4, there was a prosperous age for Israel 200 years later. How then did these

Israelite, inland farmers, with a population of about one million end up with communities outside their country more numerous than they themselves?

Okay this is my hypothesis arising from the anecdotes and facts quoted. And as usual I will state it in the most alarming and controversial way (which will probably get me lynched).

Here it is: – Most of the modern day Jews who are returning to their so called homeland of Israel are not Israelites! And the Palestinians who are sometimes called Arabs or Fellahin, who were living in Palestine and now living in Israel, or the West Bank and Gaza often in camps, with no rights in Israel, are in fact the true Israelites.

Crazy? Perhaps, but let's take the second part first. I told you about Zoe the Iranian film-maker whom I called an Arab. The Iranians or Persians, as they were originally, had an ancient culture based on Zooastrianism. Yet they have now embraced Islam but are not Arabs, they are still Persians. The Egyptians, who had a great culture based on an ancient religion, are now Muslims. They also do not call themselves Arabs but 'Masri' or 'Masrya' (female) and consider themselves North African and Middle Eastern. Arabs to them are the people who live in the Gulf.

If these great cultures have converted to Islam, what makes you think the Muslims who live in Palestine are not the original Israelites who also converted to Islam? Ridiculous? Perhaps this will convince you:

> '*The Fellahin are not descendents of the Arab conquerors, who captured the land of Israel and Syria in the seventh century. The Arab victory did not destroy the agricultural population they found in the country. They expelled only the Byzantine (Christian) rulers, and did not touch the local population. Nor did the Arabs go in for settlement. Even in their former habitations, the Arabians did not engage in farming... They did not seek new lands on which to settle their peasantry, which hardly existed. Their whole interest in the new countries was political, religious and material: to rule, to propogate Islam and to collect taxes.*'

Before I continue this quote let me tell you that originally, Muslims did not have to pay tax, only the unbelievers. You can well imagine that the Caliph had to change this policy because the mass conversion to Islam was threatening to drain his coffers.

'To argue that after the conquest of Jerusalem by Titus (AD 70) and the failure of the Bar Kokhba revolt, Jews altogether ceased to cultivate the land of Israel is to demonstrate complete ignorance.'

You will be surprised to hear that this was written by two young Jewish authors in New York in 1918. One was Ben Gurion, the first Prime Minister of Israel and the other was Ben Zvi the longest serving President of Israel. They argued that the Jewish origin of the Palestinians is revealed by their use of many Hebrew and Aramaic words in their arabic dialect. Also, like Zoe the Palistinians do not define themselves as Arabs, they see themselves as Muslims or Fellahin (farmers) while they refer to the Bedouin as Arabs. A very strong attempt has since been made to conceal these facts from the people of Israel. For more on this, go to a recent book called 'The Invention of the Jewish People' by Shlomo Sand, Professor of History at Tel Aviv University and hate figure for Jewish fundamentalists. But perhaps the following quote from Wikipedia may confirm my point.

'Recent genetic evidence has demonstrated that Palestinians as an ethnic group are closely related to Jews and represent modern "descendants of a core population that lived in the area since prehistoric times," largely predating the Arabian Muslim conquest that resulted in their acculturation, established Arabic as the predominant vernacular, and over time also Islamized many of them from various prior faiths.'

So what about the Jews who are returning to their so-called homeland? Let me clarify, there are two distinct groups of Jews, the smaller being the Sephardic Jews who came from Spain and Portugal and speak a latinized Hebrew and the larger being the Ashkenazi Jews from the Rhineland. Actually these Jews represented only 3% in the 11th century but are now 80% with most of the American Jews being fom this type.

The question is when did these two groups of Jews leave Israel? Two events are suggested. One, after Romans supressed the rebellions of AD 66 and AD 134. But remember my fact 4, there was a Golden age of Jewish culture in Israel during the time of Rabbi Judah ha-Nasi 100 years after the rebellions. So no mass exodus then. The second suggestion is, when the Arabs invaded in AD 635. Well if you read about that war, the opponents of the Arabs were the

Christian Byzantine armies who occupied and oppressed the Israelites. The main battle was in Syria, and the invasion by Islamic Arabs who consider Abraham their founder and Moses a prophet was welcomed by many of the local Jewish population. The Arabs were not farmers so it would be ridiculous to kick the locals off the land and lose all that tax income. The invasion actually led to an age of peace and prosperity for Palestine. No mass exodus then either. So who are these Jews who lived outside Israel?

I was asked to edit some film from the Steven Spielberg Jewish Film Archive. There was some amazing old footage of an incredible Jewish culture in Vilnia in the Northern Baltic state of Lithuania; also early film of Jerusalem and one film was a record of the evacuation of local Jews from the Yemen, who were flown back to Israel in 1949 in operation, 'Magic Carpet'. Originally these Yemenite Jews were quoted as an example of Israelites who emigrated during the Arab invasion. Unfortunately research threw up that they were there before the invasion. These Yemenite Jews themselves considered that they were sent by Solomon to accompany the Queen of Sheba after her little tête-à-tête with the Israelite King. I think I believe this story but perhaps the most likely is that they were converts to the Jewish religion!

Yemenite Jew   Carrying Torah   Boarding plane

Surprised by the idea of converts? Don't be: before Christianity, the Jews were out there making converts. What do you think my first fact was all about? In the Bible, Paul's letters are sent to well established Jewish communities scattered round the surrounding countries. When Paul travelled to these countries he preached in synagogues addressing them as:

"Men of Israel and you Gentiles who worship God, listen to me!"
(Acts 13:16)

Obviously Jews and converts, which he repeats with:

*"Brothers, children of Abraham, and you God-fearing Gentiles, it
is to us that this message of salvation has been sent." (Acts 13:26)*

And what about this:

*'When the congregation was dismissed, many of the Jews and devout
converts to Judaism followed Paul and Barnabas.' (Acts 13:43)*

In fact everybody who is converted to the faith in the Acts of the Apostles
is converted to Judaism:

*'In those days when the number of disciples was increasing, the
Grecian Jews among them complained against the Hebraic Jews
because their widows were being overlooked in the daily
distribution of food.'*

This problem 'with Greek Jews?' is solved by nominating 'seven men from
among you who are known to be full of the Spirit'. These seven are:

*'Stephen, a man full of faith and of the Holy Spirit; also Philip,
Procorus, Nicanor, Timon, Parmenas, and Nicolas from Antioch,
a convert to Judaism.' (Acts 6:6)*

So Paul was just one of many Jews who were going around converting
gentiles, although his was a slight variation of orthodoxy with a big advantage
over other missionaries to Judaism. Just look at this from Paul's letter in the
New Testament:

*'If those who are not circumcised keep the law's requirements, will
they not be regarded as though they were circumcised? The one
who is not circumcised physically and yet obeys the law will
condemn you who, even though you have circumcision, are a
lawbreaker. A man is not a Jew if he is only one outwardly, nor is
circumcision merely outward and physical. No, a man is a Jew if
he is one inwardly.' (Romans 2:26)*

What an advantage, you can become a good Jew even if you are not circumcised. Note it does not say you can become a good *Christian* without being circumcised.

We are told that Paul was often hounded by Jews, who said that, because he was not one of the original twelve, he was not a genuine apostle. Isn't this strange, Jews complaining that he is not a genuine apostle? Again not Christians, but Jews – obviously Christians don't seem to exist yet. It was this conversion to Paul's version of Judaism that made it easy for Christianity to spread so quickly amongst them. But that's another story.

What about Josephus, does he mention conversion to Judaism? You bet he does. He boasts about the conversion to Judaism of Izates, heir to the throne of Adiabene (part of Armenia) and his mother Helena.

Remember I mentioned an anti-Christian philosopher named Celsus; what has he got to say about it?

'If the Jews preserve their own law, they are not to be blamed for so doing, but those persons rather who have forsaken their own usages and adopted those of the Jews.'

Even the film I mentioned from the Spielberg Archive about the Jewish community in Lithuania proudly shows the tomb in Vilnius of Prince Pototski, who converted to Judaism and in 1749 was then burnt at the stake by Catholic authorities.

Now back to Simon the Cyrene, who carried the cross for Jesus; was he a Christian? How could he be, Christ was still alive? He would be a convert to Judaism, which made many converts in North Africa, especially among the Berbers. Terry Jones has a name, 'Jones' that most Welsh people have because they were suddenly made to adopt a surname. Mass conversion could explain why all members of some Berber communities are, like Brian, called Cohen. There are many examples of conversions and also examples of states bringing in laws to stop Jews preaching and converting their population.

In Carthage, where we filmed, they have uncovered a number of tombs inscribed in Latin or Phoenician with the Jewish candelabra, indicating that they are converts.

Certainly there were Israelites who migrated, many fled out of Judea to Egypt during hard times. As the tribal lands of Judah were closest to Egypt, perhaps this explains why the term Judians become used for all Israelites. I have mentioned examples of emigration, such as Mary Magdalene to Marseilles, Archelaus to Vienne, Gaul, Jesus brother James, to Compostela. These occured before the 66 rebellion and seem to be caused by persecution from strict fundamentalist Jews. This extreme fundamentalism probably began in 150 BC, after a successful revolt by the Jews against the Seleucid King Antiochus, who suppressed Jewish religious and cultural observances, and imposed Greek practices. This victory is celebrated in Israel today as Hannukkah. But unfortunately rule was established by a fierce orthodoxy, which led to many battles and persecutions, destroying the Hellenistic towns of Gaza and Gederah. The Samaritans, who had their own liturgy and insisted on holding their ceremonies in their own Temple were therefore attacked, their cities destroyed and their Temple on Mount Gerizin obliterated. Many streets in Israel today honour the name of Yohanan Hyrcanus the Jewish Titus, destroyer of the Samaritan Temple. I believe this fundamentalism led, over the next 70 years to many liberal Israelites, emigrating from the land well before the destruction by Titus of the Jerusalem Temple in AD 70.

Those Jews who went to Spain became the Sephardic Jews. They are probably mainly Israelites but could include Jewish converts like the Berbers who arrived with the invading Mahammadams. Strangely Hebrew was not known by the Jews of Spain till the arrival of the Muslims. Also when the Jews were expelled from Spain, did they go back to their homeland, Israel? No, they mainly went to North Africa or Turkey where the Sultan is said to have exclaimed: "*Ye call Ferdinand a wise king (of Spain) he who makes his land poor and ours rich!*" The French Israelites converted to Christianity and are now totally immersed in the French population. And one must assume that the Israelites from the Kingdom of Septomania around Marseilles are now totally integrated into the Catalans.

But what about the Ashkanazi Jews who once made up just 3% but are now 80% of the Jewish population, and are the main group returning to Israel from central Europe and America? Are they Israelites? Think on this: we originally find the Ashkanazis in the northern climbs of Gerrmany, Russia and as far north as Lithuania. Are we supposed to believe that people from Israel (out of all the possible countries in the world) are going to emigrate to the freezing Russian steppes? Nope, sorry guys I don't buy it. I know they are called the wandering Jews, but this is wandering gone mad. I don't think the Ashkanazi have ever stepped foot in Israel. I know there is a big attempt to cover this up but it came out years ago in a book called the 'Thirteenth Tribe' by

Arthur Koestler, an Ashkanazi Jew from Hungary, a country partly founded by a people called the Khazars. Koestler showed through extensive research, how a trading empire was set up by a semi nomadic Turkic people, called the Khazars. Their empire lay between the expanding power blocs of Christianity and Islam; and so the people were converted to Judaism by their king as a way of standing apart from both. We do have a letter from an Israelite in Spain who is pleasantly surprised to hear about this Jewish Kingdom and we have records of Jewish Priests (Kohens) going to teach the Khazars the rituals and rites of the religion. We also know that many Jews went to the kingdom, just like many British intellectuals went to live in France after the French revolution, with great feelings of optimism. How many, we don't know, and would they add to the basic state of the population? I doubt it. When the empire collapsed, the Khazars were dispersed through the countries of Eastern Europe, all the way north to Vilnius in the Baltic state of Lithuania.

I have not researched this and I may be totally wrong, but I was in Jerusalem recently during the festival of Sukkot. It commemorates the forty years during which the children of Israel were wandering in the desert, living in temporary shelters. Today they build palm shelters outside to rest in. I thought it was a great idea, because even the bars had these palm buildings outside. It was a hot day and I sat having a cool beer watching all the mass of people passing by in the most inappropriate clothing for the weather. As one young Jewish girl told me it is a real problem with the smell of some of these guys on hot days.

Take a look at one of the hats they wear, the Kolpik. This just has to be a traditional Slavic headdress for really cold weather. I can see nothing that any

of the orthodox wear that looks like it might have been worn by the Israelites except the shawl. I leave you to look at the Afghan coats, the fedoras, the knickerbockers and the Victorian frockcoats and ask you to tell me what this northern European dress has to do with the people of Israel.

By the way, guess what the word Khazar actually means? Would you believe *'wandering'*? And to top this, the name Khazar is interchangeable with Zhid so perhaps Tony these are your Yids!

What have I done? I must be mad to have got into all this. Sorry everyone, sorry. I apologize profusely for raising these awful facts and I do hope you can all live in peaceful harmony, Israelites (Palestinians) and Khazars (Jews). Oops sorry again, let's move on quickly....

21

UP YOU GO BIGNOSE

We filmed the nails being hammered in and, alternatively the arms being tied. I can't remember why it was decided not to show the nails. I suppose Terry just found it a bit too gruesome, but I can't remember now which way I wanted to play it. What I do remember was trying to get through the moment as quickly as possible. And I certainly do remember my careering film suddenly coming to a complete halt as Brian goes up. So we've put him up on the cross; that must be it. But no, we are saved by Eric as Mr. Cheeky who after announcing that 'it's not so bad once you're up,' then gives us:

ERIC: *You being rescued, then? Are you?*
BRIAN: *It's a bit late for that now, isn't it?*
ERIC: *Oh, no. We've got a couple of days up here. Plenty of time. Lots of people get rescued.*
BRIAN: *Ohh?*
ERIC: *Oh, yeah. My brother usually rescues me, if he can keep off the tail for more than twenty minutes. Randy little bugger. Up and down like the Assyrian Empire.*

So that gives us the drive for the rest of the film as all the characters arrive and appear to be about to rescue him, Revolutionaries, Otto, Judith, etc. Of course the big possible rescue is from the Centurion who arrives to 'welease Bwian'.

Now I get really upset by Christians who see this as Jesus on the cross. The source of this scene is actually Kubrick's 'Spartacus'. We are much more disrespectful to the memory of Spartacus than to Jesus here. In Kubrick's film, the Romans offer to free everyone if Spartacus is identified. When he gets up to denounce himself, the others jump up claiming "I'm Spartacus", "I'm

Spartacus." It is a truly awe inspiring moment of loyalty, humanity and comradeship, a sacrifice that brought a lump to my throat when I first saw it as a kid. What I felt a bit funny about was that we were taking the piss out of such an important film moment, and slightly reducing the impact of Kubrick's film in the future. Spartacus' crucifixion is more human, uplifting and spiritual to me than the weird ideas that try to explain Jesus on the cross.

Jesus being sacrificed for our sins is no more uplifting than an Aztec bloody sacrifice. It doesn't seem like Jesus or the Aztec have any real choice in the matter. (Even Mel Gibson's masochistic blood lust moved from one to the other seamlessly.) So to me the concept makes no sense whatsoever, and the meaning has even changed over the centuries, from a sacrificial lamb, to Abelard's loving gift, to our modern taking on of sins. The worst thing is, what does it tell us about this God, his father, that he would do something like that to his Son?

I can't imagine wanting my son even to bang his finger let alone have nails stuck in his hands and feet. Ask any parent who has had a child die. This has to be some sick God who first asks Abraham to kill his son, Isaac, as a sacrifice to prove that he loves God and then does it to his own Son.

But actually I don't think God is sick and nor are the Python's blaspheming because of what I actually believe happened at the crucifixion. Mind you, what happened on that day is not so easy to sort out as you might think. Let's try and navigate through the contradictions in the Gospels and I will point out a few oddities, leaving my fundamental analysis to the end. Remember we have Mark and the two copies (Luke and Matthew) which are called synoptic Gospels so for shorthand (syn), and then we have John (J).

This is the story: The Garden of Gethsemane (which means 'oil press') is an olive grove on the slopes of the Mount of Olives, where Jesus is arrested by a large crowd with clubs and swords sent by the Chief Priest (syn) or a Cohort of Soldiers (J). A Cohort is a Roman term for 800 soldiers! If so, a Roman official must have been involved. In fact in this Gospel Jesus asks: "Am I leading a rebellion?"

That night he is taken to the house of the Caiaphas, the Chief Priest, where there is a meeting of the Sanhedrin (syn) OR to the house of Annas, who was the father-in-law of Caiaphas who questions him and then sends him to Caiaphas (J). Peter follows Jesus to the house of the Chief Priest (syn) OR Peter follows with an un-named disciple (J) who I think is Lazarus because they seem very coy again about naming him.

'Because this disciple was known to the high priest, he went with Jesus into the high priest's courtyard, but Peter had to wait outside at the door. The other disciple, who was known to the high priest, came back, spoke to the girl on duty there and brought Peter in.' (John 18:15)

This strongly suggests that this un-named disciple is an insider as opposed to Peter who is just a witness.

That night, Jesus is questioned by the Sanhedrin and says he will destroy the Temple and is the Son of God. (Not very likely that the Sanhedrin would meet at night.) They find him guilty of blasphemy, hit him and next morning he is sentenced to death. This day is either the first day of Passover (syn) or the day before Passover (J) when they take him to Pilate. There, after questioning him, Pilate goes out to the crowd who demand his crucifixion. One Gospel adds that, because Jesus is from Galilee, Pilate says they must take him to Herod for trial. Herod wants Jesus to perform miracles, but because he doesn't, Herod sends him back to Pilate. Pilate offers the crowd an exchange of prisoners and they demand the release of Barabbas who is a rebel and a murderer.

So Jesus is whipped and a crown of thorns is put on his head because he, or someone, has suggested he is the King of the Jews. Pilate makes another appeal to the crowd but to no avail, so he washes his hands and sends Jesus to be crucified. On the way Simon the Cyrene may have been forced to carry the cross (syn).

According to Mark, at the third hour, (9am) he is put up on the cross (surely all that could not have happened before 9am). John has him put up after the sixth hour (12 noon), which is still a bit tight. Pilate put a sign on the cross in Aramaic, Latin and Greek saying he is the 'King of the Jews'.

Jesus dies at 3pm after either quoting Psalm 22, "My God why has thou forsaken me?" (Mark) OR Psalm 31, "Father into thy hands I commend my spirit." (Luke) OR "It is finished." (John) Or as several films have it, all three.

Now comes a moment in Matthew that is so odd that nobody ever dares to include it in Biblical movies or even mention it:

'At that moment the curtain of the temple was torn in two. The earth shook and the rocks split. The tombs broke open and the bodies of many holy people who had died were raised to life. They came out of the tombs, and after Jesus' resurrection they went into the holy city and appeared to many people.'

A mass resurrection of Ghosts who wander around Jerusalem. Come on guys why not film this incredible moment, or even talk about it?

According to John, the Jews ask for the bodies to be taken down before sunset (Sabbath) and so the legs are broken of the criminals. When they come to Jesus, he is already dead so they just check by piercing him with a spear, which *'brings a sudden flow of blood and water'*. (Which clearly means the heart is pumping which gives rise to theories that he was drugged).

Joseph of Aramathea returns to Jerusalem and goes to Pilate and asks for the body before sunset. Mark says Pilate is surprised he is dead after such a short time on the cross. He's not the only one! Pilate asks a Centurion if Jesus is dead, to which this Centurion answers yes. (Did he race Joseph of Aramathea back from the crucifixion site?) So Pilate gives permission for Joseph to take down the body. Why? Look at this photo from the shoot and again ask yourself, why? *(See fig 17 and 18 for colour detail)*

I think this is the most telling image about the crucifixion that exists in any film about Christ. Here Terry Gilliam, who was designing the film, has put skeletons on the cross and an executioner removing the nails, making the crosses available for the next condemned victims. Terry says the idea probably came from his morbid sensibilities but I must add that, had it not been logical he would not have done it. And his logic has produced an image the implications of which are incredible. In the Bible the site of the execution is called, Golgotha.

The Aramaic name is actually Gol Goatha, meaning mount of execution, possibly the same location as the Goatha mentioned in the Book of Jeremiah describing the geography of Jerusalem.

> *'And the measuring line shall yet go forth over against it upon the hill Gareb, and shall compass about to Goath. And the whole valley of the dead bodies, and of the ashes, and all the fields unto the brook of Kidron, unto the corner of the horse gate toward the east.' (Jeremiah 31:39)*

This all suggests a site for crucifixion where the upright stakes would be left; like Tyburn in London where a gibbet was permanently sited for hangings. Such an area we know existed in Rome and presumably Golgotha was one such site in Jerusalem. Like the photo, we believe the nails were removed for re-use as the only corpse that has ever been found with a nail, was in a heel bone where the nail was so bent that it could not be removed.

You should also be able to see in the photo that the crosses being carried cannot be the same size as those we used for the crucifixion. This must be the same for every film – so each has conspired in the false idea that Jesus carried his cross. From what we know – if a cross piece was going to be used, (and it was not essential) the prisoner was tied or nailed to it and that is what he carried to the execution site not the upright post.

But most importantly are the skeletons. To let the bodies rot *in situ* as a clear warning to others, must be the purpose of crucifixion. If this were not the case, then why would the Romans waste their time and effort building a cross? Taking the bodies down as soon as they are dead is nonsense, they may as well just chop their heads off or stab them and get it over with. Josephus tells us that at the siege of Jerusalem the Romans stuck bodies up on show to intimidate the inhabitants. So now you can understand my incredulity when Pilate gives permission for a crucified man to be taken down from his cross after just three hours.

Back to the chase, and it must seem like a bit of a chase as Joseph of Aramathea races the Centurian back to Golgotha. Presumably the Roman Centurion has to go with him to give Pilate's orders to the soldiers guarding the site. Joseph removes the body and puts it in his tomb, before sunset (syn). Or Nicodemus helps him and they wrap the body with a mixture of myrrh and aloes (J). Then they roll a stone over the entrance.

Matthew now makes a most unlikely statement, that on the Sabbath the

Chief Priest and Pharisees went to Pilate and asked to have the tomb sealed and guarded. This is most unlikely if not impossible. Religious Jews just would not do this on the Sabbath. So why does Matthew add it? The Christian critic and philosopher Celsus complained of something, which suggests why it is there. Writing in the second Century before the Gospels were formalized, he noted the diversity of manuscripts which he put down to:

> 'The perverse audacity of some people in correcting the text, or again to the fact that there are those who add or delete as they please.'

Then he writes, that the missing body in the tomb was only witnessed by followers:

> 'Their talk of a resurrection that was only revealed to some of their own adherents is foolishness.'

Okay when he read the scriptures, there were no other witnesses but next minute someone has added to the Bible that there are soldiers guarding the tomb who witness the resurrection. You can see this re-writing in other events. One suggests that Jesus was obviously not dead after such a short time on the cross, so in comes a soldier to pierce him with a spear to prove he was dead. Unfortunately the forger was not a doctor so he made an error to suggest that blood and water pumped out.

If you think the crucifixion as described in the Bible is baffling, this is nothing compared to the total confusion that follows the two nights in the tomb. So confusing that films often blur over the events.

EITHER on the morning after the Sabbath according to Luke several women including Mary Magdalene arrive and find the stone rolled away and no body. And as they wonder about this, two men in gleaming white clothes appear and tell them he has risen. They return and tell the disciples who go to the tomb and find no body, just strips of linen.

OR according to John, only Mary Magdalene arrives to find the stone moved. She does not enter but goes:

> 'Running to Simon Peter and the other disciple, the one Jesus loved, and said, "They have taken the Lord out of the tomb, and we don't

know where they have put him!"
So Peter and the other disciple started for the tomb.'

Note again the reluctance to name Lazarus, who again seems to be leading Peter into being a witness:

'Both were running, but the other disciple outran Peter and reached the tomb first. He bent over and looked in at the strips of linen lying there but did not go in. Then Simon Peter, who was behind him, arrived and went into the tomb.'

Where they find no body but strips of linen. Later at the tomb, Jesus appears to Mary Magdalene who mistakes him for the gardener.

OR if you like high drama and special fx's then look no further than Matthew:

'Mary Magdalene and the other Mary went to look at the tomb. There was a violent earthquake, for an angel of the Lord came down from heaven and, going to the tomb, rolled back the stone and sat on it. His appearance was like lightning, and his clothes were white as snow.'

Would be great on film, why does nobody dare do it? Oh and remember Matthew had guards on the tomb.

'The guards were so afraid of him that they shook and became like dead men. The angel said to the women, "Do not be afraid, for I know that you are looking for Jesus, who was crucified. He is not here; he has risen, just as he said. Come and see the place where he lay. Then go quickly and tell his disciples: 'He has risen from the dead and is going ahead of you into Galilee.'

OR you get from Mark, the original, a much more sober little number.

Mary Magdalene, Mary and Salome arrive at the tomb. The stone has already been rolled away.

'As they entered the tomb, they saw a young man dressed in a white

robe sitting on the right side, and they were alarmed.'

Significantly the specific word Mark uses for 'young man' is the same one that he used to describe Lazarus.

'You are looking for Jesus the Nazarene, who was crucified. He has risen! He is not here. See the place where they laid him. But go, tell his disciples and Peter, "He is going ahead of you into Galilee, there you will see him, just as he told you." Trembling and bewildered, the women went out and fled from the tomb. They said nothing to anyone, because they were afraid.'

That is where Mark's Gospel ends, with the body gone and a 'young man' in white saying he has risen. But someone has attempted to add more: probably to foil another criticism by Celsus.

We know that the victors write history, and we can add to this that the victors also formalize religion into the instrument of their authority. This is as true of Christianity in South America as it is for Islam in the Middle East. In Rome, Constantine and his Bishops formalized Christianity into the instrument they required, but what was Christianity before they doctored it? Our only record comes from those who were considered heretics by Constantine's Bishops. Are there features shared by the heretics about the crucifixion that give us a clue of what actually happened? Most of the heresies were Gnostic or Gnostic-influenced, repudiating the hierarchical structure of Rome and extolling the supremacy of personal illumination over blind faith. As Brian says, "You've got to think for yourself, you're all individuals."

The other common factor about the major heresies was that they were duelist, regarding good and evil as issues of ultimately cosmic import, just like our Zoroastrian Magi.

I should pause here a moment to explain dualism as it sounds like a simplistic concept, making a big thing about opposites like wet and dry, cold and hot, etc. Unfortunately it is not so simple, I still don't quite appreciate all the ramifications. The concept is extremely ancient and is basically about balance, symmetry and equilibrium. You can find it in ancient Egypt where it is called Maat, (that which is straight,) and symbolized by a winged figure or a feather. Maat was the personification of the fundamental balance and order of the universe, without which all of creation would perish in chaos.

The primary duty of the pharaoh was to uphold this order by maintaining the law and administering justice. To reflect this, many pharaohs took the title 'Beloved of Maat,' emphasizing their focus on justice and truth.

Yannis Andricopoulos in his book 'The Greek Inheritance' finds a similar concept in ancient Greece where forces were:

> '...perpetually attempting to enlarge their empire at the expense of others. They are prevented, however, from doing so by the cosmic rule of law, the cosmic Balance of Forces which ensures that no injustice is committed by the victory of one element over its opposite. ... Cosmic justice was the revelation of the eternal into the temporary and of the universal into the particular both of which set the parameters of life and limits which humans have to respect.'

Andricopoulos then relates this *Theia Dike*, 'divine justice' to the present day:

> 'If the Greeks were right greenhouse gas emmisionss cannot be allowed to spiral out of control, for the punishment is global warming and grievous climate changes; the escalating and enormous losses of biodiversity will make our own survival impossible; and the foaming desperation and hatred, the Force 12 rage of the disempowered at the world's obscene inequalities cannot continue, for the price the West will pay one day may cross the line of everything currently conceivable.'

The same complex theory can be found in the East. The Chinese concept of yin and yang is about the balance of complementary opposites within a greater whole. Everything has both yin and yang aspects, although yin or yang elements may manifest more strongly in different objects or at different times. Yin yang constantly interacts, never existing in absolute stasis. Taoist philosophy generally discounts good and evil distinctions as superficial labels, preferring to focus on the idea of balance. The moral dimension of the theory originated in the Confucian school. The concept is symbolized by the Taijitu symbol; worth a moment's contemplation.

The Dead Sea Scrolls name the leader of their community as the 'Teacher of Righteousness'. I believe this concept of righteousness is similar to the justice, balance and equilibriam expressed in the duelist concept and interestingly some believe Jesus' brother James was the 'Teacher of Righteousness'.

So that is a glimpse into the duelist heresy. The last people the new Roman Church believed were heretical were those who considered Jesus was mortal and viewed him the way Moslems see Mohammad, as a divinely inspired prophet, born naturally and died but never resurrected. Remember we are talking about original Christian beliefs, not outsiders critical of Christianity.

Now we get a division amongst the Christian heretics A few believed he did die on a cross, but most believed (Manichaeism, Arianism) that in fact he did not die on the cross. These then split into those who think he was never on a cross (who we will deal with later) and those who suggest he either was taken down before he died or there was a substitute. A Gnostic document found in the Nag Hammadi Scrolls has this statement by Jesus:

"As for my death, which was real enough to them – it was real to them because of their own incomprehension and blindness."

Interestingly, Jesus keeps telling people *'have you not got eyes to see'*, suggesting not to take an event literally but that there is more to it; a mystery.

The Qu'ran gives an ambiguous statement suggesting this later:

'They did not kill him, nor did they crucify him, but they thought they did.'

Moslem writers have expanded on this. According to most of them, there was a substitute, some suggesting that it was Simon the Cyrene. Some have written that Jesus was hiding in a niche in a wall, watching the crucifixion of a surrogate while he laughed.

Why this confused idea of substitution? Gnostics who are initiated into the mystery would laugh at all of this. Origen, the Christian Theologian writing 150 years after Christ made this statement: *'Christ Crucified is teaching for babes.'* The Gnostics believed that the literal story was an allegorical myth, encoding teachings about the spiritual path of the initiate. For instance, even the resurrection is clearly something they believe happens while you are alive:

'The resurrection is the revelation of what is and the transformation of things, and a transition into newness. Flee from the divisions and the fetters, and already you have the resurrection.'

Lazarus' resurrection is clearly an initiation emphasized by the Apostles' demand to *"Let us go and die too."* But where does all this talk of a substitute come from and is there any relation to the 'twin' concept? There is a duelist belief from the mystery religions that the Gnostics took up. The idea is that within yourself you have opposites, a lower and higher self, the Eidolon and the Daemon. Initiation leads to the overcoming of your lower self. The ass was a symbolic representation of our lower eidolon. In the mystery religion the God-

Head rides on a donkey while the crowd wave palm leaves, signifying his dominance over your lower self. In fact the very first image of crucifixion is the Alexamenos graffito, a carving on a pillar in Rome which shows a donkey headed man, crucified.

What could it mean? Perhaps nailing your carnal body to the four arms of a cross, (air, fire, water, earth) symbolically releases your daemon. Remember one of the heresies that the Knights Templars were accused of, was that they spat on the cross. Obviously initiates would understand the cross as an instrument to pin your lower self to. And let me remind you of the good Jesus and the criminal Jesus Barabbas, exactly like the Eidolon and the Daemon. Without initiation into these ideas one can see how the confused version of dualism leads to the stories of substitution and twins.

Now before I started this section I said God didn't sacrifice his son and the Python's did not blaspheme at all. My reasoning is that it is pretty obvious that Jesus never actually died on the cross!

How can I be so certain? Firstly there are no images of Jesus on the cross for 400 years after his death! The first crucifixion image we have is the donkey in the Alexamenos graffito. The original symbol used by Christians was not the crucifix but the X shaped cross of the chi-rho. This originates from paganism.

The chi-rho originated in pagan papyri as a sign used for the Greek word 'chreston' meaning auspicious.

It was Constantine who adapted the chi-rho to Christianity as part of his attempt to unite all the religions of Rome. And before that, what symbol did the Christians use? The 'fish' arising from the Pythagorean, vesica pisces. But no sign of a crucifixion or even an upright cross except in the other religion of Rome, which celebrated their God, Mithras' birth on the 25th December. During their Holy Communion they were offered wafers bearing the sign of the cross.

You can as a literal Christian believe in the crucifixion and resurrection and stay ignorant of the truth of Jesus. There is an image of a God being crucified that comes from the mystery religions.

The inscription reads 'Orpheus-Bakkos' which means 'Orpheus becomes a

Bacchoi'. Bacchoi was an initiated disciple of Dionysus. What is interesting is the support for the feet. It suggests a ritual as opposed to a real crucifixion, a death and resurrection ceremony of initiation. Could it be that the crucifixion was not the cause of Jesus death but simply a 'Passion Play'. Such symbolic rites did seem to occur. Jesus appears to be crucified in a garden where people were kept at a distance and where there was a tomb to complete the event, all of which seems to be stage-managed by Nicodemus and Joseph of Aramathea. Romans would have recognized this because they knew of the performance of the Easter rites of Attis. During this spring festival, that lasts three days, a passion play was performed in which an effigy of the corpse was tied to a sacred pine tree and decorated with flowers. It was then buried in a sepulcher but on the third night a light was brought to his grave while a priest anointed the lips of the initiates with the words: "To you likewise there shall come salvation from your trouble." On the morning of the 25th March, the vernal equinox, the resurrection was celebrated with wild glee. Another ritual called the Bacchanalia took place in a grove on one of the hills of Rome. The Senate banned it, but in spite of this it continued and those caught participating were often executed. The Senate probably acted against the Bacchants because women occupied leadership positions in the cult, contrary to the patriarchic Roman values of the time. And slaves and the poor were the cult's members who were planning to overthrow the Roman government.

> 'Uncleanliness was committed by men with men and women with women. Men were fastened to a machine and hurried off to hidden caves, and they were said to have been taken away by the gods.'

If the crucifixion was a ritual like the raising of Lazarus, how then did Jesus actually die? There are two possibilities, firstly if he was the Egyptian as I suggested he might have been:

'*The Egyptian himself escaped out of the fight, but did not appear any more.*' [*Josephus, Jewish Antiquities*]

So perhaps he escaped to India as is sometimes suggested although my research suggests that was Thomas (the twin). The other possibility accepts the theory by Daniel Unterbrink that the person who Pilate was reported as crucifying was in fact the influential Judas the Galilean. There is something very fishy in the Bible that does suggest this possibility:

'*Then Pilate announced to the chief priests and the crowd, "I find no basis for a charge against this man."*
    But they insisted, "He stirs up the people all over Judea by his teaching. He started in Galilee and has come all the way here."'
(*Luke 23*)

We know Jesus was a Nazarene not from Nazareth which probably didn't exist at the time. We also know that he was of the line of David and so from the tribe of Judah. The homeland of the tribe of Judah is Judea, not Galilee. So why is he not living in his homeland and where does Galilee come into the story at all? In fact scholars have noticed that all the passages that mention Galilee are later additions, which are oddly incorrect. For instance, Mark says that Jesus went through Sidon on his way from Tyre to the Sea of Galilee. Problem is Sidon is in the opposite direction. And Mark 1:16, reads '*And passing along by the Sea of Galilee he saw Simon and Andrew.*' In Greek the verb '*passing along*' is not used with the preposition '*by*'. So if one removed the underlined the sentence would have the correct syntax.

You will have to check this yourselves as it is all Greek to me (I was never good at grammar, that is why I went into film), but if Daniel Unterbrink is right and Pilate was not involved with the crucifixion of Jesus but with that of Judas of Galilee, then this could also clarify who arrested Jesus. We are offered in the Bible two groups, either a group sent by the Chief Priest, or a cohort of Roman soldiers (800). It is agreed in all the Gospels that those who arrest Jesus take him to the house of the Chief Priest. If a cohort of Roman soldiers arrested him in the middle of the night, can you believe that they would have dropped him off at the house of a Jewish leader and then marched away because they are not around when Peter, and an unnamed disciple, follow the arrested man to the courtyard of the Chief Priest. So I think we can say the synoptic Gospels are right and he was arrested by a group sent by the Chief Priest and Roman soldiers obviously had nothing to do with it.

Now to the heart of the matter, the Bible states that Jesus was sentenced to death that night, by the Sanhedrin for blasphemy. Even in the suspect section of Josephus it states.

> 'The teachers of the Law were envenomed with envy and gave thirty talents to Pilate, in order that he should put him to death. And he, after he had taken, gave them consent that they should themselves carry out their purpose. And they took him and crucified him according to the ancestral law.'

Either this is another forgery, or it is saying Jesus was killed by the Jewish leaders. Furthermore the Talmud of Jeschu tells us exactly how capital punishment would have been carried out according to ancestral law. Remember the quote that tried to explain how Jeschu performed his miracles with the ineffable name which:

> 'He transcribed on to a piece of parchment and concealed in an incision under his skin. By this means he was able to work miracles and to persuade the people that he was the Son of God foretold by Isaiah. With the aid of Judas, the Sages of the Synagogue, succeeding in capturing Jeschu, who was then lead before the Great and Little Sanhedrin, by whom he was condemned to be stoned to death and his dead body was hung on a tree.'

They commit the deed and the dead body is then hung on a tree. In fact, the word in the Gospels translated as cross actually has the general meaning of a stake. The dead body would then be under the control of the Jews who could conform to their ancient law.

> 'If a man guilty of a capital offense is put to death and his body is hung on a tree, you must not leave his body on the tree overnight. Be sure to bury him that same day, because anyone who is hung on

*a tree is under God's curse. You must not desecrate the land the Lord
your God is giving you as an inheritance.' (Deuteronomy 21:22)*

Where Pilate, would obviously not waste his time and money taking down
a crucified man after just 3 hours, the Jews would have to conform to their
ancient law and remove the body from the tree before sunset as mentioned in
the Bible. Now it all begins to make sense. Judas the Galilean was crucified by
Pilate, but the Sanhedrin stoned Jesus to death. Acts of the Apostles, which is a
mishmash of early writings, supports the previous statement that the Sanhedrin
caused his death:

> *'Having brought the apostles, they made them appear before the
> Sanhedrin to be questioned by the high priest. "We gave you strict
> orders not to teach in this name," he said. "Yet you have filled
> Jerusalem with your teaching and you are determined to make us
> guilty of this man's blood."*
>
> *Peter and the other apostles replied: "We must obey God rather
> than men! The God of our fathers raised Jesus from the dead—
> whom you had killed by hanging him on a tree."' (Acts 5:27)*

Again Peter tells a group in Caesarea:

> *"We are witnesses of everything he did in the country of the Jews and
> in Jerusalem. They killed him by hanging him on a tree" (Acts 10:39)*

Or even in Paul's letters:

> *'Christ redeemed us from the curse of the law by becoming a curse
> for us, for it is written: "Cursed is everyone who is hung on a tree."*
> *Galatians 3:13*

Most conclusively is the quote I used to show that Jesus was accused of
blasphemy.

> *'The high priest asked him, "Are you the Christ, the Son of the
> Blessed One?"*
> *"I am," said Jesus. "And you will see the Son of Man sitting at*

the right hand of the Mighty One and coming on the clouds of heaven."

The high priest tore his clothes. "Why do we need any more witnesses?" he asked. "You have heard the blasphemy. What do you think?"

They all condemned him as worthy of death. Then some began to spit at him; they blindfolded him, struck him with their fists.'

They have found him guilty of blasphemy and have sentenced him to death. Now 'Life of Brian' exposes the nonsense of what follows in the Bible. We are told that because they can't put him to death, they have to go to Pilate. No they don't! They don't need to go and see Pilate, or even Herod, or anyone; they can kill him by the traditional way of killing a blasphemer, the one shown accurately in 'Life of Brian'. They can stone him to death. This is the known punishment for religious blasphemers; not crucifixion, which is not for blasphemers at all but for rebels against the Roman empire! All the stuff about pleading with Pilate to kill him is obviously so much nonsense. If you doubt me then just look at what happens to Stephen when he is later brought before the Sanhedrin. Stephen tries to make a speech but:

'At this they covered their ears and, yelling at the top of their voices, they all rushed at him, dragged him out of the city and began to stone him.' (Acts 7:57)

Would you like to know what Stephen said that made the Sanhedrin cover their ears and stone him to death? Here it is:

"You stiff-necked people, with uncircumcised hearts and ears! Was there ever a prophet your fathers did not persecute? They even killed those who predicted the coming of the Righteous One. And now you have betrayed and murdered him."

So, like me, Stephen is accusing the Sanhedrin of killing Jesus. And it must have been in the way shown in 'Life of Brian', stoning!

While we are talking about 'Life of Brian' and putting people on crosses, we had to crucify the actors. What became obvious when we were making the crosses is that you need a carpenter, to make a joint to take the crosspiece;

otherwise it will wobble and even slide down. In fact, Eric originally wanted a gag that as Christ was a carpenter and the joinery was so bad, he kept tipping forward and had to give advice: "No you need to put a two by four divet there."

For our actors on the cross we had bicycle saddles, but I hear it was still uncomfortable. Probably not as uncomfortable as actually being crucified which must have been a slow painful death.

I have tried to think it through logically and think Eric has it right when Brian says '*it's too late to be saved*'. Mr. Cheeky informs him '*not at all we've got a couple of days up here.*' As mentioned, the whole point of the exercise was to put you on show, upright like a banner, struggling with pain for as long as possible as a deterrent to other rebels. And as the word translated as crucifix also means stake, we know that many had no cross piece and some criminals were even impaled, a la Vlad the Impaler.

Josephus mentions the Romans crucifying two men back to back with one upside down, as a joke. The site would already have the uprights and if a crosspiece was to be used the prisoner would be nailed to it first. If that cross piece is slipped over to the back of the upright, the weight would be pulled back and once the feet are nailed the man would almost stay up without fixing the cross piece. The other alternative is to place the slender cross piece on the top of the upright making a T shaped support. Check back to Jan van Eyck's '*The Crucifixion*', where our mysterious painter seems to have this knowledge. In a portrait, he even has a man wearing such a T cross and in the famous '*Arnolfini Marriage*' painting, there is a T cross shape in the window.

Man with PInk, by Jan Van Eyck (note T-cross)

Whoa! I better stop, I'm beginning to see T crosses everywhere.

The feet were fixed either side of the upright with two nails, one in each heel, as this was extremely painful but did not cause too much loss of blood. This is never shown in any form of art, and never will be, as it does not look very attractive to have your legs separated, it is much more aesthetically pleasing having them pinned together. But this must be pretty unlikely considering the length of nail needed to go through two crossed feet. And then there would need to be a wedge shaped footrest to nail in to, which would need to be carefully prepared for the right height of the man. All very unlikely. We know nailing the feet together was not the method used because, as mentioned, the heel bone of a crucified person was found in an ossuary in Jerusalem. Interestingly the nail had been in wood from an olive tree, which makes sense as I don't think many other trees would be found near Jerusalem. This makes most film images of Jesus on the cross, wrong. He is far too high to be on the upright of an olive tree.

Legs nailed apart, just off the ground, what else is never shown? How about the obvious. It was a problem for us, if our actors wanted to go to the toilet. Clearly crucified people, up for several days, were naked and crapped and pissed. Their legs and the upright of the cross would be covered in shit. There would be flies everywhere. The whole thing is just not a very aesthetically pleasing image to put in a film, not to mention a church.

22

THE RESURRECTION

With the film completed, we ran it at a private viewing to John Mortimer and Oscar Beuselinck representing the law. Mortimer had defended Gay News in 1977 in the infamous Blasphemous Libel case and Mike described him as:

> 'A nice friendly disarming man, with small, but not at all humourless eyes, and a ready smile. He loves the film and reckons that we are quite safe. The chances of a jury convicting Python of blasphemy on the basis of the film are very remote, he believes – but not impossible. However should an action be brought, Mortimer thinks it would take at least a year to come to court, by which time we'll have hopefully made our money and our point.'

The Pythons did make their money and their point and continue to make both to this very day.

When Graham died, I did a cut of the film introducing the missing scenes, the shepherds, Otto, etc. Terry Gilliam suggested we call it 'The After Life of Brian'. John was not sure we should release it but it turns out we could not, even if we wanted to. The company Paragon Entertainment, who distributed the film had dumped the out-takes to save money on storage.

There then followed in 1998 a Pythonesque legal battle by Monty Python against Paragon, claiming that it had failed to observe best business practice in the handling of the film. Luckily, Mr Justice Rattee ruled in the High Court against Paragon and the copyright of 'Monty Python's Life of Brian' returned to the Pythons. But then out popped the Royal Bank of Canada claiming that it had certain rights over the film because Paragon used its rights in the film as security for loans from the bank. The Pythons argued that any such rights, if they ever existed, were nullified when their relationship with Paragon ended in 1996. The Pythons won and the Bank had to swallow their loss, but unfortunately the historic out-takes were gone.

In the year 2000, a BBC history series, presented by Adam Hart-Davis, was called 'What the Romans Did for Us'. It demonstrates how John's rhetorical phrase has entered the British psyche, even to the extent of having been used in Parliament. In Prime Minister's Questions of 3 May 2006, MP David Clelland asked Prime Minister Tony Blair, "What has the Labour government ever done for us?" Blair's answer made a shorthand reference to the types of splinter political groups "Judean People's Front or People's Front of Judea."

During the Venice Film Festival, the UAAR (Italian Union of Rationalist Atheists and Agnostics) assigned the 'Premio Brian' (Brian Award) to the most rationalist/atheist movie presented to the Festival.

I suppose one should finish with the latest controversy to come from the 'Life of Brian'. In February 2007 the Church of St Thomas the Martyr in Newcastle-upon-Tyne held a public screening in the church itself, with song-sheets, organ accompaniment, stewards in costume and false beards for female members of the audience. Although the screening was a sell-out, some Christian groups, notably the conservative Christian Voice, were highly critical of the decision to allow the screening to go ahead, insisting that "you don't promote Christ to the community by taking the mick out of Him." The Rev. Jonathan Adams, one of the church's clergy, defended his taste in comedy, saying that it did not mock Jesus, and that it raised important issues about the hypocrisy and stupidity that can affect religion.

Rev. Adams is right, Jesus was probably a great man and the film or this book do not attempt to link him to any crime or dishonesty carried out by some in His name. And so I would like to conclude with three statements from the film. Firstly I hope that when you look at 'Life of Brian' again after reading this book you will say: 'I was blind and now I can see.' Secondly, as with Gnostic initiation, "you must think for yourselves, you are all individuals." And finally, given the state of the planet, remember to 'always look on the bright side of life.'

THE END

Epilogue
FATAL DISTRACTION

I read somewhere that we are only 'apes in nightclubs and battleships', so we tend to be easily distracted, and will soon forget what was in this book. In Python's following film 'The Meaning of Life' there is a point in the film where the 'meaning of life' is actually explained but we miss it because we are easily distracted. Here I reproduce it.

CHAIRMAN: Item six on the agenda: the meaning of life. Now, Harry, you've had some thoughts on this.

HARRY: That's right. Yeah, I've had a team working on this over the past few weeks, and, what we've come up with can be reduced to two fundamental concepts. One: people are not wearing enough hats. Two: matter is energy. In the universe, there are many energy fields, which we cannot normally perceive. Some energies have a spiritual source which act upon a person's soul. However, this soul does not exist *ab initio*, as orthodox Christianity teaches. It has to be brought into existence by a process of guided self-observation. However, this is rarely achieved, owing to man's unique ability to be distracted from spiritual matters by everyday trivia.

[a long pause]

BERT: What was that about hats?

Bibliography

This book owes everything to the following. I may not agree with everything in them all, but each has at least one interesting idea, which makes them worth reading.

Timothy Freke & Peter Gandy: *The Jesus Mystery 1999*
H. Lincoln, M. Baigent & R Leigh: *Holy Blood & Holy Grail 1996*
Fred Gettings: *The Hidden Art: 1978*
David Wood: *Genisis 1985*
Flavius Josephus: *The Antiquity of the Jews 70*
Flavius Josephus: *The War of the Jews 70*
Geoffrey of Monmouth: *The History of the British Kings 1966*
Laurence Gardner: *The Magdalene Legacy 2005*
Shlomo Sand: *The Invention of the Jewish People 2009*
C. Knight & R. Lomas: *Uriel's Machine 2000*
C. Knight & R. Lomas: *The Hiram Key 1998*
David Rohl: *Test of Time 1995*
David Yallop: *In Gods name 1984*
Arthur Koestler: *The Thirteenth Tribe 1976*
Yannis Andricopoulos: *The Greek Inheritance 2008*
Colin Wilson, Rand Flem-ath: *The Atlantis Blueprint 2000*
Tacitus: *The Histories 79*
Jim Keith: *Secret and Suppressed 1993*
Stephen Knight: *The Brotherhood 1985*
Robin Lane Fox: *The Unauthorized Version 1992*
M. Baigent & R. Leigh: *The Dead Sea Scrolls Deception 2001*
Peter Berrisford Ellis: *Celtic Inheritance 1985*
The Bible

Appendix 1

JOSEPHUS

Flavius Josephus (37- ca 100 C.E.)

All that we know about the life of Josephus comes from his own autobiography. He was born as Joseph ben Matthias, "in the first year of the reign of Caius Caesar" (Caligula), in a priestly family, and through his mother he was descended from the royal Hasmonaean family. He was educated at the rabbinic school in Jerusalem where he distinguished himself. As a young man he decided to learn the tenets of the three major Jewish sects of his time. At the age of sixteen, he joined the Essenes under the influence of a religious leader Banus and spent some time conducting an ascetic way of life. Then he joined the sect of the Pharisees, akin, according to him, to the school of the Stoics, and remained faithful to this sect for the rest of his life. He learned also about the Sadducees, though he gives us little information about them. We learn that he was married three times, had three sons from his second marriage and two from his third marriage, and that he had a brother, Matthias.

In the year AD 64, he was sent to Rome to obtain the release of certain priests who were sent there by the Roman procurator, Felix, for trial. During his voyage, the ship went aground in the Adriatic Sea, but he and his companions managed to be rescued and landed in the Italian city of Puteoli. He succeeded in his mission with the help of a Jewish actor, Aliturus, and the emperor's wife Poppea.

During his prolonged visit to Rome, Josephus became convinced about the invincibility of the Roman Empire and futility of fighting against it, so he decided to work toward peace in order to prevent a revolt. When he returned to Israel in AD 66, however, troubles arose when the Roman governor of Syria, Cestius Gallus, demanded taxes from the Jews, and opposition against him arose in Caesarea. In Jerusalem, Josephus opposed the nationalist party and argued against the war. That made him unpopular and he had to find a refuge in the Temple until his enemy, the extremist leader, Menachem, was murdered.

In order to stop the revolt, Gallus directed an expeditionary force against Jerusalem, but was driven out of Jerusalem and for rather unknown reasons decided to retreat. But his Twelfth Legion was ambushed in the pass of Beth-horon and defeated. Now the war was inevitable and the moderates who tried to prevent it had no choice but to join in. Josephus was sent to Galilee as a legate and general in charge of the Jewish forces with a double mission to organize a regular Jewish army, fortify the towns and citadels, and, at the same time, to pacify a popular uprising and revolt against the king, which was itself, divided into various quarrelling factions. Josephus had to deal with all these factions, with several bands of robbers who were recruited from among the poor people, as well as with interethnic fights between the Jews and the Greeks. There were some attempts on Josephus' life, but he managed to escape to Tarichaeae. Among the specific things Josephus reports about his stay in Galilee is the defence of the non-Jews living among the Jews and allowing them to practice their own religion: "Everyone ought to worship God according to his own inclinations, and not to be constrained by force." Evidently Josephus learned this attitude from the Hellenes.

When Roman General Vespasian's forces invaded Israel in the spring of 67, Josephus' forces deserted and he had to find refuge in the fortress of Jotapata where, after a siege of six weeks, he surrendered in July 67. Josephus was a valued prisoner to be sent to the emperor Nero, but he took advantage of the situation and made a prophecy that Vespasian would become emperor. Thus Vespasian kept him in his custody until 69, when his troops would declare him emperor and treated Josephus more like an interpreter than a prisoner.

With the death of Nero in 68 a period of struggle for power followed in Rome with a succession of three emperors. During this time the war with Israel was suspended. In 69, when Vespasian was pronounced emperor, he freed Josephus who assumed now the name of Flavius, the family name of Vespasian. When Titus, the son of the emperor, was named general to lead Roman forces in a renewed war against the Jews, Josephus returned to Israel. He was used by Titus as an intermediary to convince the Jews to give up their resistance and save the city by surrendering. Jews, in spite of Josephus' oratorical skills, regarded him as a traitor and fought to the end which resulted in the destruction of the Temple.

After the war Josephus was given a parcel of land near Jerusalem for retirement from active life. He decided instead to go to Rome and became a Roman citizen and client of the Flavian family. He was given a house in which Vespasian lived as a private citizen and a pension for life. He was commissioned to write the history of the Jewish people and the war. In his autobiography, he mentioned the death of Agrippa II who died in AD 93. Thus Josephus' own death probably took place around AD 100.

Appendix 2

MANY JESUS

The archetypal Jewish hero was Joshua, the successor of Moses and conqueror otherwise known as Yeshua ben Nun ('Jesus of the fish'). The name Jesus (Yeshua or Yeshu in Hebrew) therefore became almost a prerequisite for a heroic rebel. Every band in the Jewish resistance had its own hero figure sporting this moniker.

Josephus mentions no fewer than nineteen different Yeshuas/Jesii, about half of them contemporaries of the supposed Christ! In his 'Antiquities', of the twenty eight high priests who held office from the reign of Herod the Great to the fall of the Temple, no fewer than four bore the name Jesus: Jesus ben Phiabi, Jesus ben Sec, Jesus ben Damneus and Jesus ben Gamaliel. Even Saint Paul makes reference to a rival magician, preaching 'another Jesus' (2 Corinthians 11,4). Too strange to be a coincidence!

Jesus ben Sirach
This Jesus was reputedly the author of the Book of Sirach (aka 'The Wisdom of Jesus the Son of Sirach'), part of Old Testament Apocrypha. Ben Sirach, writing in Greek about 180 BC, brought together Jewish 'wisdom' and Homeric-style heroes.

Jesus ben Pandira
A wonder-worker during the reign of Alexander Jannaeus (106-79 BC), one of the most ruthless of the Maccabean kings. Imprudently, this Jesus launched into a career of end-time prophesy and agitation which upset the king. He met his own premature end-time by being hung on a tree – and on the eve of a Passover. Scholars have speculated this Jesus founded the Essene sect.

Jesus ben Ananias

Beginning in AD 62, this Jesus had caused disquiet in Jerusalem with a non-stop doom-laden mantra of 'Woe to the city'. He prophesied rather vaguely: "A voice from the east, a voice from the west, a voice from the four winds, a voice against Jerusalem and the holy house, a voice against the bridegrooms and the brides, and a voice against the whole people." – Josephus, Wars 6.3.

Arrested and flogged by the Romans, Jesus ben Ananias was released as nothing more dangerous than a mad man. He died during the siege of Jerusalem from a rock hurled by a Roman catapult.

Jesus ben Saphat

In the insurrection of AD 68 that wrought havoc in Galilee, this Jesus had led the rebels in Tiberias. When the city was about to fall to Vespasian's legions, he fled north to Tarichea on the Sea of Galilee.

Jesus ben Gamala

During AD 68/69 this Jesus was a leader of the 'peace party' in the civil war wrecking Judaea. From the walls of Jerusalem, he had remonstrated with the besieging Idumeans (led by 'James and John, sons of Susa'). It did him no good. When the Idumeans breached the walls, he was put to death and his body thrown to the dogs and carrion birds.

Jesus ben Thebuth

A priest who, in the final capitulation of the upper city in AD 69, saved his own skin by surrendering the treasures of the Temple, which included two holy candlesticks, goblets of pure gold, sacred curtains and robes of the high priests. The booty figured prominently in the Triumph held for Vespasian and his son Titus.

But was there a crucified Jesus? Certainly. Jesus ben Stada was a Judean agitator who gave the Romans a headache in the early years of the second century. He met his end in the town of Lydda (twenty five miles from Jerusalem) at the hands of a Roman crucifixion crew. And given the scale that Roman retribution could reach – at the height of the siege of Jerusalem the Romans were crucifying upwards of five hundred captives a day before the city walls – dead heroes called Jesus would (quite literally) have been thick on the ground. Not one merits a full stop in the great universal history.

Appendix 3

BUDDHISM

The similarities between the monastic practices of the Therapeutae and Buddhist monastic practices have led to suggestions that the Therapeutae were in fact Buddhist monks who had reached Alexandria, descendants of Ashoka's emissaries to the West, and who influenced the early formation of Christianity. According to the linguist Zacharias P. Thundy, the name Therapeutae is simply an Hellenisation of the Pali term for the traditional Buddhist faith "Theravada" (the "elders" of Buddhism).

There are possible Buddhist-Christian links in the life of Jesus himself. According to the Gospel of Matthew, Jesus spent his early childhood in Egypt, which was at the end of the Silk Road. Elmar R. Gruber, a psychologist, and Holger Kersten, a specialist in religious history, argue that Buddhism had a substantial influence on the life and teachings of Jesus. Gruber and Kersten claim that Jesus was brought up by the Therapeutae, teachers of the Buddhist Theravada school then living in the Bible lands. As a result of its role in trade with the East, Egypt was prosperous and enriched with religious diversity. Interestingly nard oil was part of the Ayurvedic herbal tradition of India. It was obtained as a luxury in ancient Egypt, the Near East, and Rome. It produced Spikenard, the perfumed oil used by Mary Magdalene to anoint Jesus.

Oxford New Testament scholar Barnett Hillman Streeter established as early as the 1930s, that the moral teaching of the Buddha has four remarkable resemblances to the Sermon on the Mount.

Appendix 4
MALACHI MARTIN

From 1958 until 1964, Malachi Martin served in Rome as a Jesuit priest, where he was a close associate of, and carried out many sensitive missions for, the renowned Jesuit Cardinal Augustin Bea and Popes John XXIII and Paul VI. Released afterwards from his vows of poverty and obedience at his own request (but still a priest), he ultimately moved to New York and became a best-selling writer of fiction and non-fiction.

Martin had first made explicit reference to a diabolic rite held in Rome in his 1990 non-fiction best-seller about geopolitics and the Vatican, 'The Keys of This Blood', in which he wrote:

> '*Most frighteningly for (Pope) John Paul, he had come up against the irremovable presence of a malign strength in his own Vatican and in certain bishops' chanceries. It was what knowledgeable Churchmen called the 'superforce.' Rumours, always difficult to verify, tied its installation to the beginning of Pope Paul VI's reign in 1963. Indeed Paul had alluded somberly to 'the smoke of Satan which has entered the Sanctuary'.*

This oblique reference is to an enthronement ceremony by Satanists in the Vatican. Besides, the incidence of satanic paedophilia — rites and practices — was already documented among certain bishops and priests as widely dispersed as Turin in Italy and South Carolina in the United States. The cultic acts of Satanic paedophilia are considered by professionals to be the culmination of the Fallen Archangel's rites.

These allegations have largely gone unnoticed, possibly because Martin was so crafty in his descriptions that he might even have been referring to the coronation of Pope Paul VI. But he revealed much more about this alleged ritual in one of his last works, 'Windswept House: A Vatican Novel' (1996).

In this story, he vividly described a diabolical ceremony called "The Enthronement of the Fallen Archangel Lucifer", supposedly held in St. Paul's Chapel within the Vatican, but linked with concurrent satanic rites in the US, on June 29, 1963, barely a week after the election of Paul VI. In this novel, before he dies, a pope leaves a secret account of the situation on his desk for the next occupant of the throne of Peter, a thinly disguised John Paul II.

According to The New American, Martin confirmed that the ceremony did indeed occur as he had described. "Oh yes, it is true; very much so," the magazine reported he said. "But the only way I could put that down into print is in novelistic form."

Martin claimed that Popes John XXIII and Paul VI were freemasons during a certain period and that photographs and other detailed documents proving this were in the possession of the Vatican State Secretariat.

In March 1997, Martin said on Radio Liberty's Steel on Steel, hosted by John Loefller, that two popes were murdered during the twentieth century:

Pope Pius XI, ingeniously murdered on the orders of Benito Mussolini, because of his 1931 encyclical *Non Abbiamo Bisogno*, harshly criticizing the Italian fascist state. Pope John Paul I, murdered, according to his novel 'Vatican'.

Appendix 5

THE GEORGE TAMARIN EXPERIMENT

In 1966, George Tamarin conducted the following study. He presented more than a thousand Israeli schoolchildren, aged between eight and fourteen, with the account of the battle of Jericho from the Book of Joshua:

> *Joshua said to the people, "Shout; for the Lord has given you the city. And the city and all that is within it shall be devoted to the Lord for destruction . . . But all silver and gold, and vessels of bronze and iron, are sacred to the Lord; they shall go into the treasury of the Lord." . . . Then they utterly destroyed all in the city, both men and women, young and old, oxen, sheep, and asses, with the edge of the sword . . . And they burned the city with fire, and all within it; only the silver and gold, and the vessels of bronze and of iron, they put into the treasury of the house of the Lord.*

Tamarin then asked the children a simple moral question: Do you think Joshua and the Israelites acted rightly or not? They had to choose between:

A (total approval)
B (partial approval)
C (total disapproval)

66% answered A, 26% answered C, and only 8% answered B.

Of the people who answered 'A', they gave explanations of which the three below are typical:

'In my opinion Joshua and the Sons of Israel acted well, and here are the reasons: God promised them this land, and gave them permission to conquer. If they would not have acted in this manner or killed anyone, then there would be the danger that the Sons of Israel would have assimilated among the Goyim.'

'In my opinion Joshua was right when he did it, one reason being that God commanded him to exterminate the people so that the tribes of Israel will not be able to assimilate amongst them and learn their bad ways.'

'Joshua did good because the people who inhabited the land were of a different religion, and when Joshua killed them he wiped their religion from the earth.'

The justification for the genocidal massacre by Joshua is religious in almost every case. Tamarin also ran a control group for the study. He took a different group of Israeli schoolchildren and gave them the same text from the Book of Joshua, but with Joshua's name replaced by 'General Lin', and Israel replaced by 'a Chinese kingdom 3,000 years ago.' Now the experiment gave the opposite results. Only 7% approve of General Lin's behaviour, and 75% disapproved. In other words, when their loyalty to Judaism was removed from the calculation, the majority of children agreed with the moral judgments that most people would share, that Joshua's action was a deed of barbaric genocide.

So we see clearly, in this case, that instead of providing a superior moral code for people to aspire to, religion is instead used as a justification for any barbarity up to and including genocide. When their religion is removed from the equation, the children find genocide to be bad. When their religion is included, they can overlook almost any barbarity committed in its name. The experiment was done using a chapter of the Bible and Israeli children as subjects. However the conclusions drawn from it are applicable to every other religion.

Before I knew about this experiment, I raised this chapter to Christians who came to my front door. I got the same sort of answers as Tamarin, even from Jehovah Witnesses who profess to be pacifists. In my film 'Chemical Wedding' I used a similar Biblical quote and was criticized.

Appendix 6

THE JEWISH GENE

For the book I checked my Spanish mother's genetic background. The results do suggest she had some Jewish background. This is the beginning of a long list of people who match her, the country they live in and what they think is their racial origin.

LOW RESOLUTION (HVR1) MATCHES					
Country	Your Matches	Comment	Match Total	Country Total	Percentage
Algeria	11	-	15	61	N/A
	1	Ashkenazi			
	3	Sephardic			
Argentina	1	-	1	17	N/A
Armenia	9	-	9	81	N/A
Austria	62	-	67	537	12.5%
	2	Ashkenazi			
	2	Austria-Hungary			
	1	Vienna			
Azerbaijan	1	-	7	72	N/A
	6	Mizrachi			
Belarus	27	-	34	288	11.8%
	7	Ashkenazi			
Belgium	27	-	27	256	10.5%
Bosnia and Herzegovina	3	-	3	40	N/A
Bulgaria	10	-	19	173	11.0%
	9	Sephardic			
Canada	1	-	1	132	0.8%
Central African Republic	1	-	1	99	N/A
China	1	-	1	297	0.3%
Congo, the Democratic Republic of the	1	-	1	54	N/A

It would be nice to check Brian Cohen's genetic make up as there appears to be a genetic marker for the high priests of Judaism, the Kohens (Cohens).

Kohanim are direct descendents from Moses' brother, Aaron and comprise a family dynasty within the larger Jewish levitical tribe. *Kohanim* enjoy an honoured status in Judaism, with certain designated rights and responsibilities. So it would be very unlikely that impoverished Brian would be a Cohen just as it would be very unlikely that a direct descendent of King David would be a humble carpenter.

Appendix 7

NAUGHTY JESUS IN BETHANY

And he left them and went out of the city to Bethany, where he spent the night.

Early in the morning, as he was on his way back to the city, he was hungry. Seeing a fig tree by the road, he went up to it but found nothing on it except leaves. Then he said to it, "May you never bear fruit again!" Immediately the tree withered.

When the disciples saw this, they were amazed. "How did the fig tree wither so quickly?" they asked. Jesus replied, "I tell you the truth, if you have faith and do not doubt, not only can you do what was done to the fig tree, but also you can say to this mountain, 'Go, throw yourself into the sea,' and it will be done. If you believe, you will receive whatever you ask for in prayer." (Matthew 21:17-22)

I pray that you have enjoyed this book and it will be a success.

Bonus prize answer for the crew picture on page 83 is:
right at the back, leaning on a rock is the 'Splitter'.

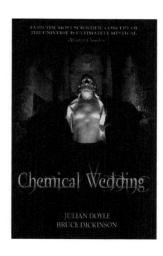

CHEMICAL WEDDING
(USA title 'CROWLEY')

THE FIRST SCIENCE FACTION NOVEL
by

JULIAN DOYLE
BRUCE DICKINSON

Jack Parsons was a brilliant chemist, founder of Cal Tech and inventor of the rocket fuel used for the US space flight to the moon.   He was also a fanatical believer in the Magic of Aleister Crowley the aging occultist who considered himself 'The Beast' incarnate.

In 1947 Jack Parsons and the now notorious, L. Ron Hubbard were performing Crowley's mystic rituals in a house in Pasadena, California. Parsons wrote excitedly to his occult leader, Crowley. 'I have had the most devastating experience of my life. I have been in direct touch with One who is most Holy and Beautiful as mentioned in your 'Book of the Law'. First instructions were received through Lafayette Ron Hubbard the seer. I have followed them to the letter. There was a desire for incarnation. I am to act as an instructor, guardian, guide for nine months; then it will be loosed on the world...'

Crowley wrote despairingly to a disciple about Parsons:

'It appears that he has given away both his girl and his money to this writer of science fiction and is now invoking the ritual to produce a MOONCHILD. I am fairly frantic...'

Nine months later while being visited by two students from Cambridge, Crowley died of cardiac degeneration. Missing from his personal possessions was his pocket-watch. His funeral took place in the Chapel of the Brighton Crematorium. The final rites were performed by the novelist Louis Marlowe reading extracts from Crowley's 'Book of the Law'. The Brighton Echo denounced the whole ceremony as a Black Mass. In 1952 Jack Parsons was blown up in his laboratory in Cal Tech, Pasadena. L. Ron Hubbard died on his yacht as leader of the now notorious Church of Scientology.

But did the issue end with these three deaths? Would Crowley, as he claimed, ever return from death to rule the world? Why did US astronauts name a crater on the moon after Jack Parsons? Is Lafayette Ron Hubbard really dead? What had been generated by the ceremony in California that seemed to signal Crowley's demise? What happened to the missing pocket-watch?

NOW A CONTROVERSIAL MOTION PICTURE
STARRING SIMON CALLOW

JULIAN DOYLE, the editor of 'LIFE OF BRIAN' is also one of the world's most versatile Film Makers. He has written, directed, photographed, edited and created Fxs all to the highest standards. He is most famous for editing the Monty Python Films and shooting the Fxs for Terry Gilliam's 'TIMEBANDITS and 'BRAZIL', which he also edited. He has recently finished directing his second feature film 'CHEMICAL WEDDING' featuring Simon Callow about the outrageous British occultist, Aleister Crowley and described by one US reviewer as *'Thoroughly entertaining although at times you wonder if the film makers have not lost all their senses'*. He has directed award winning pop videos such as Kate Bush's 'CLOUDBUSTING' featuring Donald Sutherland and Iron Maiden's 'PLAY WITH MADNESS'. He recently wrote and directed a play 'TWILIGHT OF THE GODS' investigating the tumultuous relationship between Richard Wagner and Friedrich Nietzsche and described by 'Philosophy Today' as *masterful…*

Julian was born in London and started life in the slums of Paddington. His Irish father, Bob, was one of the youngest members of the International Brigade that went to fight against Franco's invasion of democratic Spain. His mother, Lola, was born in Spain of an Asturian miner who died early of silicosis. She was thereafter brought up in a Catholic orphanage in Oviedo.

Julian started his education at St. Saviours, a church primary school. He went on to Haverstock secondary school, one of the first comprehensive schools in England. His first job was as a junior technician to Professor Peter Medawar's team, which won the Nobel Prize soon after Julian's arrival. Not that he claims any credit for that. At night school he passed his 'A' level exams and took a Zoology degree at London University. After a year at the Institute of Education, he taught biology for a year before going to the London Film School. Besides film making, Julian is well known for his Master-classes in Film Directing. While still at school, Julian had a daughter, Margarita who was brought up in the family. He then had 2 further children, Jud and Jessie.